BECOMING
a PASTOR

FORMING SELF AND SOUL FOR MINISTRY

Jaco J. Hamman

THE PILGRIM PRESS CLEVELAND

I dedicate this book to

JAMI DEVRIES HAMMAN & MICHAELA DEVRIES HAMMAN.

Thank you for teaching me how to play.

Julle vermoë om te glo is groot.

The Pilgrim Press, 700 Prospect Avenue, Cleveland, OH 44115-1100
thepilgrimpress.com
© 2007 Jaco J. Hamman

Printed in the United States of America on acid-free paper that contains
30% post-consumer fiber.

12   11   10   09   08   07   5   4   3   2   1

Library of Congress Cataloging-in-Publication Data

Hamman, Jaco J.
    Becoming a pastor : forming self and soul for ministry / Jaco J. Hamman.
        p.   cm.
    ISBN 978-0-8298-1749-2 (alk. paper)
    1. Pastoral theology.   I. Title.
BV4011.3.H355 2007
253'.2—dc22   2006035665

Contents

PREFACE

All pastors and church leaders feel that God called them into ordained or lay ministry. This feeling can be secure or in doubt. But pastors also know that responding to God's call is only the first step of an exciting process that promises to lead them more fully into who God is calling them to be.

You are involved in Christian ministry. Perhaps you are a seminarian completing your theological education and supervised ministry placements, or perhaps a seasoned pastor with many years of ministry experience. Some of you are lay leaders and teachers. At some point you received a call from God to ministry, you discerned the call, the call was confirmed by a community, and now you are living into your call.

Living into one's call is a difficult process that needs our constant attention. When we do not live into our calls, the risk of losing our calls increases significantly. All of us know someone who has lost his or her call. Some leave the ministry and others drift from church to church. Others leave the church altogether. No doubt you have discovered the challenging journey that unfolds when you answer a hesitant "Yes!" to God's call.

Becoming a Pastor: Forming Self and Soul for Ministry is a book about how you live into your call, sustain your call, and become a pastor. It addresses your formation and transformation for pastoral ministry. Notwithstanding the fact that you are functioning as a pastor, you are also always *becoming* one; you are continuously learning more about yourself,

God, and the people you love, lead, and serve. I use the word *becoming* carefully and purposefully. First, it takes for granted that you are a unique person with a history and a series of relationships and experiences that formed you. The dictionary says that *becoming* refers to origin.[1] Our families are not only determining forces in how we relate to ourselves and the world, but they are also our first school of theology. There in the presence of mom, dad, or other caregivers, we not only first learned about self and God, but we also inherited our family's culture of silence around particular painful and anxiety-provoking topics.

Becoming also communicates growth and vibrancy of an evolving, changing self, "that which is coming into existence." There are possibilities for maturation and movement, direction and discernment. The ways we learned to relate and think are not set in stone. Through grace we can grow to become more Christlike, to embody in more significant ways the love God showed us first. The Apostle Paul knew this well when he wrote to the church in Rome, saying: "Do not conform any longer to the pattern of this world, but be transformed by the renewing of your mind."[2]

Lastly, the word *becoming* also carries connotations of "that which is befitting or proper." To be becoming is to be suitable or appropriate, to act right. As pastors, we are at risk of being unbecoming of God's call. The media thrives on exposing those pastors who act unbecoming of their call and the trust placed in them. Whether sexual misconduct, financial mismanagement, or other forms of malfeasance, you and I need to guard ourselves against many forms of boundary violations and other temptations.

I imagine ministry as walking a narrow path. Family commitments, ministry obligations, and personal needs are just a few of the forces that restrict the path of our call. My concern is not whether you and I will stray from this path, but rather how long we might stray before realizing that we need to return to the path set by our call. Many of us do not realize we are wandering off, and by the time we do realize, the sign warning us of a boundary violation is only visible in our rearview mirror. Few of us can describe how we came to the point where we are now, but the pain that we and our families, victims, and our congregations experience is palpable. On the ministry path, our call functions as a beacon, a gyroscope, a guiding light. It is also a source of energy, allowing us to do things we never thought we could do or keeping us from doing things that feel "natural."

One way to live into your call is to constantly return to your call story and the path set by your call. Some of you undoubtedly find walking a narrow path risky and a burden too heavy to carry. Some might find the thought of straying from our God-given path disheartening. Some of you might even say: "Straying will never happen to me." Be warned, denial is not a river in Egypt! Despite the risk of being unbecoming, ministry, as with life, can be exciting and rewarding. *Becoming a Pastor* will show you directions to and the boundaries of such a life.

In these pages, the journey of becoming a pastor and the transformation needed for fruitful ministry are understood in very specific ways. This transformation involves six capacities or core competencies that must be achieved in order to become a mature congregational leader. I assume that some form of theological education, whether formal or informal, is needed, and I address theological education only tangentially. Rather, I argue that you are becoming a pastor when you nurture and grow in various aspects of your self—the only self you bring to your ministry—the self that engages persons and the world, and, of course, the self that enters into relationship with God. More specifically, you *become* yourself when:

- *You develop a deep sense of inner security:* You are self-confident and can risk transparency, authenticity, and even the uncertainty of not knowing; you can tolerate being needed, yet find it essentially unnecessary.

- *You nurture your imagination:* You can see beyond the obvious; you can empathically imagine what your parishioner with cancer is experiencing; you can see that the teenager's rebellious behavior is a way of showing the distance between his mom and dad, their marriage being the primary concern; your teaching and preaching speak of creativity.

- *You embrace your dark side:* You engage your anger that lurks but does not speak; the envy that you hide with self-sacrificing cynicism or sarcastic humor; your shame that communicates you are vulnerable and insecure.

- *You become aware of the emotions you experience:* Perhaps these include depression or being burned out, or the sexual yearnings you have for a certain parishioner; you can measure the temperature of your spiritual life and the nature of your relationship with the Triune God; you do not flee into false relationships as you try to get rid of your anxiety and internal chaos.

- *You can "see" others:* You can allow others, including God, to be who they are and not who you think they are or who you want them to be; persons become subjects and not objects.

- *You engage life and ministry with a sense of playfulness:* You laugh and have fun, your sermons are creative, and your words not always calculated; the smile on your face removes that frown and serious-looking brow; your shoulders are no longer carrying the weight of the world and you have a bounce in your step.

It is being transformed in these six areas of experience that describes becoming a person who can be effective in pastoral ministry. *Becoming a Pastor: Forming Self and Soul for Ministry* introduces these areas of being present to self and others and engaging internal and external realities. But since knowledge rarely leads to change, I will suggest in this book that you spend time in certain relationships or activities, such as with an artist who uses her imagination often, or reading poetry. At times I will ask you to meditate on a certain verse of Scripture, or to journal your thoughts. I will ask you to visit a children's museum or playground and do some playing and "people watching." Altering your sense of self and changing your soul both require work that has already started.

IN GRATITUDE

I extend my gratitude to:

- The pastors and leaders who invite me into their lives, some of them giving me permission to use their stories and creative reflections in this book.

- The students and faculty of Western Theological Seminary; Stellenbosch University Faculty of Theology; Pretoria University Faculty of Theology; the members of the Mid-west Region of the American Association of Pastoral Counselors; and my colleagues at the Society for Pastoral Theology. They all received portions of this book as course material or in a workshop setting and provided helpful feedback.

- The Board and Administration of Western Theological Seminary for granting me sabbatical leave (January through September 2006) during which this project was completed.

- Colleagues in ministry who read drafts of each chapter and offered affirmation and constructive criticism: Kobus Anthonissen, George Brown, Corky DeBoer, Pierre Goosen, Cobus Greyling, Abigail Fyten, Angie Mabry-Nauta, Vicky Menning, Cheryl Molhoek, Carolyn Raar, Stanley Rock, Randy Smit, Beth Smith, William Stroo, Herbert Tews, Cindi Veldheer DeYoung, and Gordon Wiersma.

- The following transformational educators in Australia, New Zealand, and South Africa: Paul Windsor (Carey Baptist Theological College, Auckland); Gerard Kelly and Anthony Maher (Catholic Institute of Sydney); Brendan Daly and Stuart Sellar (Good Shepherd College, Auckland); John Woodhouse and Richard Campbell (Moore Theological College, Sydney); John Reid (Morling College, Sydney); Julian Muller and Malan Nel (University of Pretoria); Christo Thesnaar (University of South Africa); Jeremy Brown; Xolile Simon; Ignatius Swart (University of Stellenbosch); Douglas Purnell (St. Ives Parish, Sydney); Mary Caygill and Phillip Culbertson (St. John's Theological College, Auckland); Elaine Wainright (University of Auckland).

- The following persons who created space for me to write: Reneé de Vries, who allowed our family to make her home ours; Gys and Marlene Steyn, for homes filled with hospitality close to nature where I could reflect, converse, write, and play; Peter and Natalie Miller, who reminded me that friendship spans time and distance; Douglas Purnell, an imaginative pastor-teacher, a good conversation partner, and a great cook; Michelle, my life partner, for unconditional love, support, and affirmation.

- Ulrike Guthrie, my editor at *The Pilgrim Press*. Uli, thank you for seeing the potential within a proposal. Working with you is life-giving and transformative.

Introduction

CREATED TO SEEK TRANSFORMATION

You and I were created to seek experiences and relationships that promise transformation of our sense of self. Most often the transformation is in the service of emotional, relational, spiritual, or even cognitive growth, but sometimes the transformation we seek actually inhibits or undoes holistic growth. The Book of Genesis introduces God as the Creator who formed this world and then transformed creation when God realized Adam was alone. Genesis 3:1–7, a section of Scripture we often refer to as "the fall of humanity," plays a central role in how we see human nature. Interpreting these verses often leaves us feeling guilty and in need of salvation (the guilty self) or naked and ashamed and in need of covering our nakedness (the tragic self). Especially verse 6, however, provides an additional image, that of being created to seek transformative experiences:

> When the woman saw that the fruit of the tree was good for food and pleasing to the eye, and also desirable for gaining wisdom, she took some and ate it. She also gave some to her husband, who was with her, and he ate it. (Gen. 3:6)

The phrase "and also desirable for gaining wisdom" is a *hapax legomenon*, used nowhere else in Scripture. Some might say that it is dangerous to make too much of such a one-of-a-kind phrase, but I would disagree. Not having multiple contexts that can inform our discernment opens the possibility for new understandings of the text. Tradition consistently interprets this verse in terms of guilt, sin, temptation, and lust,

1

a legacy at times ascribed to Augustine. However, verse 6 describes Eve as a person wanting to transform herself by gaining knowledge. Her primary motivation was not "I want to disobey God," rather, she acted on one of the deepest forces God placed in each of us, the desire to transform her self. By seeking this additional understanding of Genesis 3, I am not pretending sin does not exist. *Becoming a Pastor: Forming Self and Soul for Ministry* exposes and addresses many sinful attitudes and behaviors we pastors enjoy, ranging from a pharisaic rigidity to clandestine use of pornography to masochistically working ourselves to death.

Scripture says the fruit was desirable (Hebrew *hamad*). Even though hamad can mean desire or lust, which has sexual connotations, it also means a deep longing. Reflecting on verse 6, commentator Claus Westermann writes that "[Humanity] is created with a strong desire to know, and *to enhance its existence* through knowledge."[1] Westermann does not develop this thought of seeking enhancement any further, but Adriaan Van Selms, in his commentary, does give us a glimpse of what that enhancement might look like. Van Selms states that Eve sought spiritual growth or awakening.[2] The transformation she sought was soul transformation. Thus, the allure of the fruit is not to be found in the fruit itself, and it certainly does not reside in sexual pleasure. Rather, it is found in the promise that was awakened in the very hearts and souls of Adam and Eve that they could become new beings. Satan exploited this deep desire for transformation within the souls of Adam and Eve.

Some might think that Adam and Eve had it all, but wanted more. I see them merely living into the image of the God who first formed and then transformed creation. Sadly Adam and Eve, as you and I often do, sought transformation from a person and a relationship that could not offer them what was promised and what they desired. Imagine what would happen to theology and our understanding of human nature if an additional message from Genesis 3 preached from pulpits were that Adam and Eve sought self-transformation and that we do too!

In Genesis 3 we thus have at least three paths to follow: the path of guilt, the path of shame, and the path of the transformation of self and soul. Of course, these paths are not mutually exclusive and *Becoming a Pastor* follows all three. However, the basic premise of this book is that we were created to seek experiences that transform self and soul.

Psychology, always seeking ways to understand who we are and what motivates us, knows the potential for transformation we carry. Picture this: An infant, merely a couple months old, lies in her crib and looks at her mother's face. The mother has a smile on her face. Within seconds the baby girl smiles too. The mother is then asked to portray a neutral, "still face." Mother stops smiling. Within moments the baby girl's smile disappears. The infant's face is now expressionless, if not somewhat uncertain. Then the mother is asked to show a sad, downcast face. Within seconds the baby girl's face changes from being expressionless to looking depressed. This experiment, first photographed by psychologist Daniel Stern twenty years ago, showed that unresponsive behavior from the mother caused negative emotional reactions, indicative of frustration, depression, or shame in the infant.[3] Mother's responsive behavior, of course, had the opposite effect. The mother's sense of self transformed the infant's self-experience. In a matter of moments the baby girl went from being happy and cooing to being sad and silent, all this merely by looking attentively at her mother. The mothers photographed by Stern assured the well-being of their children. As a mother or primary caregiver engages her or his infant, gazing into each other's eyes and responding to basic needs, the mother or caregiver communicates to her or his infant *a way of being* that becomes the infant's sense of self.

Complementing Stern, other scholars of psyche and soul have identified mothers and caregivers as transformational agents, for the relationship between infant and mother forms the relational structure of the infant's sense of self.[4] It is this sense of self that determines how the infant relates to his or her inner world as well as to the outside world. Born to seek out transformational agents and experiences, you too desire relationships or experiences that will alter your self experience. It is this very search for transformation that might have prompted your discernment to enter seminary, your desire to pursue ministry, or your hand reaching out for this book. You learn from your mentor(s), a supervisor, or possibly a spiritual director; you listen to music and engage culture. You read Scripture and nurture your personal relationship with God. You have experienced many significant relationships that have transformed your sense of self. Some of us obsessively seek transformational experiences, selling our souls to partners or ideologies. Some of us build our identities around doing things, for when we take action we experience less anxiety. We do this, not only to remember existentially the preverbal relationship we first had with our mothers or primary caretakers, but also because our souls constantly seek out transformational experiences.

The fact that we were created to seek transformational experiences that alter our sense of self should not be confused with our sanctification. Sanctification is that process describing the restoration or renewal of persons that follows our salvation and justification in Christ. Sanctification is the work of God in which God's people can cooperate. The Westminster Larger Catechism describes our sanctification in terms of grace, as the work of the Triune God, and as a process of renewal, strengthening, and being risen to a new life.[5] With the help of God's Spirit we become more Christlike as our intellect, affections, will, soul, and body are transformed. Our becoming and our sanctification have much in common, despite being qualitatively different. Both processes imply a developmental path that does not lead to perfection; both have moral value and address the inner nature and outward presence of our beings.

The Christian faith, since the time of those forebearers of faith sometimes called the church fathers, has rejected consistently the tenet that we can become Christlike by ourselves. As Jesus said: "Remain in me, and I will remain in you. No branch can bear fruit by itself; it must remain in the vine. Neither can you bear fruit unless you remain in me" (John 15:4). This then is the paradox we have to hold: *We seek transformation but we are not sanctified by ourselves.* When we collapse this paradox, either by placing emphasis on only one of these processes or by arguing that they are the same process, we diminish both. Rather, through the work of God's Spirit and through the incarnational presence of Christ in other persons and in the church, we are transformed in body, soul, and mind. We too pray the prayer of the Apostle Paul to the Thessalonians: "May God, the God of peace, sanctify [us] through and through. May [our] whole spirit, soul and body be kept blameless at the coming of our Lord Jesus Christ" (1 Thess. 5:23). The process of your becoming a pastor and your sanctification are inextricably connected, for becoming is not merely seeking transformation; it also describes God's work of grace in our lives. Many of us are becoming even as we are sanctified. Let me introduce you to two pastors, very much like us, who are being transformed in their ministries.[6]

A SENSE OF RESPONSIBILITY

Pastor Andrew, the newly appointed associate pastor for youth and families at Faith Community Church, has a history of anxiety. During his seminary years, Pastor Andrew would become sick to his stomach the days of his preaching lab, anticipating with dread the experience of preaching to his peers. A similar dread came over him whenever he had to visit someone in hospital. At other times he developed skin rashes, which he could tie to his anxiety. It was during his seminary years that he was diagnosed with irritable bowel syndrome.

When Andrew discerned his call to Faith Community, his thoughts often went to Pastor Bill, the senior pastor he met during the interview process. Pastor Bill radiates a sense of inner peace and maturity. At times Andrew would compare Pastor Bill to his father and he silently wished that his father was more like Bill.

One night a call disrupts Andrew's evening meal, a call that informs him that one of the teenagers in the youth group has overdosed on over-the-counter medicine. No sooner is the call over than Andrew gets sick to his stomach. Andrew knows it is not brought about by the food he ate. He rushes to the hospital feeling a mixture of dread and intense guilt.

His inner voice reminds him that he should have seen this coming, that he could have prevented this painful happening. Thinking about it, he recalls that the teen had been somewhat distant during their last youth gathering. He should have asked her whether something was bothering her. *How could he have failed to notice her distress? What will the other parents think of him when they leave their children in his care?* The meeting at the hospital is brief, since the teenager is sleeping and the mother wants to make some phone calls. Andrew is frankly relieved that he can leave after only a few minutes, but then feels guilty about not being a good pastor to her. When he returns to his apartment later that evening, the food left on his plate repulses him. He throws it in the trash and wonders if he should call Bill, the senior pastor. Seeing that it is past eleven already, Andrew decides to tell Bill about the events at their regular meeting the next morning.

Walking to Bill's office, the same dread Andrew felt while going to the hospital the previous night comes over him again. His inner voice tells him that Bill does not want an associate who cannot prevent a parishioner from hurting herself. *How blind must he be?* Andrew is therefore quite surprised that Bill does not respond the way his inner voice anticipated. Rather, Bill asks about the girl and about Andrew, saying: "Man, you probably could not sleep last night with all the adrenaline in your body!" Bill continues: "You know, Bonhoeffer writes in his *Life*

Together that one of the more difficult things to carry as Christians is the autonomy of someone else. He actually calls it a burden. Surely wanting to take your own life is an autonomous act, even if depression is involved." A strange thing happens. As Andrew listens to this description of being burdened by someone else's choices, he feels relief. He confesses to Bill that he became sick to his stomach. They talk and pray together as they reflect on what Bonhoeffer might have meant when he said that we carry the burden of others' autonomy. Andrew compares this burden with the burden of responsibility he has carried for as long as he can recall. He tells Bill that he prefers the burden of someone else's autonomy to the burden of accepting responsibility that is not his to own. "I'll stop stealing others' responsibility," he says. As their meeting ends, Andrew is aware that he does not feel particularly burdened. He drives to his apartment thinking more of Bonhoeffer's comment on what burden we actually do carry.

Andrew, of course, did not consciously think or realize that Bill was functioning as a transformational agent to him. Like an Elisha, he "inherit[ed] a double portion of [Elijah's] spirit" (2 Kings 2:9). But Andrew's self-experience was completely altered by his conversation with Bill. When Andrew left Bill's office, the anxiety-driven self-talk was gone, and he "knew" that there was nothing he could have done that would have prevented this painful event. All he could do was carry this burden, which actually felt manageable. Andrew decided to make a quick stop at the teenager's house, as she had been released into the care of her mother. He felt mildly confident as he walked to the door . . .

You and I also seek out significant people and experiences that offer the promise of the transformation of our selves because we were created with such a desire.

- Who are your transformational agents?
- What experiences might function in a transformational manner?
- What parts of your self are in need of transformation?
- What experiences do you seek that actually prevent your emotional growth and spiritual maturation?

For anyone becoming a pastor these are important questions to reflect upon. For some of us such reflection will bring revitalization to our sense of call and for others it will help sustain longevity of call. Pastor

Cassie, to whom I will introduce you next, like many pastors who graduated in recent years, is thinking of leaving the ministry; she could benefit from a revitalization of her call.

LEARNING NOT TO BE PERFECT

Pastor Cassie's life has changed for the worse since she accepted her call and consequently she often thinks that doing something else would be a good thing. Over the months she has become an angry, resentful person, slowly isolating herself. Cassie often hears the words "You are such a nice girl. Why are you not married?" If her congregation only knew how she hates those words . . . Yes, she knows that they mean it well, but somehow those words ringing in her ears have never been a pleasant experience. Serving a small, rural congregation initially felt like a sign of God's faithfulness touching her life. But now she longs for an independence she once knew. She gave up a well-paying career in the corporate world when she entered seminary. Her friends wondered what had gotten into her when she told them she was going to seminary, but she knew she was called to this vocation and nothing else. "I am not a nice girl!" is her silent scream.

Cassie knows that these comments annoy her so much because they are a half-truth. She likes people and people seem to love her. However, she knows that is not the issue. The reference to her being a "girl" as she nears her fourth decade of life is irritating and her not being married is a painful reality. However, what really gets to her is the fact that she allows others to take advantage of her. One parishioner who especially confronts Cassie in this way is Delia, a homebound parishioner. Though Cassie always visits Delia with a plan to leave within an hour, typically she stumbles out of Delia's house two or three hours later, angry with herself that she could not find a way to leave and feeling guilty that she did not even listen carefully to what Delia said. Delia repeats herself so often anyway; every time Cassie hints that the conversation should end, Delia shares another sad story about her life. Despite the fact that she feels disconnected from Delia, Cassie typically feels that she cannot end the conversation at that point, leaving Delia in such a sad place. On her last visit, she finally managed to get away because she had another meeting to attend. It did mean, however, that she went to the meeting without eating dinner. Cassie promised herself not to visit Delia the next month, but that inner conversation brought pangs of guilt to her soul.

The inner voice that tells Cassie that Delia expects a weekly visit frustrates her and has become her intimate enemy.

Realizing that she cannot continue in this manner, she decides to visit with a professor who was also her advisor during her seminary years. Her professor listens attentively as Cassie laments her frustration with the congregation and especially with Delia. The professor just nods as Cassie says, "I let others take advantage of me," and then replies, "Cassie, it seems to me as if your problem is that you are afraid to disappoint someone, even yourself. And now you tell of your resentment." Her professor's words resonate with Cassie and she remembers her childhood. Her mother would always say, "Cassie is the perfect child." At some point Cassie thought it was a compliment, but now she realizes that it weighs heavily on her. She tells her professor that she wants to learn how "not to be perfect." She realizes it is this matter, and not Delia's loneliness and hunger for conversation, that she needs to work on. They decide that Cassie will journal her self-talk and what she believes God expects of her in ministry. They covenant to meet again in a few weeks.

ANTICIPATING *Becoming a Pastor: Forming Self and Soul for Ministry*

I trust that you are being pulled into these pages, already engaging the thoughts and possibilities they carry, and that you are curious about what's to come. The chapters of this book are all interrelated; for example, playfulness, which is addressed in the last chapter, is impossible without a sense of inner security, which is addressed in the first chapter, since play brings forth powerful emotions we need to hold. Like a web, the capacities discussed here are all woven together, each a thread that helps create the whole. Even though there is a logical unfolding of the chapters, each chapter is independent and paging ahead if one chapter interests you more than another is possible.

As I write this book, I am in my fifteenth year of being actively engaged in ministry, primarily hospital chaplaincy, pastoral psychotherapy, and more recently, teaching. Along the way, I met Donald Woods Winnicott, a creative and innovative theorist who introduced me to the capacities that form the foundation of *Becoming a Pastor*.

Donald Winnicott (1896–1971), a British pediatrician and psychoanalyst who saw himself as an "amateur theologian," was a key figure in establishing the post-Freudian school of object relations theory. Object relations theory focuses on early childhood, primarily the first three to four years of one's life. No longer are we driven by instincts (Freud), but we search for and are shaped by our initial relationships. Winnicott is described as "the master of the middle, the in-between," having had Anna Freud and Melanie Klein, opposing psychoanalytic pioneers, as mentors.[7] Even though the middle position is often unexciting and moderate in nature, Winnicott kept it alive by remaining in the tension field formed by opposite views without reverting to dichotomous thinking.

Winnicott's primary theoretical aim was to map out the territory traversed by the developing infant and to observe the gradual formation of the self capable of an experience that is real. This search for the real, which I can imagine is something similar to experiencing a life of abundance (John 10:10), Winnicott sees as a "primitive task" that is never completed.[8] With his playful spirit, I can hear Winnicott say: "Sir, madam, you are cordially invited to continue your work on achieving the capacity to believe, a task you already started in your infancy." Personally, *Becoming a Pastor* describes my chosen path of transformation as I live into my call and grow towards maturation. This journey, which begins new every day, remains exciting.

Since some spiritual and emotional preparation for what's to come will enhance your engagement of the book, a brief overview of the chapters can inform that process.

The first chapter identifies a deep sense of inner security, self-confidence, and general well-being as a core trait of a spiritually, emotionally, and relationally mature person. We meet Jesus as such a person in his "I am the bread, the way, the vine . . ." statements. This first chapter addresses the *capacity* to believe, which is distinguished from *believing in* God or an ideology in that the capacity to believe does not need an object to believe in and it is internally focused. The chapter addresses your inner space, the very nature of your soul, that deeply personal foundation determining your sense of self. *How would you describe your inner space? When and how do you engage your inner space? As a person of faith, believing in God, who and what do you allow into your inner space?* The capacity to believe also speaks to a deep emotional and relational "hunger" some of us have. Typically we try to satisfy this hunger by excessively consuming food and drink, material possessions, images and thoughts, or even consuming the emotional lives of others. Not to be confused with a narcissism that leaves us vulnerable, the capacity to believe describes the true self that proactively and creatively engages real-

Becoming a Pastor: Forming Self and Soul for Ministry concludes with a brief postscript asking: What now? The postscript's goal is to empower you as you embark on a journey of formation and transformation, a journey of nurturing the six core competencies I discuss. This journey is an exciting and lifelong process and makes a life of ministry worth living!

AN INVITATION AND A WARNING

Many of us live most of the time as strangers to ourselves. *Becoming a Pastor* invites you to meet yourself, to revisit a friend of old and to discover hospitality to others. *Strangers to Ourselves* is the title of a thought-provoking book by the French linguist and psychoanalyst Julia Kristeva.[10] Kristeva argues that we remain strangers to ourselves, and thus a "foreigner or alien" lives in each of us. It is our relationship with this stranger, she contends, that fuels hatred and rage to the stranger we meet from a foreign country. Besides the strong emotions of hatred and rage, we experience mental impoverishment when we deny the stranger inside. Such denial further opens the way to act out an inner anxiety. *How do you hear Kristeva on being a stranger to yourself? What might the price be for you if you decide to continue to live not knowing yourself? How will your preaching, teaching, and caring change if you no longer live as a stranger to yourself?*

Kristeva offers a serious warning for us who preach. Talking about the plight of a stranger, she states that a stranger experiences "void or baroque speech." The community, Kristeva writes, has no interest in the contribution of a stranger:

> Your speech, fascinating as it might be on account of its very strangeness, will be of no consequence, will have no effect, will cause no improvement in the image or reputation of those you are conversing with. One will listen to you only in absent-minded, amused fashion, and will forget you in order to go on with serious matters.[11]

Imagine a ministry that bears little or no fruit. Imagine preaching Sunday after Sunday and seeing no results. Imagine welcoming new members into your community when you cannot embrace the stranger in you.

When we meet the stranger who is us, some of us lose our voice while others hide behind formalism. Some speak with excessive sophis-

four years of one's life. No longer are we driven by instincts (Freud), but we search for and are shaped by our initial relationships. Winnicott is described as "the master of the middle, the in-between," having had Anna Freud and Melanie Klein, opposing psychoanalytic pioneers, as mentors.[7] Even though the middle position is often unexciting and moderate in nature, Winnicott kept it alive by remaining in the tension field formed by opposite views without reverting to dichotomous thinking.

Winnicott's primary theoretical aim was to map out the territory traversed by the developing infant and to observe the gradual formation of the self capable of an experience that is real. This search for the real, which I can imagine is something similar to experiencing a life of abundance (John 10:10), Winnicott sees as a "primitive task" that is never completed.[8] With his playful spirit, I can hear Winnicott say: "Sir, madam, you are cordially invited to continue your work on achieving the capacity to believe, a task you already started in your infancy." Personally, *Becoming a Pastor* describes my chosen path of transformation as I live into my call and grow towards maturation. This journey, which begins new every day, remains exciting.

Since some spiritual and emotional preparation for what's to come will enhance your engagement of the book, a brief overview of the chapters can inform that process.

The first chapter identifies a deep sense of inner security, self-confidence, and general well-being as a core trait of a spiritually, emotionally, and relationally mature person. We meet Jesus as such a person in his "I am the bread, the way, the vine . . ." statements. This first chapter addresses the *capacity* to believe, which is distinguished from *believing in* God or an ideology in that the capacity to believe does not need an object to believe in and it is internally focused. The chapter addresses your inner space, the very nature of your soul, that deeply personal foundation determining your sense of self. *How would you describe your inner space? When and how do you engage your inner space? As a person of faith, believing in God, who and what do you allow into your inner space?* The capacity to believe also speaks to a deep emotional and relational "hunger" some of us have. Typically we try to satisfy this hunger by excessively consuming food and drink, material possessions, images and thoughts, or even consuming the emotional lives of others. Not to be confused with a narcissism that leaves us vulnerable, the capacity to believe describes the true self that proactively and creatively engages reality. This chapter introduces the structure of the chapters to follow: You will be introduced to the capacity that speaks of your inner security; you will be helped to recognize the competency in your own person and ministry; and, you will gain practical guidelines on how to cultivate and strengthen authentic self-confidence as a core competency.

Chapter 2 speaks to imagination as a core competency for ministry. It addresses imaginatively living in the in-between world, the one between subjectivity and objectivity, between your own thoughts and the thoughts you receive from others. It describes a way of looking at things. Imagination is hearing the mother complain that her teenage son is rebellious and seeing that the son is crying out against a mother and father's distant relationship. It is listening to a person describe the details of her chemotherapy and envisioning empathically the helplessness and loneliness she is experiencing. *How does imagination inform your preaching, teaching, and caring? How do you nurture your imagination? What is the cost to you personally and to your ministry if you can only see the objective, rational world?*

The third chapter addresses the core competency and crucial integration that is required when we realize that we hate the same persons we love. For us as Christians, who often are called upon to "love," embracing our own aggression and destructiveness is a difficult process of maturation. *At church, how do you stay emotionally connected as you engage conflictual relationships or situations? When you do become angry, how do you manage your anger? What boundaries do you find difficult to keep?* The integration of love and hate is named as central to achieving the capacity for concern, that potential that fuels a desire to help or rescue. Lack of this capacity comes forward in someone who does the emotional/spiritual work of others, since not doing so is experienced as causing hurt. This, of course, is the high road to burnout. When we allow love and hate to embrace in our own selves, it helps us remain in a covenant relationship with a prodigal people.

Chapter 4 describes the ability to recognize and contain powerful emotions in a one-body relationship (your own) and to enter into appropriate and responsible two-body or multibody relationships when needing to do so. This chapter addresses the paradoxical capacity of being alone in the presence of other people. Ministry is impossible without relationships, which implies that you are always surrounded by persons, yet you are fundamentally alone with your thoughts, actions, and desires. The capacity to be alone is to know something that you are not telling. Or to know something and do tell, for that is the appropriate thing to do. *How do you contain "juicy bits of information" about parishioners and others, keeping confidences? How do you discern whether to share information or to intervene or not? What do you do if you sense "sexual chemistry" between yourself and a parishioner? How much spiritual, emotional, and/or relational hurt will you carry before you reach out to someone who can become a transformational agent to you? How will a lack of the capacity to be alone affect your ministry?* In a world where clergy misconduct is a sad reality and where pastors hurt spiritually and emotionally, gaining the core competency to be alone in the presence of others is essential to becoming a pastor.

The fifth chapter addresses the difficult challenge of entering into relationships mindful of the preconceived notions of the other person you bring to the relationship. All of us carry such beliefs and we rely upon them to protect ourselves in relationships where the other person is essentially autonomous and an unknown mystery. *What preconceived notions do you have about the single parent, the divorced individual, the victim of spouse abuse, the homeless person you encounter, a person of color, or a gay person? Who do you see as "us" and who do you see as "them"?* In the words of the Jewish scholar Martin Buber, do you experience the other as a "Thou" or an "It," a subject or an object?[9] The capacity to discover the other/Other, discussed in this fifth chapter in the metaphor to use or be used, is crucial for the experience of intimacy and mutuality, to relate to another person or God using your innermost and whole being. It calls for openness and an attitude that invites dialogue with others as they educate you about their joys and hopes, their fears and concerns.

The sixth and concluding chapter addresses the core competency of being playful. The capacity to play relies on all the other capacities. *Becoming a Pastor* invites us to be playful—not to be confused with being childish. Playfulness is suggestive of a secure inner space, imagination, comfortableness with the strong emotions play can induce, the ability to contain those emotions in a one-body relationship, and more. *Where and how does a playful spirit inform your ministry? When does the playful child become childish and egocentric? How can you maintain a playful spirit amidst seriousness?* To have a playful spirit will enable you to live into your call despite the inevitable changes that will occur within you and in your ministry context. Such a spirit, of course, is also central to experiencing longevity of call.

Becoming a Pastor: Forming Self and Soul for Ministry concludes with a brief postscript asking: What now? The postscript's goal is to empower you as you embark on a journey of formation and transformation, a journey of nurturing the six core competencies I discuss. This journey is an exciting and lifelong process and makes a life of ministry worth living!

AN INVITATION AND A WARNING

Many of us live most of the time as strangers to ourselves. *Becoming a Pastor* invites you to meet yourself, to revisit a friend of old and to discover hospitality to others. *Strangers to Ourselves* is the title of a thought-provoking book by the French linguist and psychoanalyst Julia Kristeva.[10] Kristeva argues that we remain strangers to ourselves, and thus a "foreigner or alien" lives in each of us. It is our relationship with this stranger, she contends, that fuels hatred and rage to the stranger we meet from a foreign country. Besides the strong emotions of hatred and rage, we experience mental impoverishment when we deny the stranger inside. Such denial further opens the way to act out an inner anxiety. *How do you hear Kristeva on being a stranger to yourself? What might the price be for you if you decide to continue to live not knowing yourself? How will your preaching, teaching, and caring change if you no longer live as a stranger to yourself?*

Kristeva offers a serious warning for us who preach. Talking about the plight of a stranger, she states that a stranger experiences "void or baroque speech." The community, Kristeva writes, has no interest in the contribution of a stranger:

> Your speech, fascinating as it might be on account of its very strangeness, will be of no consequence, will have no effect, will cause no improvement in the image or reputation of those you are conversing with. One will listen to you only in absent-minded, amused fashion, and will forget you in order to go on with serious matters.[11]

Imagine a ministry that bears little or no fruit. Imagine preaching Sunday after Sunday and seeing no results. Imagine welcoming new members into your community when you cannot embrace the stranger in you.

When we meet the stranger who is us, some of us lose our voice while others hide behind formalism. Some speak with excessive sophistication that no one can follow or we speak with dazzling eloquence, living with the illusion that the audience is captivated. Some become a dominating presence, never empowering the body of Christ to function as a body. Some choose to live a disembodied life, prizing the life of the mind. Yet others become a mere presence from whom no contribution can be asked. And some of us welcome the stranger home, enriched by having a new relationship.

Of course, full knowledge of self is not possible in this life, and ordination implies being set apart, a stranger within community, of sorts. Yet, you are invited to strengthen six competencies and to become aware of your own strengths and weaknesses as you seek growth and learning. I invite you (and me) to become a pastor. If you accept this invitation as an individual, you will benefit greatly, but the transformation will be much richer if you, in turn, invite a few colleagues with you on the journey.

one

THE CAPACITY TO BELIEVE

[We] may teach the concept of, say, everlasting arms.
We may use that word "God," we can make a specific link with
the Christian church and doctrine, but it is a series of steps.
Teaching comes into place there on the basis of what the
individual child has the capacity to believe in.

—D. W. Winnicott, Home Is Where We Start From

The pain of looking into one's own depth is too intense
for most people. They would rather return to the shaken and
devastated surface of their former lives and thoughts.

—Paul Tillich, The Shaking of the Foundations

Thinking of the fear I've had for so long . . .
Strangled by the wishes of pater,
Hoping for the arms of mater
Get to me sooner or later . . .

—Simply Red, "Holding Back the Years"

To become a pastor embraces the invitation to enter deep into your self. It accepts a paradoxical view of reality, recognizing that the outer world can only be engaged from your inner landscape. Becoming is about seeking personal inner transformation or revitalization before you seek it for others. As a congregational leader, you are called to mature into an authentic person secure enough to enter deep into your emotional, spiritual, and relational life. Achieving this ability allows you to create space for friends and strangers as you welcome them to the body of Christ and beckon them on a similar journey into themselves and towards a deepening understanding of God. Being able to nurture the core of your being—your inner space—is a capacity you need to achieve as you lead the body of Christ with effectiveness and fruitfulness. It is an achievement, because most of us have had experiences in life depriving us of the secure sense of self. However, we as religious leaders are often at risk of unwittingly substituting a life task such as this one for the content of our faith traditions, by becoming "good" at doing what others expect of us, or by hiding behind the power and prestige of our positions.

Some theologians and religious leaders deny that our sense of being has any importance, arguing that what one believes in—the knowledge you carry about God—is the essential matter. Intellect triumphs over affect. Belief, however, needs to come "home" to your self. *And in what condition is the foundation of your inner being?* Affect and intellect are inextricably linked. As many pastors and hospital chaplains have experienced, you too probably have been with persons in crisis who then also enter a spiritual crisis when they discover that their belief in God is not integrated into their persons. Suddenly God cannot come home . . .

The word "capacity" stems from the Latin *capere*, which literally means to contain or "to be capable." Brooke Hopkins, a professor of English, reminds us that *capere* is related to the adjective *capax*, which means "roomy or capacious."[1] The use of "capacity" therefore implies not only potential or an ability to do things, but also refers to one's inner space as capable of holding persons and ideas. One is not born with such capaciousness. Rather, the capacity to believe is nurtured over time within life-giving and life-affirming relationships and community. The word "belief," Hopkins reminds us, finds its roots in the Old Teutonic meaning of "to hold dear," "to trust in," but also "gladly, willingly,"—as in "beloved." The capacity to believe suggests a space where things can be held, to hold something dear, an activity that each one of us as individuals needs to do. The capacity to believe is the capacity to trust.

Since Moses, many leaders in the church have voiced their insecurity and doubt: "Who am I, that I should go . . . ?" (Exod. 3:11). We often want to pacify ourselves in ways such that others do not see or experience or are not affected by our insecurities that are showing up as physical symptoms, relational discord, boredom, meaninglessness, and poor decision-making that is affecting our lives and ministries. Sometimes we project a false sense of security and strength as we hide behind pulpit, power, and frenetic activity. Other times we are painfully reminded that we never live up to our own expectations.

As the theologian Paul Tillich warns us in the words at the beginning of this chapter, looking into the depths of who we are is a challenge most people avoid, and yet one that greatly determines how we live into our calls. Being self-aware is a capacity you need to achieve to be an effective and fruitful leader. Inwardness is neither encouraged by our society nor by most families and often feels like a taboo. If you choose to engage your inner space, no doubt you will discover that engaging the core of your being can feel like dishonoring your mother and father, since introspection inevitably takes you to your childhood home. It can also feel like narcissism or egocentrism. When we try to evade our inner world, the childhood we may not even remember, we will rarely feel alive. Feeling alive in ministry, as in life, is very different from going through the motions and reacting to whatever is happening or expected of you in ministry. The path that leads to feeling alive is a courageous path to choose.

One of Tillich's most influential books is *The Courage to Be*.[2] In this book Tillich encourages us to become mindful persons who find meaning in being (living inwardly, our female element) and not just in doing (living outwardly, our male element). In North American society, we find meaning in doing and therefore miss the deeper sense of being or experience a depleted sense of being. For Tillich, courage is the realistic self-affirmation of one's being despite those elements in our existence that make such self-affirmation difficult. Having a large inner space implies a deep and profound connection not only to self, but also to others in rich relationships. In addition, it suggests a deep connection to one's vocation. What may look like a "focusing on the self," in the end actually becomes focusing on self to clear the cobwebs, allowing you to be present to others. It is not to be confused with navel-gazing, narcissism, or even egocentrism, which Martin Luther referred to as the sin of bending back into ourselves (*incurvatus-in-se*). The courage to be invites you to embrace your deepest fears and doubts, whether you fear death, emptiness and meaninglessness, or guilt and condemnation. *The Courage to Be* addresses our existential anxieties, which tend to surface under stress, rather than pathological anxiety requiring a psychological diagnosis. Accepting that physicians and psychologists will address pathological anxiety, Tillich argues that addressing the deeper personal anxiety is a ministerial task we can neither escape nor conquer, leaving all persons in the tension-filled position of being both courageous and anxious. Like Moses, we stand before God, but we stand in fear (Exod. 3:6). Clearly, working towards the courage to be is a lifelong task we may only complete in our resurrection from the dead, but nonetheless one we do well to embark upon with courage and trust.

Growing towards a secure inner space, or as I will shortly argue, achieving the capacity to believe, becomes synonymous with gaining self-knowledge and being self-aware or sensitive. Self-knowledge can be defined as understanding what you are feeling and thinking, possibly making some connections to your past, but always mindful of how those feelings and thoughts impinge upon your self and determine the nature of your behavior, motivations, and all your relationships, including your relationship with God. It is a central aspect of us being "woven together" in imago Dei, as the psalmist prays: "Search me, O God, and know my heart; test me and know my anxious thoughts" (Ps. 139:23). We can know ourselves because God knows us. Many theologians and scholars, men like John Calvin, Paul Tillich, and Karl Barth, and women like Hildegard of Bingen, St. Theresa of Avila, and Ann Ulanov, have stressed the importance of self-knowledge. Without self-knowledge one cannot "know" others, for as Parker Palmer argues, "I will see them through a glass darkly, in the shadows of my unexamined life . . ." But Palmer continues:

> We teach who we are. Teaching, like any other truly human ac-
> tivity, emerges from one's inwardness, for better or worse. As I
> teach, I project the condition of my soul onto my students, my
> subject, and our way of being together. Teaching holds a mirror
> to my soul . . .[3]

The way you lead is determined by your inner space. One's inner space, describing the core of your being, can be dead or alive, small or large, insecure or secure, fragmented or integrated, in chaos or ordered, empty or filled, still or moving, hateful or loving, unwelcoming or hospitable, heavy or light, sinking or rising, sad or happy, depressed or vibrant, in discord or in harmony, serious or playful, and unknown and mysterious or known and being discovered. As such, the inner space is a sacred space. These opposites indicate a continuum and all of us can find ourselves between these extremes all the time. As you nurture your inner space, or as you deprive the very core of your being, you will move along this continuum.

I describe your inner landscape through the metaphors of the inner space and the capacity to believe. I assume that you have experienced two "births": as an infant and when you confirmed Christ as your personal Sovereign and Savior. Margaret Mahler, the child psychologist who wrote *The Psychological Birth of the Human Infant*, reminds us, however, that we are in need of a third birth, that of becoming a self. She asks, "Who are you if you never experienced a psychological birth?"[4] Surely you can answer this question, even if you have to think about the answer first, and despite the fact that you may not have the emotional language to describe your inner landscape.

So in this book we first imagine the inner space and I indicate the relationship between the inner space, the experience of basic trust, and the capacity to believe. I then address how the object relations theorist, Donald Winnicott, who is intrigued by how we are formed in relationships, describes the capacity to believe. We envision the inner landscapes of Jesus and the Pharisees. This first chapter concludes with practical guidelines on how to cultivate your inner space and achieve a sense of inner security and self-confidence also referred to as the capacity to believe. As you enter into this chapter and the challenge it will bring for you to enter your inner space, know that you are not alone. You are engaging not only me and the scholars I refer to in dialogue, but more important, the God who has searched you, who perceives your thoughts from afar, who knows your comings and your goings, who is behind you and before you, the God who laid a hand upon you, and the Spirit that is with you (Ps. 139).

THE UNBECOMING LEADER

The inner space is not a theoretical concept. You know it intimately even if you cannot tell about it. Our eyes reflect it and our words and actions mirror it. For what we reflect and mirror can be either becoming of our call or unbecoming thereof. This, then, is the image of an unbecoming leader—someone whose capacity to believe is compromised. The inner voice of the unbecoming leader echoes: "There is something fundamentally wrong with me." It feels as if he or she has, and sometimes is, a basic fault. The unbecoming pastor will not be able to lead a congregation towards spiritual, emotional, and relational maturity. The unbecoming leader:

- Is not secure enough to pray or initiate significant conversations about ultimate concerns
- Finds an identity in doing, as doing becomes a defense against being
- Is compliant to the needs of others
- Is often concerned about what other people might think of him or her
- Cannot contain or address personal needs, allowing them to become powerful desires
- Has an overdeveloped intellect that values thoughts more than feelings
- Knows what is best for others
- Splits reality into black or white, right or wrong
- Is envious of the giftedness of others
- Is very critical and judgmental of self and others
- Uses dogma, tradition, and authority as rigid defenses against inner insecurity
- Knows melancholia or depression, loneliness, anxiety, shame, and alienation
- Has a gluttonous nature: food and drink; buying books that are never read; taking in (pornographic) images or the emotional lives of others; working long hours towards burnout
- Portrays poor self-care
- Uses humor to hide insecurities
- Preaches and teaches without any imagination or creativity
- Carries undischarged aggression that can erupt in volcanic fashion or frequent conflict
- Cannot be spontaneous and playful

How do you recognize the unbecoming nature that most of us carry? And when and how does it manifest in you?

WE HAVE AN INNER SPACE

Long before poets and psychologists gave us language to talk about the inner space, the twelfth-century Christian mystic and prophet Hildegard of Bingen (1098–1179) had a vision she called "the cosmic wheel." In this vision, God is portrayed as a man stretching out his arms holding a large sphere, the whole cosmos. Inside the sphere stands another person, representing humanity or possibly Jesus. Also in the sphere are the sun, stars, wind, various animals (a dog, deer, fish), and clouds. In the lower left-hand corner, Hildegard is sitting drawing the vision she saw. The vision tells us that God carries and sustains all of creation and that we live an embodied existence. It envisions God as having a space large enough to contain all of creation. "The cosmic wheel" challenges us, asking us whether we have a space large enough to hold God, persons, and nature.

I envision my inner space—which of course is a spiritual, emotional, and relational reality and not a physical space—in my chest. Sometimes I think it can be my heart, for there I hold what is dear to me. If I look into this sacred space, I see the faces of my wife and two daughters; I see God, other family members and persons; and I see scenes of the natural world. Sadly, however, my space welcomes primarily persons who think like I do, who act like I do, and who come from a similar socioeconomic background. *Who resides in your inner space? Is your space small or large? Secure or threatened? How hospitable is your space?* Do imagine that your space is growing in size.

One psychologist who writes about the inner space is the developmental psychologist Erik Erikson (1902–94). He argues that women— and men, who need to cultivate it—have an "inner space."[5] The inner space refers to the womb, but also metaphorically to one's sense of being, which starts with the earliest experiences of differentiation as an infant. It carries connotations of construction and destruction, of "dangerous potentials." Observing the play activity of children, Erikson found that boys and girls use space differently, girls emphasizing the inner space by building enclosures and boys preferring outer space by building towers, which they then would topple. Erikson associated these different play styles with the difference between being (the feminine element) and doing (the masculine element).

The inner space is greatly affected by an infant's early experiences. These experiences can leave us with a sense of basic trust or a sense of basic mistrust, determined by the provision we received in infancy. Basic trust implies that one has learned to rely on the sameness and continuity of the outside providers—also that you will not be annihilated by your inner urges and that you are trustworthy.[6] Basic trust is a certain kind of confidence that care will arrive and that loving and aggressive feelings can be contained. One who settles on basic mistrust will withdraw into oneself in particular ways when at odds with oneself or others. Erikson associates the virtue of hope with basic trust. He defines hope as "the enduring belief in the attainability of fervent wishes, in spite of the dark urges and rages which mark the beginning of existence. Hope is the ontogenetic basis of faith, and is nourished by the adult faith which pervades patterns of care."[7] Basic trust thus makes faith possible in adulthood.

Trust and mistrust has an incorporative element—taking in—since a baby experiences the world primarily through her mouth. Drawing on the insights of Erikson and offering a model of human development, pastoral theologian Donald Capps argues that gluttony, understood as excessively taking in and which has an addictive quality, is suggestive of mistrust and the vice linked with Erikson's first stage of development.[8] Because of mistrust's gluttonous quality, we take in excessively. In the words of Frederick Buechner: We "raid the icebox for a cure for spiritual [and we can add, emotional and relational] malnutrition."[9] Of course, living in a gluttonous, all-consuming culture where the corporation or company gives a lifestyle but takes your life, sets our families up to raise children with a sense of basic mistrust.

The image provided by Erikson, where a self is formed through the care it receives, is biblical. In Psalm 131, ascribed to David, David writes:

> But I have stilled and quieted my soul; like a weaned child with his mother, like a weaned child is my soul within me. O Israel, put your hope in the Lord, now and forevermore. (Ps. 131:2–3)

For David, there is a close relationship between how we are raised and the nature of the faith and hope we have as adults. It is therefore not surprising that sociologists like Sarah Hrdy, in her book *Mother Nature: A History of Mothers, Infants, and Natural Selection*, identifies daycare for children as the biggest threat we face in the West.[10] She asks what kind of mothering children receive, since that primary relationship greatly forms the core of one's being and determines why we engage all of reality, including our call to the ministry and our relationship with God.

THE CAPACITY TO BELIEVE

As stated in the introduction, D. W. Winnicott provides a model for optimal early development and argues that we develop from dependence, through relative dependence, towards independence, for we never can be truly independent.[11] The first category describes the very early stages of emotional development where the infant is totally dependent upon his or her mother or the primary caregiver. The care provider creates a facilitating environment through dependability, love, empathy, enough frustrations, and by protecting the infant against a broken world's impingements. The infant takes in (through the process of introjection) the different ways of negotiating relational life. These introjections then guide the infant in negotiating the outside world. Artists often sing about introjection. The British group Simply Red, quoted at the opening of this chapter, sings about father and mother. Artist Michael Kelly Blanchard describes it beautifully: "There are faces that hang on the wall of my soul . . ." And in Pink Floyd's song "Mother," mother is saying: "Mother's gonna put all her fears into you . . ." Harry Guntrip, a pastor and analyst, uses more technical language when he says:

> Bad-object relationships in infancy and childhood prevent the child from developing a strong and consolidated "ego-structure," a firm sense of definite selfhood with positive characteristics and creative powers. Instead of inner sureness as being a properly self-possessed person with sufficient inner strength and resources to face and meet life with, the individual whose early ego-development has been stunted feels unequal to every task and feels that he will "'go to pieces" under every pressure.[12]

What faces are hanging on the walls of your soul? What fears were put into you? How do they facilitate a secure sense of self? When do you feel that you cannot face and meet life? How would you know that you are going to pieces? The answers to these questions were determined early in your life.

During this initial phase the mother-infant dyad is central, with the mother becoming "preoccupied" with the infant and the father playing a supportive role. The mother is identified with the infant and intuitively "knows" her infant's needs. This can easily be seen in a parent who can differentiate the infant's different cries, whether it is for food, warmth, a diaper change, or fear. Another basic characteristic of this first category is that the mother does not let her infant down, implying that the environment (mother) meets the infant's instinctual needs. The mother, giving herself over to the infant in a predictable manner, becomes a good-enough mother and assures her infant's going-on-being.

A mother cannot always meet her infant's needs and the infant then feels deprived. The baby cries out of hunger, for example, but the mother's breast does not appear immediately to bring relief. The delay that now exists between developing a need and having the need addressed introduces the move towards relative dependence as the infant adapts to the new reality. Winnicott believed that mothers gradually should refrain from meeting all of their infant's ego-needs, as the "too good" mother, who always anticipates and provides her infant's needs, causes just as much harm as the parent who neglects the infant. The baby now has to wait to be fed and learn to tolerate a waiting period previously found unbearable. And so the mother gradually introduces the infant to the world.

Through new mental mechanisms, the young child also learns to identify, first with mother and then with father and others. Identification (or the process of introjection) establishes a sense of "Me" and "not-Me" in the child, a sense that there is an "inside" that can influence an "outside."

The third category Winnicott identified was growing towards independence. In health, relative independence introduces the child to ever-widening circles of social life. Striving towards independence is central to toddlerhood and adolescence, but it is also central to adulthood, since "towards independence" indicates that an independent position is never really reached. The environmental relationship is a given, even if adults continue the process of growing out of relationships of dependency.

The poet Alfred Lord Tennyson (1809–92), like other poets and artists, knew the importance of the mother-child relationship. In his poem "In Memoriam A.H.H." stanza XLV (1850) Tennyson writes:

The baby new to earth and sky,
What time his tender palm is prest
Against the circle of the breast,
Has never thought that 'this is I;'

But as he grows he gathers much,
And learns the use of 'I,' and 'me',
And finds 'I am not what I see,
And other than the things I touch.'

So rounds he to a separate mind
From whence pure memory may begin,

As through the frame that binds him in
His isolation grows defined.

This use may lie in blood and breath,
Which else were fruitless of their due,
Had man to learn himself anew
Beyond the second birth of Death.[13]

Winnicott reminds us that our self develops in a holding (or facilitating) environment where the child was held appropriately and where external anxieties did not impinge on the child. However, there are also selves that develop in families where infants need to learn early to take care of themselves, since the emotional care and physical provision they need are lacking. Imagine an infant whose mother struggles with depression and who learns early that she can make her mother smile. Imagine a young boy who grows up in a house where his father's aggressive outbursts assure that everybody walks on eggshells. Or imagine the child who grows up in a tension field, as mother and father fight over custody arrangements during their divorce. Children like these do survive, but only thanks to the development of what Winnicott calls a false self that is always compliant to the environment.[14]

We thus have at least two selves, a personal private self that is part of our creatureliness and a socialized or polite self. The private self is called the true self and carries the potential for emotional, spiritual, and relational individuality. Winnicott called the socialized self, which is compliant to outside demands, the false self. The false self leads to emptiness, futility, guilt feelings, and deadness. Where there is maternal and environmental failure, that is, where good-enough mothering is not found, the secure, spontaneous, and creative true self of an infant never develops. Instead, a false self appears that hides the true, spontaneous self. The false self is thus a defensive organization in which there is a premature taking over of the nursing functions of the mother. When a mother (or the caretaker) is not attuned to the needs of the infant, the infant becomes attuned to the needs of the mother. The infant adapts to the environment while at the same time protecting and hiding the true self, or the source of personal impulses. Personal needs and desires (called forth by the true self) are placed aside as the needs of others take precedence. The false self is a restless self, often having an inability to concentrate, as it needs impingements from outside reality so that life can be filled by reactions to these impingements.

The development and character of the false self show degrees of compliance affecting every person. At one extreme, the false self sets up a self that other people may interpret as secure. This can be seen in the pastor who is heralded as a great preacher but whose inner world speaks of insecurity, anxiety, and doubt. On the other side of the spectrum the false self is built on identifications of individuals who had a big impact during childhood. It is important to indicate that the false self is also found in health, where it is represented by the whole organization of a polite and mannered social attitude. Here, the false self consciously becomes compliant to others. Much has gone to the person's ability to forego primary process thinking—the thinking of the inner world—to gain a place in society that can never be attained or maintained by the true self alone. Thus, the false self can be found in psychological illness and in psychological health. The false self and the true self are paradoxical in nature, for the false self inhibits the true self from appearing even though the false self assures the survival of the infant. Also, the true self is inward turning whereas the false self, due to its compliant nature, is outward turning. The false self is a primitive defense mechanism, defending the true self, who often lives in hiding. The false self is not alone in protecting the infant, however, for the primary caretaker(s) of the infant and the environment must protect the infant against the unthinkable anxiety of being annihilated, which should be understood as the death of the true self and the strengthening of the false self. When our true selves are threatened and our capacity to believe diminished, we will go to great extremes—even personal and professional suicide—to defend ourselves against being hurt again.

PASTOR TIMOTHY'S DOUBLE LIFE

Pastor Timothy sought out pastoral counseling three years after entering the ministry. His general complaint was stated in the words: "I am tired. Maybe God did not want me to be a pastor after all." Working sixty- to seventy-hour weeks, he still felt he was not serving his two-hundred-member congregation well. Pastor Timothy can name many shut-ins and families who "need me," but whom he cannot find the time to visit. Disappointing his congregation in this way awakens a deep sense of guilt in him. He also notes that he is often entangled in conflict with certain members around ethical issues.

Pastor Timothy has gained much weight, admitting that fast food restaurants hold a strange "peace and quiet" for him. His contemplation of Scripture is minimized to his sermon preparation, where he makes liberal use of online resources. He describes his relationship with God as "almost nonexisting," rarely engaging God in conversation and in prayer. When he never mentions his marriage the counselor asks him about it. Timothy sounds helpless when he says: "We are not intimate anymore." What places significant pressure on him, however, is that Dorothy, his wife, wants to have a family. He states: "I do not know whether I love her anymore. Maybe we married too soon . . ."

Pastor Timothy describes himself as a "perfect child" who has always been "good." He achieved academically, which denied him involvement in sports. He also adds that "I never embarrassed my parents." Pastor Timothy's parents divorced when he was four years old, "making me the man of the house." His mother went back to school and worked full-time, never marrying again. Initially, Pastor Timothy stayed with his mother one week and then with his father the next, but that "turned out to be too disruptive for all." He then moved in with his mother, "who never found herself after the divorce."

Pastor Timothy cannot understand why he feels so depleted, being left with a sense that he is not good enough as a pastor: "I'm doing everything expected of me, and maybe even more than most pastors!" And in a matter of mere minutes Pastor Timothy has described his double life. Outwardly he seems to be doing well, even if he thinks he should be doing better, but inwardly he is slowly dying. He is living "as if"—as if he is at peace with himself, as if he is enjoying his ministry, as if his marriage is on solid ground, as if he engages God regularly. Yes, he is living, but has no sense of being alive.

Pastor Timothy echoed the words of Dietrich Bonhoeffer, who, in his *Letters and Papers from Prison* (1972), wrote a poem called "Who Am I?" In the poem, written shortly before he was hanged by Nazi Germans, Bonhoeffer states that his fellow prisoners and the wardens know him very differently from the way he knows himself. They see calmness; he experiences "trembling with anger." They experience a cheerful and proud person; he is "struggling," "yearning," "tossing," and "weary and empty at praying." Bonhoeffer writes:

Who am I? This or the other?
Am I one person today and tomorrow another?

Am I both at once?
A hypocrite before others,
and before myself a contemptibly woebegone weakling?
Or is something within me still like a beaten army, fleeing in disor-
der from victory already achieved?
Who am I? They mock me, these lonely questions of mine.
Whoever I am, Thou knowest, O God, I am thine.[15]

"A contemptibly woebegone weakling . . ." Even Bonhoeffer's false self knew how to keep his true self diminished with harsh inner judgment. The false self could bury his fears and longing so deep that nobody noticed, but he knew! Pastor Timothy too is aware of the cost of his decisions: "I cannot even think of changing the way I have been going. If I do, no doubt people will be very disappointed in me. They might even ask me to leave . . ."

Like many pastors, Pastor Timothy entered ministry with the silent hope that his true self would be able to find expression. However, he now finds himself ruled by his false self, modeled in an exaggerated way after Pastor Timothy's identifications with his family of origin. The false self is keeping him from sharing with his congregation the state of his inner space and of his marriage. He feels exploited by his congregation and a fraud for not sharing with them who he really is. His false self protects him against inevitable pain and the risk of being rejected when he freely begins to tell about his inner landscape. Here the false self functions in a positive manner. However, it also kept him from seeking help early on in this process of alienation. Pastor Timothy is discovering that the false self always breaks down under stress, since it lacks the creative mind to find solutions. He feels the anxiety when he knows there is something wrong, but he cannot name what he feels.

ACHIEVING THE CAPACITY TO BELIEVE

Winnicott states that a strong true self and a healthy false self, the kind of self that develops in a home with good enough parenting, can achieve the capacity to believe.[16] This metaphor describes the nature of one's inner space as secure enough to worship God with all one's body, heart, mind, and soul and to engage the world with self-confidence. Always playful with words, Winnicott argues that there is a difference between believing in God and having the capacity to believe. The Who? (or person) who believes greatly impacts the What? of belief.

The capacity to believe and *believing in* describe two different processes; the one is maturational and the other is the parents and family and society giving the content of belief. The first process, achieving the capacity, not only determines the nature of the second process, but is also completed by the second, when belief in is encouraged. The difference between the capacity to believe and believing in can be stated as follows:

CAPACITY TO BELIEVE	BELIEVING IN
Requires a facilitating or holding environment (nurtured growth; loving care; human relationships)	Requires a Messenger (accepted as a gift; grace)
Internal world holds the external world	External world being held by the internal world
Qualitative (an aspect of human development)	Quantitative (Triune God or other object; dogma or ideas)
Needs no object or ideology (Who believes?)	Needs an object or an ideology (What do you believe?)
Personal (individual)	Cultural, traditional, communal
Openness and flexibility; can carry uncertainty and risk not knowing	Fixed-ness and rigidity; seeks clarity and certainty
Comfortable with ambivalence	Polarized truth or knowledge (right and wrong)
Indicates the ability to keep mental images alive (object constancy)	Requires a constant object
Female element of being in our person	Male element of doing in our person
Loving of self	Loving of others
Feeling alive	Life giving

The paradoxical tension between the capacity to believe and belief in cannot be resolved. It is not a choice between one and the other. Rather, emotional, relational, and spiritual maturity requires that you engage both the inner reality of the capacity to believe and the outer reality of believing in. As persons of faith, we can never escape being a person who believes in God. Sadly, many Christians think that if only they believe in "the right God," it will speak miraculously into their person. Of course there is a mutual relationship between believing in and the capacity to believe, and our faith in God does speak into who we are. However, our faith (or belief) in God does not undo our personal life history, even if it restores our relationship with God. Belief in God does not remove the false self that was born when good enough parenting did not occur or when life wounded our inner spaces.

Looking at the chart, how do you evaluate your capacity to believe and your belief in?

DISCOVERING WHO I REALLY AM

Reflecting on his capacity to believe, Pastor Ken, a pastor who regularly engages his inner world, had to admit that his space feels small and insecure. Pastor Ken's mother returned to full-time work shortly after his birth. He states: "My mother's choice to work instead of staying home to raise me has created both a gap inside me and a desire to produce something in order to find worth in myself." He describes the false self that hides in his imagination and finds meaning in doing, while he is plagued by inner doubts about whether he is worthy of being a pastor. He states: "As I have grown, I have felt the need to be older than I really am. I was constantly trying to 'earn' respect and freedom. . . . As I grew older, it became apparent that something within me, namely, the cumulative voices of my parents and other authority figures, continued to tell me that my worth does not come from who I am, but from what I do."

As Pastor Ken works towards achieving the capacity to believe, he relies on the creative nature of his true self to assist him. Here it is not his imagination that goes into hiding, but rather creative authenticity that is shown. He wrote a song called "Who We Really Are" that revisits the birth of his false self and small, insecure inner space.

Who We Really Are

Momma's gone . . . child grows too fast
The need to push the pain away
Time reveals . . . uncovers layers that
Aren't really stronger anyway

Child is gone . . . kept moving faster still
Can't stay in places underground
Tension grows . . . can't separate my end
From where a part of you begins

Like moving head to heart
The space between us breathes of life
I want to find you there
Discover who you really are

Another voice . . . is growing louder now
It speaks from broken memories
I begin . . . now standing closer still
To shame and anger buried there

A part of me . . . prefers to close my eyes
Indifference my only friend
A people speak . . . I recognize myself
And layers start to fall away

Like moving head to heart
The space between us breathes of life
I want to find you there
Discover who you really are
I want to find us there
Discover who we really are

The song honors the birth of the false self, its impact on Pastor Ken and his relationships, and his deep desire to discover who he is. But, significantly, it also presents the creativity of Pastor Ken's true self.

What broken memories can you recall? How would you describe the birth of your false self? Who would you like to discover in yourself and in others? Where do you identify with Pastor Ken?

JESUS'S SECURE, WELCOMING INNER SPACE

We believe in a God who has a secure identity, an "I am" (Exod. 3:10–14). Yahweh, as we refer to God, has connections with the Hebrew word for "being," which is *hayah*. God has an identity of being, which we learn to understand first as the act of creativity and then the desire to be in relationship. We discover, however, that Yahweh's *hayah* speaks with authority as God distinguishes Godself from other gods. It is no surprise that Jesus refers to himself as "I am . . ." We hear Jesus say: "I am the Vine, the Bread, the Son of God . . ." Holding Jesus as an example can be dangerous, but Jesus, in his words and actions, does show us the nature and quality of his inner space. Compare his inner space with that of the Pharisees, for example, and we see that Jesus has a "roomy" inner space, welcoming women and children and the poor, secure enough to go against tradition. He ate with them so often that he is called "a glutton and a drunkard, a friend of tax collectors and sinners" (Matt. 11:19). And he reminded us that "in my Father's house are many rooms" (John 14:2).

The Pharisees, however, seem threatened and rigid, afraid of becoming unclean, while outwardly, they could pray on street corners. They show us that their inner spaces are small and insecure. We see in them that small inner spaces lead to rigidity, a lack of compassion and hostile aggression. The Pharisees' rigidity, for example, would not allow for Jesus and his disciples to pick grain on the Sabbath (Matt. 12). Today I perceive similar small inner spaces and a lack of compassion as Christians harangue gays and lesbians in the body of Christ and as Christians remain nonresponsive to the poor, to the oppressed, and to the ecological disaster we face as we exploit the earth.

Do you have room for the poor and the prisoner, the person with AIDS, the gay or lesbian person? Or are you afraid of becoming unclean, defending yourself by judging others? Whose does your inner space reflect—the inner space of Jesus or of the Pharisees?

Jesus, as the theologian Emil Brunner reminds us, is a mirror in which we can discover our humanness.[17] Unlike a mirror, however, we not only see who we are as sinful beings and who we are called to be in Christ, but we also discover our essential need for relationship. Someone who looks deep into the Jesus-mirror is Michael Newheart, a professor of New Testament. Here he reflects on Jesus's proclamation, "I am the bread of life" (John 6:35). With serious playfulness, Newheart writes:

> This is the feast that I have longed to eat, the bread of self-acceptance, the wine (not whine) of self-confidence. I am the bread of life, Jesus says. Something both attractive and repulsive about that saying. I AM. I am. I Am. Jesus, this man who lived, died, ate, drank, eliminated, says I AM, not i . . . am but I AM. I marvel at, long for, yearn for such confidence, such sense of self, such, such, such self-possession, grasp of who he is. My own ego, lack of self-confidence, know who i am but don't love i am. Anxiety about who I am. What do I fear? There is no fear in I am. I want that, I want it.[18]

You are an "I am." *Do you know your "I am"? How do you love "I am"? How does Jesus as the I AM come home to your I am?* You are invited to the feast of self-acceptance, where the Bread of Life awaits you.

SEEKING A SPACE LARGE ENOUGH

Kari Dodd, a second-career seminarian called to be a Lutheran pastor, reflects on Jesus feeding the multitudes using only a few loaves of bread and a few fish (Matt. 15). She is keenly aware that whatever Jesus touches, multiplies. She is also consciously engaging her inner space and her ability to discover the true self in others, while allowing others to discover her true self. With the creativity that speaks of a burgeoning true self, she describes her inner space:

A space large enough

can I hold a space open large enough to allow someone I want to be larger than me to be for a moment a minute a month a year smaller than me so they can feel their smallness their vulnerability so they can again realize within themselves their Jesus math that one plus not enough is good enough

can I hold a space open large enough to allow someone I want to be smaller than me to be for a moment a minute a month a year larger than me so they can feel their largeness their strength so they can again realize within themselves their Jesus math that one minus enough is good enough

the Jesus math, the Jesus math
subtracting and multiplying and dividing and adding
the Jesus math 5 + 2 + Jesus
the Jesus math

can I allow others to hold a space for me that's large enough to allow myself to be smaller and larger for a moment a minute a month a year larger and smaller than I used to be so I can feel my largeness and smallness so I can realize again within myself my Jesus math that one plus one minus one divided one multiplied + Jesus is good enough

the Jesus math
the Jesus math

subtracting and multiplying and dividing and adding
the Jesus math 5 + 2 + Jesus the Jesus math

I'm not ready yet for me nor for you for the space to be large enough
to enter Jesus math but the day is coming and is already here where
Jesus math exists and is right outside my grasp
the Jesus math 5 + 2 + Jesus the Jesus math

Kari is wrestling with herself and the nature of her inner being. *When is your inner space large enough for even the smallest of people? How do you reckon with the Jesus math? Who do you know with a large inner space that can guide you along the way?* Like a mother's face shapes the sense of self in her infant, your face becomes the face of God to others. *What aspects of God are they discovering in your face?*

CULTIVATE YOUR CAPACITY TO BELIEVE

It is grace to have the capacity to grow and to be transformed. The paradox of achieving the capacity to believe is that to be, you need to do, even if doing in itself cannot facilitate the capacity to believe and might even indicate the lack thereof. The broken reality that received you greatly impinged on your person even as it formed you.

As a religious leader, however, you are also called to nurture your inner space to be secure enough to carry you into your ministry. Therefore, each chapter of *Becoming a Pastor* will end with the acronym GRASP to offer practical guidelines as to how you can nurture your self and be proactive in your own formation for ministry. I envision these guidelines as ways of engaging life, of being, rather than exercises we do. Through examining your covenant with God, specific Relationships, Actions, contemplating Scripture, and Prayer (not necessarily in that sequence), you can participate in the transformation God is working in you through God's Spirit.

Examine Your Covenant with God

You received the content of your faith from your parents and pastors, from teachers and churches, from friends and society, but because the content is held within you, you have a unique relationship with God. Clinical Pastoral Education supervisor Dennis Kenny created an instrument that helps us discover the nature of our relationship with God. He calls it our "covenant with God."[19] When our covenants go unexamined,

Kenny writes, they can become hindrances in life and ministry, for they become binding and inflexible.

Each covenant has roots that tie us to our family of origin. It describes the atmosphere within your family or the air that came forth from one of your parents. Our roots are then communicated in a silent life prayer and also indicate our unforgivable sin—the taboo your family identified (and not the theological argument whether a sin exists too big to be forgiven). Lastly, we enter into a covenant with God, a statement that typically begins with: "God, I will be your child if . . ." This covenant—and you will discover we have many—has specific ramifications for life, faith, and ministry.

Pastor Timothy, whom we met earlier, completed the exercise as follows, "My roots are: I became an adult child when my parents divorced. I learned early in life never to disappoint people and to live with a deep fear of rejection. My inner space was wounded and remained small and insecure, making me better at doing ministry than being someone. My life prayer is Oh God, please let me be someone." When asked who that "someone" would be, he said, "Someone who can risk saying no without a deep fear of disappointing others or being rejected. My unforgivable sin is to be an irresponsible child and disappoint others. My covenant with God is: Dear God, I will be your child and not be rejected when I do what people ask of me."

The ramifications of Pastor Timothy's covenant with God are clear as he finds himself on the brink of burnout. He will continue to work long hours and neglect his self-care and marriage, however, until he finds a transformational person or experience that will alter his sense of self. As Pastor Timothy finds himself alienated from himself, his marriage, and his congregation, the very rejection he fears stares him in the face. Now, Pastor Timothy prays: "Dear God, I am your child, whether I feel I disappoint the congregation or not. As your child, you ask of me to be aware of my limitations and keep healthy boundaries."

1. What are your roots?
2. What is your silent prayer?
3. What is your unforgivable sin?
4. What is your covenant with God?
5. What are the implications for your life, your ministry, and your relationship with God?

6. Do take your discernment in prayer to God and in conversation to a trusted mentor or friend.

Relationships

Created in the image of God, we are formed and transformed in relationships. It is in relationships where we receive our wounds and where healing and transformation occurs.

- Engage in conversation, and possibly enter into a relationship with a mentor, a coach, a spiritual director, a counselor, or even a supervisor—someone who has worked towards achieving the capacity to believe. Choose a person with an inner space larger than yours. Allow this person to see your inner space and together envision yours becoming more secure.

- Volunteer at a shelter, a community kitchen, or similar ministry where you can enter into relationships with those who are very different from you. Be invited into the lives of others.

Action

As stated, the paradox of achieving the capacity to believe is that to be, you need to do.

Read an author who wrestles with his or her inner space. Be informed about someone's inner transformation. *How do the inner spaces of these authors speak to yours? What can you learn from them about this path of introspection and growing towards inner security?* I recommend these books:

- Anne LaMotte. *Traveling Mercies: Some Thoughts on Faith.* New York: Pantheon Books, 1999.

- Michael Newheart. *Word and Soul: A Psychological, Literary, and Cultural Reading of the Fourth Gospel.* Collegeville, Minn.: Liturgical Press, 2001.

- Parker Palmer. *The Courage to Teach: Exploring the Inner Landscape of a Teacher's Life.* San Francisco: Jossey-Bass, 1998; or *A Hidden Wholeness: The Journey Toward an Undivided Life.* San Francisco: Jossey-Bass, 2004.

Observe the relationship between an adult and an infant or toddler. This can be at a mall or a playground, even a kindergarten classroom.

How do you think the relationship between the adult and the child is a facilitating environment for the self of the child as it seeks to mature into a secure identity?

Create and engage the creativity of others: Take a piece of paper. Draw a large plus sign (+) on the paper with markings from 1 to 5, 1 being close to where the lines cross and 5 being the end of each line. Discern how large and secure your inner space is. A circle around the four 2s, for example, would indicate a smaller inner space than a circle drawn around all the 4s. Name one thing you can do to enlarge your inner space by one point on this scale. Pastor Timothy drew his inner space as follows:

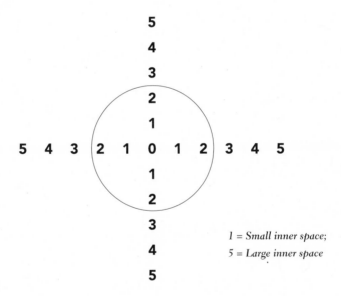

1 = *Small inner space;*
5 = *Large inner space*

He reckoned he can move to a 3 by creating a schedule for visiting the members of his congregation and discussing it with his elders. He will publish the schedule in the Sunday bulletin so that it's known to the whole congregation. On the schedule he will indicate Tuesdays as his day off.

You can also write a poem or a song or a prayer about your inner space. Sculpt or paint or imagine your inner space. Use your "painting mind," to quote one pastor.

Journal: Some people enjoy keeping a journal, others do not. Keeping a journal about your dialogue with this book and how it speaks into your life, or about what you have to do, however, can assist your transformation. Be as candid as you can. A journal, as one spiritual director said, is "a place to wrestle with angels and struggle with demons."

Scripture

Allow Scripture to speak into your life. Read:

- Romans 12:2–3. "Be transformed [*metamorphusthe*] by the renewing of your mind. . . . Think of yourself with sober judgment. . . ."
- Galatians 4:19–20. "My dear children, for whom I am again in the pains of childbirth until Christ is formed [*morphoothe*] in you, how I wish I could be with you now and change my tone, because I am perplexed about you!"

How are you being transformed to become more Christ-like? What areas of your life are in need of transformation? Where and how do you engage in "sober judgment"?

Reflect on Psalm 139. As you search your inner landscape, what are you finding that God already knows? How can you receive the courage to look at yourself from this psalm?

Read:
- Exodus 3:14; Isaiah 43:10–11, 45:18
- John 6:35, 48 (Bread), 8:12 (Light), 9:5 (Light), 10:7 (Truth), 10:11 (Good Shepherd), 11:25 (Resurrection), 14:6 (Way and Truth), 15:1 (Vine)

God and Jesus refer to themselves as "I am . . ." Made in the image of God, how does the I AM (God) speak to your I am?

Reflect on Luke 7:36–50. What do you discover about space: physical space, inner space, spiritual space? What are the differences you perceive in Jesus and in the Pharisee? How would you describe the "faith" that saved the woman? With whom do you associate in this text? Why do you make this association?

Prayer

Doing the kind of inner work I ask of you in this chapter takes us to many "raw moments," those moments where we are vulnerable in the presence of our wounds and our God. Prayer can be like the arms of God holding

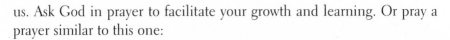

us. Ask God in prayer to facilitate your growth and learning. Or pray a prayer similar to this one:

> Dear God, thank you that I can be in relationship with you, the I AM. Thank you Jesus, for showing us a way to be. I pray—O Spirit of God—that you will give me the courage to look at my inner space. Open my eyes to who I am and to who you called me to be. Let me be someone who is an instrument in your hands. I pray this in Jesus name, Amen.

CONCLUSION

To become a pastor is to be someone. And being someone should not be confused with believing or knowing or doing. Stated differently, we can say that it is unbecoming of someone in religious leadership not to have a secure sense of self. The insecure leader will never risk transparency, authenticity, and the uncertainty of not knowing. Rather, it is becoming of a pastor to tolerate being needed, yet you find being needed essentially unnecessary. If the only relationship parishioners have with you is with the pastor-as-actor (or elder-as-actor) in the absence of a real self to engage, spiritual growth and maturity will remain elusive. Becoming a pastor is creating space for others to grow, something that is only possible if your inner space is nurtured. In this chapter I introduced you to two selves, one that lives inward and the other outward, one that is spontaneous and creative and the other compliant to the needs of others. Feeling alive requires of you to be aware of both these selves, and to nurture the true self, the one most deprived and thus insecure.

I encouraged you to experience a third birth to a secure emotional-spiritual self. You discovered that you have an inner space, a spontaneous and creative true self and a compliant false self. Like the rich young man in Luke 18, you are challenged with whom you invite into your inner landscape, not with what you know or what you can do.

It might have surprised you that you have "many selves," each demanding your awareness and cultivation. In conversation with a friend, he reminded me of the theologian H. Richard Niebuhr, who, in his book, *The Responsible Self* (1963) quotes the poet Eunice Tietjens on the nature of the self as characteristic of internal division and even conflict. Tietjens writes:

I am too many selves to know just one.
In too complex a schooling was I bred,
Child of too many cities who have gone
Down all bright cross-roads of the world's desires,
And at too many altars bowed my head
To light too many fires[20]

Many selves. One true and one false. One secure and the other insecure. One creative and the other compliant. Many selves, each to be known. It is these selves that challenge us in ministry, for we preach, teach, and counsel who we are. To revisit Palmer's statement earlier in this chapter: Ministry, like any other truly human activity, emerges from your inwardness, for better or worse. As you preach and pray, you project the condition of your inner space onto those around you. Ministry opens a window to your inner space.

It may be that your deprived true self, as it seeks freedom to thrive, is the self that led you to the ministry. For ministry holds the potential to find love and healing and address other personal concerns. However, ministry also becomes a fiery furnace that consumes. You need to achieve the capacity to believe to engage life and ministry to the full. The capacity is foundational to our being, for with it we can risk doubt. And doubt, Frederick Buechner says, is "the ants in the pants of faith. They keep it awake and moving."[21] With the capacity we can welcome others like Christ did; we can risk imagining God's reign coming to earth; we can love and we can contain our hate; we can allow others to be; we can play; and our belief in God and the work of God's Spirit is greatly deepened. Truly, revitalization of the church begins within!

The saying, "the glory of God is a person fully alive," is ascribed to the second-century bishop of Gaul (France), St. Irenaeus. It takes much cultivation of the inner landscape to become a person with such "alert readiness" and "alive waiting" (as one theorist writes). Imagine yourself, fully alive and mature as Christ (Eph. 4:13)!

two

THE CAPACITY TO IMAGINE

Creativity is then the doing that arises out of being.

—D. W. Winnicott, *Home Is Where We Start From*

Imagination is the passport we create
to take us into the real world.

—John Guare, *Six Degrees of Separation*

The people sat waiting out on their blankets in the garden
But God said nothing
So someone asked him, "I beg your pardon:
I'm not quite clear about what you just spoke—
Was that a parable, or a very subtle joke?"

—Crash Test Dummies, "God Shuffled His Feet"

To become a pastor is to regularly engage the world of the imagination. It is to live creatively *between* different realities: inner-subjective and outer-objective, I and O/other, and self and Text. Only in this in-between world can we discover what it means to be a person and a partner, a parent and a participant, a parishioner and a pastor, a prophet and a preacher. One definition of imagination is having the ability to see what is not there and to know the unknown or the unuttered. Like the artist who sees a beautiful flower on her white canvas, or the sculptor who sees a mother and child in a piece of granite, you see God using you to tend God's flock, you see the Spirit of God moving between and among the members in your community, or you see the personal loss or relational pain behind the person who is criticizing your leadership. Another definition of imagination can be that it is the gift of moving between past, present, and future. You move effortlessly between tradition, the now, and the future that is unfolding.

As Winnicott reminds us, living imaginatively or creatively is the *doing* that arises from *being*. Without a secure sense of being—the capacity to believe—imagination is a frightful experience of the unfamiliar, best to be avoided. Living imaginatively, however, is not to be confused with being artistically creative or with being a prodigy. Rather, the capacity to imagine speaks to the way you engage the outside world. It tells something of your ability to perceive reality, even that part of reality that is not yet real or realized. As such, every person can achieve the capacity to imagine to some degree.

For us in religious leadership, the capacity to imagine is crucial. Ministry, after all, is a place of creating. Despite the philosopher Ludwig Feuerbach's disdain of religion and his view that we merely project or externalize aspects of ourselves that we then call God, he is correct when he says that the imagination is the original organ of religion. Think of how you use your imagination to see beyond what is there: You see the reign of God coming; you study, interpret, preach, and teach God's Word and words; you re-vision the Word that became flesh and lived amongst us; you communicate empathy, imagining yourself into the shoes of someone else; you find hope in desperate places; you lead the body of Christ in today's world; and, you find ways to live with the inevitable disappointments in ministry. All of these tasks of leadership require imagination. Indeed, ministry without imagination is unfathomable. We rely on our capacity to imagine, to create and reason, to speculate and inspire, to associate and perceive, to learn, comprehend, think, and understand, to memorize, to philosophize, to analyze, and to risk change. Having developed fairly late in our evolution—possibly as recently as 77,000 years ago—our capacity to imagine has become a central force defining how we engage the world. In the previous chapter I stated that when we lack the capacity to believe, the intellectual function becomes very strong. As one author puts it, we experience "intellectual overgrowth." The imagination cannot thrive where intellectual overgrowth is in place since such overgrowth brings the illusion of security in objectivity. Because of our intellectual strength, however, we never achieve the capacities to believe and to imagine and thus cannot critically imagine our selves or imagine being a midwife to the lives and souls of others.

This chapter addresses living imaginatively and creatively in everyday life and ministry. I do not necessarily envision you creating an art piece or writing a poem, even though I will encourage you to risk creating something. I imagine you reaching out creatively inward and to the outside world, rather than always being reactive to the outside world. I want to urge you to cultivate a prophetic imagination similar to the prophet Elisha's. In 2 Kings 6 we read the fascinating account of Elisha's imagination challenging the imagination of two leaders, the king of Syria and the king of Israel. Elisha's imagination kept him from being caught; it helped him to remain less anxious when all those around him were troubled; it beckoned him to pray when others became angry in their proclamations; it showed him chariots of fire when others were blind; and, Elisha's imagination created a table with food where enemies ate together when the king of Israel excitedly wanted to kill his enemy.

I provide a framework for the formation of imagination and argue that you lead your community with at least three different imaginations: one that appears when you retreat deep into yourself; a second that thrives in the world of power and money; and a third that draws on elements of both the personal and the objective. The chapter focuses on this third imagination, the kind of prophetic imagination Elisha portrays, how it develops and how it can be distinguished from imagination that is so personal that it has difficulty communicating itself, or one that is so real that it has no mystery. The chapter ends with suggestions on how to work towards achieving the capacity to imagine.

THE UNBECOMING LEADER

As with the capacity to believe, the capacity to imagine is not a theoretical concept. I remember well that even as a child I was aware that some sermons would put me to sleep within minutes whereas others kept me awake. Neither my mother's elbow nor my father's peppermints helped if the sermons were as dry as a valley of bones. I now think of the sermons that kept me awake as imaginative sermons! Sadly, I also remember how rare those sermons were. I slept through most sermons as a teenager and even now as an adult, I can regress in worship services to be the teenager of old. *What kinds of sermons hold your attention and energize you to leave the worship service revitalized?*

No doubt, you have experienced many preachers whose sermons reflected the inability to imagine. Sometimes, especially when you are stressed and/or tired, you too probably lack imagination. For us in religious leadership, however, it is unbecoming not to nurture our imagination or to be unimaginative. We cannot hide the lack thereof, for others experience it in our words and actions. The unimaginative, unbecoming leader:

- Has an overdeveloped intellect
- Is fundamentally uninterested in the subjective, relational, and spiritual lives he or she and others live
- Needs to be right and is unwilling to engage in dialogue
- Does not realize there is tension between the objectively perceived and the subjectively conceived, questioning objective truth
- Cannot appreciate or understand symbolism and the importance of ritual
- Values power more than creativity
- Thinks that what people need is another thought and readily proceeds to provide that thought
- Due to the lack of compassion and empathy, misnames the feeling states of parishioners
- Cannot imagine that abuse occurs in "good" Christian families
- Does not empower the many members of the body of Christ to portray their many functions (Rom. 12:4–6)
- Never has enough time to complete tasks to satisfaction
- Knows despair, cynicism, and meaninglessness intimately
- Cannot complicate an issue by viewing it from different perspectives
- Is easily bored and impatient, finding "rest" in daydreaming, playing solitaire on the computer, or surfing the web or television channels
- Takes the "No" he receives from the congregation personally
- Cannot see the painful motivations people might have behind their destructive actions
- Confuses letting go and risking change with abandoning tradition and commitments
- Has little or no creative vitality, but is always exactly compliant to others
- Allows the difficulties of life and ministry to become problems
- Cannot enter a resting state of being after a day's doing

This unbecoming leader is a tragic person who may, in the extreme, suffer from what psychoanalyst Christopher Bollas calls "normotic illness." Leaders who are ill with normotic illness are "so firmly anchored in objectively perceived reality that they are ill in the opposite direction of being out of touch with the subjective world and with the creative approach to fact." They are often "abnormally normal, too stable, secure, comfortable, and socially extrovert."[1] Not only is this leader uninterested in subjective life, but he or she will not be creative in communicating the Christian faith in a modern metaphor. Sadly, leaders ill with normotic illness have lost the capacity of introspection, which discovers deep emotions, and find security only in relationships that lack depth and durability, which of course are rife in ministry. In close intimate relationships and during times of stress and conflict, however, their relationships are shallow and break down easily.

The leader with normotic tendencies is the elder who visits a family during a crisis, only to avoid them in weeks and months that follow as they embark on an emotional and spiritual roller-coaster. Or it is the pastor who responds to a passionate drama performed by the youth group by saying: "It was *interesting* that they chose red as a background to the stage . . ." Or, the chairperson of the finance committee whose vision for ministry is greatly impaired by bank statements. It is the deacon who reacts to the custodian's complaints that the children's ministry is "making a mess" in the fellowship hall, suggesting that the children's ministry move to a room without a carpet, saying, "The room will clean without difficulty." The leader with normotic illness is the one who, when powerful emotions arise and spirited conversation takes place, uses her knowledge of Robert's Rules of Order to smother the spirited conversation into a rational debate a few persons engage in as others become uninterested listeners and feel unheard.

Bollas sees individuals who have normotic tendencies as being "unborn," since the final stages of emotional birth never occurred. What a sad image, a person who never really comes alive and is always predictably together, unless alcohol or anger becomes a "cure" for normotic illness. Due to their interest in things and facts, normotic leaders avoid ritual and symbolism, which invite numerous and rich interpretations. Sadly, persons who lack the capacity to imagine do not understand parables. Like the Pharisees of old, they can and indeed with enthusiasm and commitment do follow the letter of the law. The truth is that most religious leaders carry some normotic traits. This is not so much a judgment as an invitation to engage your imagination to temper these traits. It is grace that we were created with the ability to be transformed, to learn how to live creatively. It's a grace that we can change.

RE-VISION YOURSELF

Imagine this. Suppose tonight, while you are sleeping, a miracle occurs: You achieve the capacity to imagine. Of course you don't know that the miracle occurred because you were sleeping. Miraculously, any normotic tendencies you had are of the past. *When you wake up tomorrow morning, how would you know that the miracle of achieving the capacity to imagine happened? What would be the smallest sign the miracle occurred? What if your normotic tendencies disappeared? How would you look at yourself differently? How would others notice the miracle occurred? How would you enter the committee meeting differently? How would you pray differently? What new aspects of God would you discover? Describe your leadership once the miracle has occurred.*

THE CAPACITY TO IMAGINE

Neuroscientists tell us that our ability to imagine is a function of our brains, making it possible for us to entertain what is real and what is not so real, to conjure up images that soothe or images that induce fear and anxiety. Through technologies such as magnetic resonance imaging (MRI) and positron emission tomography (PET scans), we can see how the brain comes alive with electrochemical activity during imaginative activity. A network of many millions of neurons, with axons, dendrites, and neurotransmitters between synapses, creates pathways for information to be processed at great speeds, making imagination and memory possible. These pathways of learning imply that the more we "practice" a mental exercise such as imagination, the more creative our minds become! As you pondered the questions I asked about your miracle night, your brain came alive and new possibilities entered your being. You relied on the left hemisphere of the brain that is concerned with logic, data facts, numbers, linear thinking, lists, and analysis, and you needed the right hemisphere, supporting the intellectual functions of rhythm, spatial awareness, imagination, color, day-dreaming, and creative activity. A neuropsychological understanding of imagination is beyond the scope of this project, but talking about the imagination without referring to the brain seems unimaginative. Brain studies tell us that not only do we love and hate and experience compassion, empathy, and kindness with our brains, but our brains keep on forming new pathways of learning. All we need to do is to expose ourselves to creative activity, which the brain then records and can use in future information processing.[2]

Object relations theory provides an additional understanding of the formation and role of the imagination. Donald Winnicott, who sees creativity as an innate drive and argues for the capacity to imagine, describes the infant who first experiences her environment as "creating" the breast that nurses her. As the baby is held and cries out in hunger, the mother places the breast before the infant, who discovers what has been there all along. This paradox, that a baby creates what exists, cannot be resolved. Thus, in a moment of illusion and omnipotence—which later in adult life can return to us as narcissistic grandiosity and a desire for control—the infant believes she creates the breast.

At first, when the mother presents the breast or the father the bottle almost as soon as the baby cries, the sense of omnipotence is not frustrated. Frustration, however, needs to be introduced and happens naturally as the hold the baby has on her mother, father, and other caregivers loosens. Frustration gives birth to mental activity. After a few weeks, we thus find that the baby is allowed to cry a while before the breast or bottle arrives. This change, which Winnicott describes as moving from a *me-world* to a *not-me world*, is the baby's first experience that there is a world out there that is not created by her in her sense of omnipotence. From now on, the infant lives "between" different realities, the subjective me-world and the objective not-me world.[3] The false self, which we addressed in the previous chapter, is formed to protect the infant against the impingements of and lack of attention by the not-me world. This differentiation between the me and the not-me is crucial in the maturation of a person. It is also here that the infant relies on the imagination to bridge the me and the not-me world and to defend against existential anxiety.

My daughters, for example, immediately started using pacifiers to negotiate the anxiety they experienced as they moved between their subjective (the me) and objective realities (the not-me). When waking and going to bed or when my wife or I would leave them at their play group, their pacifiers help them with the transition. Some children might suck their thumb or use a blanket, a pillow, a soft toy such as a teddy bear, or even a lullaby. Like the breast before, these items are discovered (or one can say created) by the infant even though it was provided. Winnicott calls pacifiers and blankets and teddy bears transitional objects, for they bridge the me and the not-me worlds. Parents and family members honor these transitional objects. For example, mothers know intuitively the blanket is a security blanket that should not be washed regularly, despite the fact that the one corner is sucked on. And father knows that there has to be space in the car to take the teddy bear or pillow along on vacation. No doubt you have experienced the high anxiety in an infant when you have removed, or threaten to remove, the transitional object from a child, indicating that some part of the child is found in the object.

Transitional objects contain personal aspects of the infant (some of the me) even as they were made of certain materials (not-me). Winnicott describes this paradox as follows:

> Of the transitional object it can be said that it is a matter of agreement between us and the baby that we will never ask the question "'Did you conceive of this or was it presented to you from without?" The important point is that no decision on this point is expected. The question is not to be formulated.[4]

A transitional object is owned by the child, who affectionately cuddles and loves the object. The object also survives the child's aggression, when the child might throw it away from herself, only to return as the loved object. A transitional object is experienced as giving warmth and as having a vitality of its own. Since it is owned by the child, a parent or someone else cannot change the object at will and one child's object rarely becomes another child's object.

Transitional objects live between objectivity and subjectivity in an area that Winnicott called at different times the transitional space, the transitional sphere, the intermediate area of experiencing, the potential space, or the cultural field. All these descriptions refer to the same space. There is a "third part of the life of a human being, a part that we cannot ignore," Winnicott writes, "an intermediate area of *experiencing*, to which the inner reality and the external world both contribute." It is a "resting-place" for a person, "that which is allowed to the infant and which in adult life is inherent in art and religion."[5] He continues: "The intermediate area . . . is the area that is allowed to the infant between primary creativity and objective perception based on reality-testing." It is the home of illusion, "without which there is no meaning for the human being in the idea of a relationship with an object that is perceived by others as external to that being."⁶ In this space, something is both found and created. No doubt, you have experienced the paradox inherent to the transitional space, when you were "pulled in" by an author, a movie, or by a specific drama, or you have "lost yourself" in music. The author, actor, or musician created a space—not to be confused with the inner space of the previous chapter—and you entered the experience without moving or leaving your body. We have created language to describe entering the transitional space.

Scripture, of course, often describes the intermediate area of experiencing, since it is the only place where you can find God. Psalm 42 tells us of the soul thirsting for God as a deer longs for flowing streams. The Dutch theologian Abraham Kuyper reflects on Psalm 42 and writes:

> My soul pants, yea, thirsts after the living God. Not after a Creed regarding God, not after an idea of God, not after a remembrance of God, not after a Divine Majesty, that, far removed from my soul, stands over against it as a God in words or in phrases, but [God as a Self], after God in [God's] holy outpouring of strength and grace, after God who is alive . . .⁷

Kuyper longs neither for a God who is a mere reality on paper, part of the not-me world, nor for one who is only memory, part of the me-world. Rather, he longs for the Living God who is alive. *How do you know God? As an idea? As a piece of dogma? As someone alive and exuding strength and grace?*

Where Freud and others viewed religion's use of illusion as infantile, something delusional and false, Winnicott sees the capacity to imagine and its fruit illusion as essential to healthy living. Furthermore, it makes the use of symbolism possible. Children literally grow out of their transitional objects, but as we grow out of it, we grow into other manifestations of transitional phenomena: the worlds of creativity, literature, art, music, religion, and ritual. To enter these worlds is a developmental achievement, a sign of health.

As stated, the creativity we are interested in is not necessarily the creativity of an artist. In an essay called "Living Creatively," Winnicott talks of the doing that arises *out of* being as an important achievement for every person. Winnicott describes creativity, the fruit of the capacity to imagine, as "the retention throughout life of something that belongs to infant experience: the ability to create the world . . . . Using creativity means seeing everything afresh all the time 'with new eyes'."[8] It is our sense of being that allows us to be creative and that allows us to look at our potential for construction and destruction. Some babies, however, have to spend all their energies to get the attention of their mother or father or someone. They have to do, and the false self, always reactive to the environment, is strengthened. Creative living, therefore, implies living a life that is not merely compliant to the outside world. It is living a responsive, not reactive life. It is being who you are and not always being who others "ask" you to be or who you think you need to be to be loved. Creative living is about feeling alive and having meaning.

"[For] creative living we need no special talent," Winnicott writes.[9] Every person, irrespective of age and of physical health, can live creatively. The imagination has no bounds. Such living, however, is greatly diminished when stress and anxiety sets in. *Since every person can live creatively, the question is how will you, as a leader in your community, live a life of feeling alive and not merely living?* One answer that can be given to this question is to say you will spend more time in the transitional space, that area of experiencing between subjectivity and objectivity. Living creatively, however, also implies that those who live exclusively a normotic existence find you a little bit insane, for you can enter deep emotion and engage realities not visible with the naked eye. Furthermore, living creatively requires of us to be embodied and disembodied in mind and soul at the same time. For some, being a body is an unthinkable thought and for others being disembodied conjures up similar anxieties. As the analyst Michael Eigen states, we walk a tightrope, "sometimes we move within and between these two poles, now immersed in thought, now in body experience."[10] It is imagination that allows us to be embodied souls.

TO RESPOND IN COLOR

Art therapist Shaun McNiff reminds us that creative activity can assist us in making deeper connections with ourselves and with others. Through art you can engage the world "through the heart rather than the habitual mind," and experience how "creative imagination carries your relationship to a different place."[11] Paula, a seminarian in her senior year, is discovering the freedom and vitality that comes from making "deeper connections." Through artistic expression, she is allowing her true self to speak into her life and in the process is learning how to be herself and be less compliant in ministry. Here Paula encounters a colorful God in worship and takes that God into life:

Balancing

balancing
in the grey between
extremes
our colorful God emerges
and we learn
marigold, fuchsia, cobalt
our bodies dance in the timelessness
of worship
stepping, spinning, twirling
we awkwardly find
the beat, it's in us,
on us, through us
not of us
or by us
yet, there it is
underneath the white
and black calling us
to respond
in color

How are you living a life of color? When does it become difficult for you to abandon the polarities of black and white? When does worship become a place where you can dance? Who is Paula's "colorful God"? Reflecting on this poem, what can you learn about yourself as someone called to be a leader in the body of Christ?

"Balancing in the grey between," Paula discovered a "colorful God." Such a discovery only happens when one enters the transitional space, where our capacity to imagine makes new ways of seeing and being in the world possible.

LOCATING MINISTRY

The Dutch-American psychologist of religion, Paul Pruyser, in his book *The Play of the Imagination*, builds on Winnicott's work about the transitional space when he too invites persons to live creatively.[12] He reminds his readers that there is an etymological relationship between illusion and play, both finding their origin in the Latin verb *ludere* (to play). To live creatively is to be playful, a theme we will revisit when we discuss the capacity to play.

Pruyser names the transitional object as the transcendent, for it "is beyond the ordinary division we make between the mental image produced by the mind itself and the objective perceptual image produced by the real world impinging upon our sensory system."[13] God is not a real object we can perceive in reality, pointing to a material object. But God is also not a creation born from our desires and wish-fulfillments. For Pruyser, following Winnicott, illusion becomes something unique: neither hallucination nor delusion. Rather, we *experience* God somewhere between subjectivity and objectivity in the transitional space.

Pruyser develops the tripartite view of reality that Winnicott introduces when he names an in-between world that can be found between the me-world and the not-me world. This in-between world, which Pruyser calls the illusionistic world, is the imaginative world of creative living and is neither subjective nor objective, but contains elements of both. The three worlds we then live in are: the autistic world, the illusionistic world, and the realistic world. The autistic world does not refer to autism, but rather to the me-world of pure subjectivity. We often enter into this world—as a coping mechanism—when we are ill or when we have experienced a traumatic event. The realistic world, in turn, refers to the not-me world of objective reality. The three worlds (see table on the following page) represent three distinct ways of being in the world.[14]

If you read 2 Kings 6:1–23 with this tripartite view of reality in mind, you will see that the kings of Syria and Israel oscillate between the autistic and realistic worlds. Their rage, seeing themselves as all-powerful, their cold decisions to kill, and their engagement of an internalized enemy, whether Elisha or the other nation, all speak of their regression into their autistic world. However, they also engage the realistic world with the search for the factual, their resourcefulness, their work ethic, and their reactivity to what is happening around them. The servant boy, doing his work and then struck with fear, also portrays these two worlds. He is invited into the illusionistic world, however, when Elisha opens his eyes to see imaginative entities, the chariots of fire. Elisha clearly lived by his prophetic imagination. He seems less anxious as his life is in dan-

AUTISTIC WORLD	ILLUSIONISTIC WORLD	REALISTIC WORLD
untutored fantasy (dreaming)	tutored fantasy (stories, parables, myths)	sense perception (sight, smell, touch, taste, hearing)
omnipotent thinking	adventurous thinking	reality testing
utter whimsicality	orderly imagination	undeniable facts
free associations	inspired connections	logical connections
ineffable images	verbalizable images	visible referents
hallucinatory entities or events	imaginative entities or events	actual entities or events (icons)
private needs	cultural needs	needs of others
symptoms (bodily reactions such as asthma, migraine headaches, irritable bowel syndrome, depression, and anxiety)	symbols (as representations that conceal and reveal)	signs, indexes
dreaming	playing	working
sterility	creativeness	resourcefulness
internal object (imago)	transcendent objects	external objects

ger; he acknowledges a reality besides what one feels or sees; his act of feeding the enemy is not only creative but also deeply symbolic; and there is playfulness in how he leads the Syrian army between blindness and sight.

Deacon Philip, like the kings of Syria and Israel, is someone firmly rooted in the objective world. His world is especially governed by economic principles. As the song reminds us: "Money talks, but it don't sing and dance and it don't walk . . ." Money—and therefore Deacon Phillip—rarely enters the transitional world of song and dance. He sees ministry as something you *do*.

Deacon Phillip has been chairperson of the finance committee for nearly fifteen years. He is a successful businessman in town and tithes a tenth of his pretax income to the congregation's ministries. At a recent meeting, two women came forward with a request to receive financial support for a new ministry: offering childcare to young and single parents one evening each week. They wanted to offer some care and relief to the many parents in the congregation who work all day and have no relatives in town who could offer childcare. The women envisioned hiring college students to look after the children, while they would offer their supervision as a service to the church. They were asking for $2,800 to cover all expenses.

Deacon Phillip had immediate concerns: First, their request was not part of the budget that was approved by the congregation. Second, he heard nothing in the proposal about charging the parents a fee for the services. And third, he was not sure that the church should enter the "childcare business" since it would raise the liability of the church. The women responded by saying that he was correct, this was an extraordinary request not in the current budget; that they envisioned offering the service for free since some of the families were financially struggling; and, they knew of no other congregation in town who offered such a service and, according to their understanding, the existing liability insurance would cover this ministry as a ministry of the church. They continued by saying that they had prayed over this for weeks and sensed that God had placed this ministry on their hearts. Certainly the parents who could benefit from this ministry were excited about the prospect. The rest of the finance committee listened and looked in silence at Deacon Phillip, who was becoming visibly uncomfortable. His response was to say that this would put the budget even further "in the red" and that "I do not think it could be done without another congregational meeting." Suddenly he announced: "If you cannot accept my leadership of this committee, I'll resign . . ." As Deacon Philip retreated in silence, his breathing became audible in the room.

Within a matter of minutes Deacon Philip oscillated between a full engagement with the realistic world to withdrawal into his autistic world. He could not meet the women in the transitional space where hope, possibility, creativity, and new opportunity reside. Furthermore, he could not find any empathy and compassion for the young parents and single mothers who would benefit from the ministry. To meet the parents in the transitional space, he had to leave the realistic world and refrain from retreating into his autistic world where he became again the small boy scolded by his father. After what felt like a stalemate position, the vice-chair of the finance committee motioned to table the request for a future meeting, suggesting to the women that they also look into alternative ways of funding the ministry. The women left the meeting feeling unheard and defeated. As they closed the door behind them, Deacon Philip announced the next agenda item: Who, besides the pastor, should cosign checks if he was not available . . .

When leaders cannot enter the illusionistic world, the transitional space where ministry becomes possible, sisters and bothers in Christ become disremembered and a congregation's ministry smothers under the reality principle.

Ministry takes place in a third world between inner reality and outer reality, between self and other. Faith, hope, love, prayers, sermons, music, care, discernment, Bible study, compassion, kindness, forgiveness, healing, justice, reconciliation, and many other elements of religious leadership are all elements of the illusionistic world. So too is a sanctified life of love, joy, peace, patience, kindness, goodness, faithfulness, gentleness, and self-control impossible without entering the transitional space as a third world (Gal. 5:22). As a leader in the church, you need to be firmly rooted in self (chapter 1) and reality (chapter 5), while spending much time in the illusionistic world. Becoming a pastor implies that you have to mediate the seen and the unseen; that which is and that which is yet to come; that which is before and that which is after; and that which is received from tradition and new traditions being formed. You are perpetually at risk of being too esoteric and subjective (autistic) or too objective (realistic). When either of these extremes occurs, you will become a dismembered member of the body of Christ.

The Old Testament scholar Walter Brueggemann in his book *Interpretation and Obedience: From Faithful Reading to Faithful Living* draws upon the work of Winnicott and Pruyser. Brueggemann states that faithfulness is neither autonomous, autistic, and thus disobedient, nor realistic and no longer an interpretive act. Rather, he too locates ministry in the illusionistic or transitional space:

> The locus of the church's ministry in the United States is a situation in which the third world of illusional processing is denied, rejected and dismissed. Faithful ministry is to engage people in that imaginative process which is largely resisted but upon which hangs our future as a viable society.[15]

As a leader in the church of Christ, you are called to be a missional presence, bringing the good news of Jesus Christ to all people. Living in the illusionistic world, however, is risky—even too risky for some. "Some of us," Brueggemann writes, would rather "have a propensity for the 'real world' of 'truth,' imagining that we know and wanting simply to announce it." Others "have a propensity for grace that comes too cheaply, because we know how much hurt there has been and we want to reassure." In congregations where life has become predominantly programmatic, living in the illusionistic world is both difficult and brave. Here, creativity can be smothered by what is expected. The third world of the imagination, however, is determined not by what is expected, but by symbols, narratives, playfulness, and entering deeply into people's lives.

Being a presence in people's pain ends the moment we refuse to enter into the murky waters of spiritual and emotional pain or when we give advice and, in a moment of narcissistic grandiosity, believe that our words can fix. Rather, when we understand the "playful freedom we call God's holiness," we invite people into "the third world of imagination" where people can be re-imagined because God keeps imagining us.

How are you aware that you oscillate between the realistic world and the autistic world? How do you consciously seek out ways to enter into the third world of prophetic imagination? When do you enter the autistic world? Where do you see yourself and your ministry four years from now if you can enter and invite others into this third world of prophetic imagination?

CULTIVATE YOUR CAPACITY TO IMAGINE

Grace is about being created with the capacity to imagine. *But how does one go about achieving this capacity if life itself never bestowed you with the capacity to be imaginative?* Merely reading this chapter will not make you more imaginative, even if it stimulated your imagination at times. Cultivate your imagination and participate in the transformation God is working in you. Do so by using a few of the many entrances to the transitional space, the only location of the imagination. Examining your relationship with God, establishing relationships that can speak into your life, engaging in mindful activities, studying Scripture, and strengthening your prayer life (GRASP) can assist you in practicing ways of actively nurturing your imagination.

Examine Your Covenant with God

You have a covenant with God that speaks of your capacity to imagine. As we saw in the previous chapter, each covenant has roots that lie in our family of origin. Our roots are communicated in a life prayer rarely verbalized, which also indicates our unforgivable sin. These elements become the building blocks of our covenant with God. Reflect on the silent and overt communication you received from your family regarding living creatively, about not always honoring the reality principle or not withdrawing into personal isolation.

Pastor Timothy, whom we met in chapter 1, identifies his roots regarding the capacity to imagine as: "During the divorce of my parents, I retreated into my own world, spending much time first playing by myself and then reading on my own. It was a safe place. Here I followed my father, whom I never saw angry, for he became silent long before any anger might set in." Pastor Timothy's life prayer is: "Dear God, please allow me to retreat into my own safe world or grant me freedom in the realistic world." His unforgivable sin would be "to stay in my own safe world and not engage the world out there." Pastor Timothy's covenant with God is: "Dear God, I will be your child if I remain realistic and not retreat into my own imaginative world."

Thinking about the capacity to imagine as the ability to live in an in-between world:

1. What are your roots?
2. What is your silent prayer?
3. What is your unforgivable sin?
4. What is your covenant with God?
5. What are the implications for your life, your ministry, and your relationship with God?
6. Take your findings in prayer to God and in conversation to a trusted mentor or friend.

Relationships

Created in the image of God, we are formed and transformed in relationships. Therefore:

- Engage in conversation, and possibly enter into a relationship with someone for whom creative living is more important than doing well.

- Ask someone who regularly engages the transitional space (an artist, a writer, a poet, a musician) how they manage living between inner-subjectivity and outer-objectivity.

Action

Read an author whose imagination and creative living can inform your imagination. Any poetry book, novel, or short story would be good. *What do you learn about the author's imagination? In what ways is your imagination informed? What are you learning about becoming a pastor?* In addition, I can recommend the following books:

- Walter Brueggemann. *Interpretation and Obedience: From Faithful Reading to Faithful Living.* Minneapolis: Fortress Press, 1991.
- Julia Cameron. *The Artist's Way: A Spiritual Path to Higher Creativity.* New York: J.P. Tarcher/Putnam, 2002.
- Donald Capps. *The Poet's Gift: Toward the Renewal of Pastoral Care.* Minneapolis: Fortress Press, 1993.
- Edwin Friedman. *Friedman's Fables.* New York: Guilford Publications, 1990.

Observe people's tendency to engage only the objective world or see them retreat in silent withdrawal.

Create and engage the creativity of others by bringing something into existence:

- Paint, do pottery, sculpt, or write (a reflection, a poem or a haiku, a short story, a sermon, a prayer).
- Visit any gallery. *How are you "pulled in" by the paintings or other pieces of art? Why does some art "speak" to you more than others? What is happening between you and a specific art object?*
- Watch a film/movie. Be guided by the movie reviewer in your local newspaper or by an acquaintance as to what movie might be a good one to watch. *What is the message the director or producer wanted to communicate to you? How is your knowledge of human nature enriched? What emotions in the film do you recognize and which ones resonate with yours? How does the film address issues of peace, justice, reconciliation, healing? Where do you see God in the movie? What aspects of yourself do you discover in the characters on the screen?*

- Listen to music. Use some of the preceding questions to guide your reflection on the music.

- Enroll in an art class or similar activity. Find resources that will assist you in living creatively (an art course, a dance class, voice lessons, pottery, knitting classes, writing something creative, taking photographs, playing a musical instrument, drumming with others, etc.).

- Cook a meal and invite friends or possibly even a stranger to the dinner. Be surprised by the person and the taste and smell of the food.

- Tidy up boxes and drawers, taking out what is not needed and putting away neatly what should be kept. Or rearrange furniture in your home.

- Prepare your next sermon with enough time in hand to share it with a few members in your congregation before you preach it on Sunday. Allow their comments, ideas, and creativity to inform yours. Rewrite your sermon. One pastor meets with ten to fifteen parishioners every Wednesday morning. He shares his general thoughts and Scripture references; they in turn share insights and life experiences and make other suggestions. All agree that these meetings strengthen and enliven the pastor's sermons and each participant's spirituality.

- Journal: Write down your own creative ideas or the moments where your imagination was stimulated by someone else's.

Scripture

Discover the prophetic imagination in the Book of Joel:

- Name the locusts that are ravaging your personal life, your ministry, the life of your congregation, your community (Joel 1:1–15).

- What does "return[ing] to the Lord" look like for you (Joel 2:12–14)?

- How is God already repaying you and your congregation for the damage the locusts caused (Joel 2:25–27)?

- How is God pouring God's Spirit out over you and the congregation? What prophesies are being given? What dreams are being dreamt? What visions are received (Joel 2:28–30)?

- Notice how a flowing river that nourishes is a central image in Scripture (Gen. 2:10; Ps. 46:4–6; Joel 3:18; Rev. 22:1). Imagine a river that is flowing forth from your inner space (or your congregation). How would you describe the quality of this water? Is it life-giving or brackish and unable to nourish life? What ministries or acts of love are "water" to a dry valley around you? Who is represented as a dry valley?

Prayer

Margaret Guenther, a spiritual director, reminds us that in an acquisitive, competitive, and consumerist culture, the ability to pray becomes a skill to be mastered and one more thing to do, rather than a way of being.[16] I invite you to talk with God numerous times during the day: when you are in silent contemplation; when you study Scripture; when you are driving to engage in ministry; when you exercise; when you wait at the checkout line in the grocery store. Prayer invites us into a reality, a kingdom that is coming, visible now only through faith's imagination. Pray the most imaginative prayer in Scripture (Matt. 6:9–13) as if for the first time:

> *Our Father who art in heaven, hallowed be your name.*
> *Your kingdom come, your will be done*
> *On earth, as it is in heaven.*
> *Give us this day our daily bread.*
> *And forgive us our debts, as we forgive our debtors.*
> *And lead us not into temptation, but deliver us from evil:*
> *For yours are the kingdom, the power, and the glory, for ever. Amen.*

CONCLUSION

A few years ago I was invited to speak to a congregation. I informed them that my topic would be "Living in the Third World." When I got to the building on that Sunday, it was decorated with an African theme. The leaders, who knew that I was born in South Africa, thought the talk would be about what it was like growing up in an Apartheid society. I in turn, was prepared to talk about the third world of creative imagination! That day I discovered that I need to be clear about living in the third world of imagination as living in the transitional space. I also discovered that some people would rather hear about a country on another continent and in another time, rather than be confronted with their own life and how they engage creative living.

Craig Dykstra, vice president for religion at the Lilly Endowment Inc., has identified "pastoral imagination" as "something very special — a kind of internal gyroscope and a distinctive kind of intelligence" that "good ministers" possess.[17] Similar to artistic imagination in that it can create and cultivate, pastoral imagination is an ever-present hermeneutic that speaks into knowledge of self and other, of systems and knowledge of God's grace. Dykstra recalls numerous ministers and theologians, "extraordinary people," who shaped, taught, cared for, helped, and befriended him. They, as many other pastors who sustain effective ministries over many years, all share one common trait, "an imagination, a way of seeing into and interpreting the world which shapes everything a pastor thinks and does."

For Dykstra, adding "pastoral" to imagination takes the capacity to imagine into new realms since pastoral ministry requires specific capacities of mind, spirit, and action. Pastoral imagination is akin to the imagination of "the legal mind" and to "artistic imagination" in that it perceives, understands, and engages the world in a specific way. Pastoral imagination differs from artistic imagination, for example, in its depth and breadth of engagement. Ministry demands complex, substantive knowledge of persons and systems, of call and culture, of theory and theology, of experience and history, and of what is and what is coming. Only pastoral imagination as an imagination that can enter the transitional sphere can span all these realities.

Dykstra concludes his reflection on pastoral imagination when he states that

> There is, I think, operating in the everyday work of our best ministers an amazing intelligence peculiar to the pastoral vocation that imbues their every thought and action. Such an intelligence has certainly been characteristic of all the really good ministers it has been my privilege to know, and the ways they have employed their pastoral imaginations has made a real difference in their congregations, in their communities, and in the lives of all to whom they have ministered.

It is your pastoral imagination that allows you to enter painful situations with compassion rather than an urge to fix. And that creates a worship experience that invites others into the transitional space where renewal, transformation, and creative living become a possibility. With imagination you need not fear the constant adaptation required of life and ministry. Without imagination, you cannot engage questions first raised by Dietrich Bonhoeffer, who said that "people as they are now simply cannot be religious anymore . . ." Bonhoeffer asks: "*How do we speak about God—without religion . . . ? How do we speak in a secular way about God . . . ? In what way are we religionless-secular Christians, in what way are we ek-klesia, those called forth . . . belonging wholly to the world?*"[18]

Becoming a pastor and living creatively, as the poet Emily Dickinson reminds us, is the slow process of discovering the miracle before you and the miracle behind you:

> 'Tis Miracle before Me—then—
> 'Tis Miracle behind—between—
> A Crescent in the Sea—
> With Midnight to the North of Her—
> And Midnight to the South of Her—
> And Maelstrom—in the Sky—[19]

What miracles surprised you in the past? What miracles need to happen? Where can you see God's reality breaking into your world? Winnicott said: "Happy is [the person] who is being creative all the time in personal life as well as through life partners, children, friends, etc."[20] Blessed indeed, is the one engaging the transitional space.

three

THE CAPACITY FOR CONCERN

Concern refers to the fact that the individual cares
or minds and both feels and accepts responsibility.

—D. W. Winnicott, "The Development of the Capacity for Concern"

My expressive, loving family practiced denial.
It forbade anger, ignored sorrow, and created a culture
of silence about hard things. . . . Some of us lost great
chunks of ourselves along the way.

—Kathleen O'Connor, *Lamentations and the Tears of the World*

I've been unfair and unkind,
Turned away from your suffering far too many times . . .

—Patty Griffin, "Standing"

To become a pastor is to recognize and contain one's own destructive tendencies. It requires the ability to look at one's own life and repair the broken lives and relationships one sees there. It is to care enough about others that you can imagine how they experience your dark side. Isn't it ironic that we, leaders in the body of Christ, have to protect those we lead from ourselves, even as we protect the body of Christ from devouring itself? Being mindful of your destructiveness and engaging in acts of reparation and restitution requires not only an imaginative mind, but also a secure enough self to enter deep into your own dark side.

Such mindfulness or concern addresses the integration of *love*—representing all constructive impulses—and *hate*—representing all destructive desires—into one's being. I use hate to describe a wide range of behaviors, some healthy and others gross violations. As pastors our hate can range from healthy boundary setting—saying no when others want you to say yes—to mild annoyance or frustration and flaming white anger or significant boundary violations. Some might say that "hate" is a politically incorrect word to use in a world where hate crimes are far too prevalent. Or that the word "love" has become so insipid that it is meaningless. I want to redeem and reframe these words, however, so that love and hate can be acknowledged as central to who we are as persons and as leaders in God's church.

The capacity for concern describes your ability to feel and own your ruthlessness and your lack of compassion and it anticipates reparation and restitution of lives and relationships. This ability is greatly determined by the holding environment that received you (chapter 1). Many of us in leadership experienced the destructiveness of others—possibly even the aggression of parents or other caregivers—and acts of reparation never came. We learned early that our brokenness is best protected by our own ruthlessness and lack of compassion. But even before we experienced others' destructiveness, we, as children, portrayed much aggressiveness. Young children will, in a state of excitement, bite, hit, pull hair, and hurt someone, seemingly without the other person provoking the child or the child being aware that the other person is being hurt. Some of us never grew past this point of early aggression.

Concern-as-reparation is true soul care and without it one can hardly envision ministry. Achieving concern is one way to live into the Apostle Paul's urging to engage in a "ministry of reconciliation" (2 Cor. 5:18). The need to have a ministry where the holistic reparation of lives is a goal makes pastoral ministry one of the most difficult vocations imaginable. Without first integrating the love and hate in your own person, those you serve will experience you as ruthless and aloof, emotionally disconnected from your own issues and from their problems. Some of us will frequently find ourselves entangled in intense conflictual relationships or we might catch ourselves doing the emotional and spiritual work for others. Worse yet, without the integration of love and hate in our persons, we put others at risk of becoming innocent victims of our unbecoming behaviors and attitudes. Certainly, without the integration of love and hate in your own person, you will not assist those in the body of Christ to love their enemies.

I am reminded that anger and aggression stem from the Latin *aggressere*, meaning "to approach." Aggression, as pastoral theologian Kathleen Greider reminds us, speaks of energy and agency, of vigor and enterprise, of boldness and resilience.[1] Aggression takes us into ourselves and towards others and anticipates concern as acts of reparation. The picture I paint of ministry suggests that the capacity for concern is not a philosophical reflection on love, hate, and destructiveness. Furthermore, it does not have only extreme situations of misconduct in mind, even if such situations do make the headlines of our newspapers. One's aggressiveness is seen in concrete behaviors such as declining a seemingly appropriate request; in leaving a family while they are still anxious; in initiating painful conversations as a family anticipates the death of a loved one; in telling people you are their pastor, thereby indicating that you cannot be their friend. Of course, one's love for those you serve is seen in the very same acts!

In this chapter I am moving beyond the "destructiveness-is-a-sin" tradition, the inevitable result of valuing thoughts more than feelings in a disembodied life. I am not envisioning an end goal of being free from destructiveness—anger, for example—for that would not be possible. Rather, I am asking you to get to know your own ruthlessness and to welcome it as your intimate enemy. The more you engage this stranger-that-is-you, the less likely it is that your dark side will become destructive towards yourself and others and the more likely it is that you will engage in acts of reparation and restitution.

Think of a recent moment where you first became angry and then withdrew in silence, possibly with a loud inner dialogue. Meditating on Scripture, say Ephesians 4 and its urging of us to remove all bitterness and anger, might be helpful. It will show you your sinful behavior, but might not help you repair the relationship with the person in mind. Rather, such a meditation can repress deep emotions, allowing them to surface at a later stage, probably towards someone you love: a partner, spouse, your children, or the nameless person who is driving so irresponsibly. Maybe the resentment only slithers deep within you and eats away at you, so that you have to feed the hole left by the resentment with food and drink and sexual images.

As in the previous chapters, I am encouraging you to listen back into your past and look deep into your present. Envision being a different kind of person, which will make you a different kind of leader. I am asking you to rediscover some of the scars on your heart, left there by words that wounded and someone else's ruthless destructiveness. Inevitably, you will recall what pastoral theologian Christie Neuger calls "narratives of harm," those stories most of us can tell where we were hurt by others.[2] First, I identify a pastoral leader who lacks the capacity for concern and will also give some of the reasons why it is difficult for us to talk about love and hate. I then will discuss the capacity for concern as the ability to accept responsibility for your own destructiveness and to engage in acts of reparation. Overfunctioning is identified as a form of destructiveness many pastoral leaders carry. We look at shame as a form of hate received from someone where reparation remained absent. The chapter concludes with providing suggestions for how to cultivate and nurture your capacity for concern.

THE UNBECOMING LEADER

When you lack the capacity for concern, it speaks powerfully into your ministry. You will be reactive to what is happening around you and rarely engage in proactive ministry. Furthermore, your effectiveness in ministry will be minimized as you constantly do the personal work of others or of the body of Christ. You may burn out or "flame up" in a scandal, leaving ministry in shame as your destructiveness is exposed to the world. The unbecoming leader:

- Disowns or denies his or her destructiveness only to show anger and aggression periodically in violent volcanic-like moments of weakness or inward withdrawal
- Portrays poor self-care (or is destructive to one's body)
- Disciplines others by shaming them
- Is passive aggressive, portraying hostile actions that are not obviously destructive, such as being late, using the thoughts and ideas of others without recognition, and not addressing conflict in the congregation
- Has a diminished sense of his or her sinfulness
- Never addresses the pervasiveness of personal, familial, interpersonal, and societal violence (issues of gender, race, power, poverty, injustice, and oppression)

- Reacts to the destructiveness of others or in life by rationalizing and giving answers, by becoming punitive, by moralistically quoting Scripture, or by resorting to verbal and even physical retaliation
- Overfunctions, that is, does the emotional, spiritual, and relational work of others
- Rarely encourages difficult and even painful conversations with individuals and families
- Cannot make constructive use of destructive powers
- Allows temptations to escalate into sinful behavior

Most of us can recognize ourselves somewhere in this picture. *What behaviors and attitudes are most prevalent in your life and ministry? How do you think these behaviors and attitudes affect your interpersonal relationships? How do they influence your relationship with God? Who taught you these behaviors and attitudes as ways to respond? How are these attitudes and behaviors impacting a ministry of reconciliation?* For some of us, admitting our destructive potential is the first step toward achieving the capacity for concern.

CAN YOU ADMIT YOUR RUTHLESSNESS?

Owning your own destructiveness as a fundamental part of who you are might be one of the most difficult achievements in life. Few of our families empowered and taught us how to express our emotions. Most probably, your family in some way told you to filter your emotions and to be "nice." Therefore, admitting your destructiveness asks of you to emotionally and relationally "betray'" your family. In the words of the singer-songwriter Marc Cohn, you have to admit that you were handed things "that you'd gladly sell or trade."[3] You already know that betrayal of parents is a taboo God despises (Exod. 20; Matt. 5). Kathleen O'Connor, quoted at the beginning of this chapter, recognizes how ill-prepared she is to express deep emotion and to engage deep emotions of others when she writes:

> My expressive, loving family practiced denial. It forbade anger, ignored sorrow, and created a culture of silence about hard things. From generation to generation, we practiced denial: we looked on the bright side, walked on the sunny side, and remembered that tomorrow is another day. . . . [A]nger lurked but

could not speak. . . . Some of us lost great chunks of ourselves along the way.[4]

How difficult it is to imagine that our families gifted us with traits and skills we use effectively in our ministries even as they handed us qualities that render us a mere presence to ourselves and others as we continue to support cultures of silence. *What kind of denial did your family practice? How was anger and sorrow expressed? What part of you do you have to reclaim as you become a pastoral leader?* The capacity for concern, envisioning us as compassionate persons with the ability to engage in acts of spiritual, emotional, and relational reparation, is truly an achievement.

Additional reasons that make owning our destructiveness difficult are theological and spiritual. Most of us can quote a Proverb stating that only foolish persons become angry (Prov. 14:17, 29; Eccl. 7:9); we remember Jesus telling us in the Sermon on the Mount that an angry person will be judged (Matt. 5:21); or we refer to the Apostle Paul urging us not to sin in our anger (Eph. 4:26). Andy Lester, in a book I offer as suggested reading later in this chapter, reflects on verses like these and concludes that "the dominant belief about anger in the Christian tradition is that all anger is sinful and evil, leading to estrangement from God. This anger-is-sin tradition declares that anger was not present in humans at creation, but has its roots in the original sin of pride and disobedience that set us over against God."[5]

Lester challenges this tradition, encouraging us to see anger as a normal human emotion caused by the way our brains function and the different ways we experience our environments. He reminds us that love and anger are not opposites, but that "in many situations anger is the most loving and therefore, the most Christian response"[6] Lester encourages us to understand familiar texts anew:

Rather than squelching anger, I suggest the commandment to "love your neighbor as yourself" should often motivate us to be angry. For Christians, a faithful response when our deeply held beliefs—central to our integrity and moral commitments—are contradicted or transgressed is to be threatened and feel angry. Anger can be the logical and ethical requirement of loving others as God loves us.[7]

We become angry *because* we love, not *in contradiction* thereof. Anger is in the service of love and does not oppose love. Anger motivated by deeply held Christian beliefs, however, is far removed from the reactive interpersonal anger that most of us know so well and other forms of destructiveness that this chapter addresses. However, the Christian faith wants to help us reclaim our humanity in the presence of our Creator. It does not seek our dehumanization by asking us to deny a core aspect of who we are. Honoring your father, mother, pastors, and teachers, then, is not keeping silent and honoring denial, but rather achieving the capacity for concern and reclaiming the parts of your self that got lost along the way.

How do you view anger and aggression in general and yours in particular? When and how does your aggression and destructiveness show? How do you typically feel and react after your destructiveness surprised you and others? How can you envision yourself moving beyond the anger-is-sin tradition?

Recent works by Lester, Kathleen Greider, and David Augsburger not only argue strongly against the anger-is-sin tradition, but also for a theology of anger and hate.[8] Looking at neuroscience and different psychologies and sociologies, and through thoughtful interpretation of Scripture, these authors can help you gain a broader understanding of how we as Christians should think about anger, aggression, violence, and the many ways of hating we carry. They also engage in exegetical discussion of the commonly used texts that prohibit anger, showing that the Bible sees anger as a basic human emotion, and that we have to make an ethical assessment on the basis of *why* the anger occurred and *how* the anger was expressed. Anger can only be understood in context, ours and the specific verse. Lester, for example, shows how the same word used to describe Jesus's anger at the Pharisees in Mark 3:5 (the Greek word *orgé*) is the same word used to describe the selfish anger of the older brother in the prodigal son story (Luke 15:28)[9]. We need to discern the Scriptural contexts to understand how the Bible views anger.

How does your scriptural understanding of sin and anger prohibit or assist you in consciously engaging your own destructiveness? How do you think God views the various forms destructiveness takes? How do anger, violence, and justice relate to each other in your own faith? What would constructive anger look like for you and your community? Because of family, spiritual, religious, and societal taboos, admitting and especially consciously engaging your destructiveness is a true achievement!

RANK YOURSELF

I assume that for most of us consciously engaging our destructiveness is a difficult task, rarely modeled to us. Imagine a sliding scale in the form of an upright ladder. On this scale the bottom rung indicates zero, that is, relationships that are strained and even ruptured due to anger and hostility or the inability to repair relationships. Zero indicates a withdrawal into silence or an outburst of aggression that stops a conversation or brings an emotional break in a relationship. It leaves you and the other person where spiritual, emotional, and relational growth is impossible. The top of the ladder, ten, conversely, symbolizes the integration of love and hate in your person and the ability to repair a relationship between you and someone else. (Ten recognizes that you cannot control another person's choice to withdraw from you even as you attempt to repair the relationship.)

Recall a recent experience with a loved one or someone else where you became very angry or significant tension entered the relationship. *Where on this scale do you place yourself, being mindful of your emotions and reactions during the experience? What do you have to do to move up just* one *step on this ladder, that is, grow towards an integration of love and hate in your person? If you move from a four to a five, for example, how will you respond differently in a similar situation?*

Pastor Timothy recalled a conversation with an elder who "suggested" that "I am not a good pastor, for I am not visiting all the shut-ins." The conversation ended rather abruptly when Timothy responded: "I need to work harder at getting to all the folks." Timothy, however, left furious and promptly went home where he got into an argument with his wife. He caught himself avoiding the elder the next two weeks. On the scale above, Pastor Timothy places himself at a three. He could see himself going to a four if he calls the person who functions as his mentor and discusses what happened with him, so that his wife does not have to receive his anger. Or, he can say to the elder, "You know, not reaching every person is a concern I too have. Will you take a look with me at all my responsibilities and help me prioritize them in light of my job description? There might be expectations for ministry even I carry that are not humanly possible."

Growing towards the integration of our constructive and destructive capacities is important, for if we are not mindful, we become a person shaped by our destructiveness. Frederick Buechner describes such a person in provocative terms:

Of the Seven Deadly Sins, anger is probably the most fun. To lick your wounds, to smack your lips over grievances long past, to roll over your tongue the prospect of bitter confrontations still to come, to savor to the last toothsome morsel both the pain you are given and the pain you are giving back—in many ways is a feast fit for a king. The chief drawback is that what you are wolfing down is yourself. The skeleton at the feast is you.[10]

Buechner reintroduces us to the gluttonous false self and to the kings of Israel and Syria we met in the previous chapter (2 Kings 6). Our gluttonous self carries an insatiable hunger; the monarch in us wants to destroy.

THE CAPACITY FOR CONCERN

Earlier, I defined the capacity for concern as *the ability to feel and own your ruthlessness, that is, your aggressiveness and lack of compassion, and to engage in acts of reparation and restitution where broken or strained lives and relationships are mended.* This definition and the title of the chapter come from Donald Winnicott, who wrote an essay entitled "The Development of the Capacity for Concern" in 1963.[11] Winnicott experienced the power of the reparative act, the central dynamic in the capacity for concern, when, at the age of three, he demolished the wax face of one of his sister's dolls. His dad warmed the wax and reshaped the face. For Winnicott, this 1963 essay was the culmination of a number of essays on the roots of human aggression and destructiveness as healthy maturational processes. Winnicott writes that concern implies integration and growth, especially in respect to relationships into which one's destructiveness has entered. Normally, Winnicott argues, a person feels guilty when he or she has been destructive, a feeling most often only discovered retrospectively or observed by others. Associating guilt feelings with anxiety that erodes a sense of feeling alive, Winnicott describes the guilt feelings young children feel when they hurt someone they love. Thus, Winnicott believes that when you hurt someone you love, guilt feelings set in that can be removed when you repair the damage. Of course, one can also just passively wait for the guilt feelings to dissipate.

Winnicott's paper on concern reflects close observation of children and adults and describes behavior and attitudes you have most probably experienced:

- A mother complains to you that her newborn is biting her breast, making breast-feeding very painful. She feels like a "bad" mother for sometimes resenting a feeding session and other times not wanting to engage her child. Her infant, of course, is oblivious to the hurt he is causing his mother.

- You hold a six-month-old infant who pulls your hair or grabs your nose or glasses. Your eyes tear up from the jolt of pain, but you coo with the infant, who is enjoying this experience.

- A toddler, who transgressed the rules of the home by pressing the television's buttons or by drawing on a wall, comes to you and suddenly gives you a hug or expresses her love to you.

- You ask the four-year-old to apologize for hurting his younger brother. He vehemently refuses and locks his lips, but his whole body says "I'm sorry."

- A teenager responds to the destructiveness that entered her parent's marriage by getting herself into trouble with the law and cutting her wrists and arms with broken glass.

- You are at odds with your partner or spouse. You know that you have to talk things over but find yourself withdrawing in silence as you entertain angry thoughts and rehearse the conversation that never takes place.

All of these experiences speak to various achievements of the capacity for concern, that awareness of hurt caused and a desire to repair the break in a relationship caused by someone's ruthlessness. As such, the capacity for concern is an *innate* sense of morality we carry when we realize that our "me-world" engaged the "not-me world" in a hurtful manner or that we received someone else's destructiveness. In both circumstances, reparation of the "damage" caused is needed. Concern is not possible without the realization that we cannot control others in our omnipotence and as such is an integral part of settling on a sense of self. Ironically, we discover the other person through our destructiveness!

Winnicott was adamant that, if an *external* sense of morality is forced upon a child too soon in an attempt to control or even break the child's willful ruthlessness, it can come at the cost of the capacity for concern. Most persons, however, have an *internal* sense of morality as the capacity for concern developed to some extent.[12] They experienced a holding environment early in life that survived their primary destructiveness and ruthlessness. With aggression being an integral part of play activity, mother or father or a caretaker tolerates the child's ruthlessness, even if being jumped upon really does hurt and wears one out. The ruthlessness of the child is not forced to go into hiding where it is kept in place by a compliant false self. When the ruthless fantasies and behavior of a child cannot be held by his or her caretakers or by society, or when acts of reparation remain unacknowledged, despair sets in and the child uses destructive behaviors to force someone or society to acknowledge his or her significance. When our primary caretakers cannot hold our early destructiveness, our dark side is awakened.

Around loving and hating, central to our relational lives and essential to feeling alive, Winnicott identified a "benign circle" or pattern that plays out between an infant and a mother or caretaker. This pattern carries the potential for much destructiveness and continues into adult life: 1) A relationship is complicated by love and hate being present at the same time. 2) A conscious awareness of this tension is formed: "I am hurting the person I love (or someone else)." 3) An internal sense of guilt sets in as the infant struggles with the ambivalence such an awareness brings. 4) The capacity to give and to restore develops as the infant works through the guilt feelings. 5) Reparation of the hurt and reparation of the relationship with mother takes place if the reparation is accepted.

Without the capacity for concern, one cannot fully engage another person. Every time you have experienced being "nice" to someone with whom you were very angry, when you continue a conversation through conflict, or if someone who criticized you offers an unexpected compliment, this pattern repeats itself. The capacity for concern becomes a dance we learn early in life that teaches us to love and extend restitution. "Over and over again in the ordinary infant-mother relationship," Winnicott writes, "this hurting-made-good takes place, and gradually the infant comes to believe in constructive effort, and to be able to bear guilt and so to be free to love instinctually."[13]

As expected, this pattern repeats itself in our relationship with God. Every time we confess our sinfulness, we admit our ruthlessness in the form of violating boundaries of loving self and neighbor set by God. The paradox within confession is that we repair our relationship with God even as God repairs the relationship. God accepts our confession as an act of reparation and we are restored and freed to live anew. Long before

God holds our ruthless transgression of God's law, however, we had a caretaker who held our destructiveness without retaliation.

The capacity for concern thus calls forth "spontaneous gestures," those acts of reparation that say "I hated you but also love you and I know that I hurt you." From a sense of guilt comes a constructive act. Young children, no doubt you have discovered, are much better at these spontaneous gestures than adults. It seems that the older we become, the less ability we have to repair our broken or strained relationships. Spontaneous gestures, which are an integral part of relational life, require the awareness that you can impact persons and nature in hurtful and harmful ways. The ease by which we enter into war and conflict and the way we deny our destructive impact on nature and the atmosphere are sad statements about us being concerned selves. Yet, our capacity to repair is just as vast as our capacity to destroy.

Engaging in acts of reparation is the sign of a mature person and that "personality-building" has taken place. "This involves," Winnicott writes, "becoming more and more able to acknowledge one's own cruelty and greed, which can then, and only then, be harnessed to sublimated activity."[14] The cost of losing our destructiveness is our humanness, the very image of God we are. For we believe in a God who wanted to destroy Israel, was it not for Moses's interceding (Exod. 32:9–11); a God who showed remorse for having destroyed people and the earth through water (Gen. 6:11–13; 9:7–17); and a God who sacrificed and resurrected a Son so that we might not perish, but have eternal life (John 3:16). We are made in the image of this God! One can thus say that we become more human when we recognize our destructiveness and when we engage in acts of reparation. All acts of reparation, whether only in your mind or a concrete act, change the nature and quality of your relationships. As a religious leader, many acts of reparation are asked of you, such as:

- Acknowledging your aggression or intention to become destructive
- Repairing broken relationships with others, especially with other pastoral leaders in the congregation
- Recognizing that what you despise in the other person is alive in you
- Extending a warm smile in a "cold" relationship
- Discovering or protecting the humanity of someone

- Affirming someone for who they are
- Feeling deep compassion
- Expressing empathy
- Extending an appropriate and caring touch
- Loving another person
- Receiving love, care, or a compliment
- Helping another person discover his or her ruthlessness
- Assisting others to repair their relationships with you
- Resisting the desire to steal, to enter into inappropriate relationships, or to visit a pornographic web site.

Recognizing your own destructiveness and engaging in acts of reparation takes courage. Sometimes acts of reparation take place in one's mind, but most often they are concrete acts. *Where and to whom are you currently destructive? What boundary violations, ranging from sexual misconduct to financial mismanagement and plagiarism, are tempting at this moment? What relationships are strained at this time and in need of an act of reparation?* Situations like these create much pressure where the creative reparative response becomes far from simple and even elusive.

When we do not achieve the capacity for concern, Winnicott believes we never risk being excited and we find that our souls can never reach a "state of quiet." We live a life where self-soothing, symbolizing, playing, and the capacity to be alone (see the next chapter) is impossible. Without the ability to repair and offer restitution, we can only risk living as false selves, always compliant to the outside world while inwardly denying our destructiveness. We then live as persons who are not whole, for whole persons love and hate and repair.

Mature leaders are not only able to acknowledge their personal destructiveness, but can tolerate it, that is, hold it in suspension. Suspending one's ruthlessness means you have a moment of hesitation before you act. It is the hesitation of an infant who holds a spoon, assessing whether it can be mouthed. This moment of hesitation is that moment before an object becomes alive with experience, a subject; it is a moment requiring mindfulness about your own feelings, thoughts, and behaviors. *What kind of leader am I if I remain in a state of ruthlessness? What is the nature of the holding environment that created me? How can I become aware that my destructiveness hurts others? When does my "I speak the truth in love" leadership style reflect the capacity for concern and when does it hide my destructiveness behind pious words? What acts of reparation and restitution did I offer someone recently? Where did I receive such acts? How will others, especially those closest to me, know that I am working towards achieving the capacity for concern?*

You can grow into a person who can remain emotionally available to others, rather than experiencing an incapacitating degree of guilt feelings, envy, competition, rivalry, hurt, aggression, and withdrawal. This person can survive the everyday failures and relational aggressiveness that are part of everyday life.

THE VIOLENCE IN OVERFUNCTIONING

Most of our destructiveness does not make the newspaper headlines. Yet many persons experience our destructiveness firsthand. Overfunctioning is one of the most destructive and violent acts in which we religious leaders engage. Overfunctioning is a way of managing personal and often unconscious anxiety by getting involved in the emotional, relational, and spiritual lives of others. An overfunctioner does the spiritual, emotional, and relational work of others as *doing ministry* overrides *being a facilitative presence.* Overfunctioning becomes an act of violence because the other person or group is denied the opportunity for growth and new learning. It is especially destructive to the body of Christ, for overfunctioning assures that the body of Christ will never function as one body with many members as suggested in Romans 12.

The irony is that when we as leaders become violent in our overfunctioning, the people we serve might respond with appreciation. Some people, however, will indicate that your presence is too much. A family is facing the death of their matriarch. Family members traveled great distances "to be there for her." Pastor Natalie is spending long days at the hospital. She has moved into the role of being the liaison person for the family as they negotiate with the medical staff and the hospital. Pastor Natalie is not aware that she repeats a way of being in relationship, being the mediator, she first learned in her family of origin. Not once has she facilitated a conversation with the family as to what it means for them that their beloved "Gran" is dying. She has not asked "Gran," who at times is lucid, how she is moving towards death or whether she is concerned about the family she is leaving behind. She did invite some remembering from a few family members while they drank coffee, but did not invite the family members to share their memories *with* Gran. Pastor Natalie knows that there are tensions between different members and does not want to escalate the tension that is already present. The family responds with gratitude, asking incessantly whether she can place everything on hold to be "present" with them.

Deacon Pete, another overfunctioner, was called in to assist a family who had "financial concerns." He visited with them, gathered all their invoices, and left. Later, he returned with a plan whereby the family would be out of debt in three years, while still having some money left to spend on whatever they want each month. He also gave them a check from the church that would cover their overdue heating bill. The family responded with gratitude that hid their shame. However, the family still cannot say how they ended in the position they are in; they cannot draft a monthly budget and seem unable to prioritize their expenses. They learned nothing through Deacon Pete's involvement and discovered little about themselves or about God. As you can imagine, acts of aggressive overfunctioning take on many diverse forms, most of them rarely recognized, examined, and addressed. Overfunctioners typically:

- Know what is best not only for themselves, but for others as well
- Move quickly to advise, fix, rescue, and take over when stress and anxiety manifests in a system
- Worry about other people
- Feel responsible for others
- Have difficulty staying out of and allowing others to struggle with their problems (in other words, they become uncomfortable seeing others struggle)
- Do the spiritual, emotional, and relational work for others when they can be empowered to do that work themselves
- Have goals for others they do not have for themselves
- Have difficulty sharing their vulnerable (or underfunctioning) side, especially with those they believe have problems
- May be labeled as people who are "always reliable" or "always together"
- Talk more than listen
- Probably took on responsibilities as a child that were meant for someone emotionally much older[15]

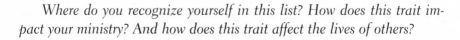

Where do you recognize yourself in this list? How does this trait impact your ministry? And how does this trait affect the lives of others?

THE TRAUMA OF SHAME

A journey into our destructiveness inevitably leads us to our own shame. Shame is the painful feeling of being exposed, being made vulnerable, being uncovered and left unprotected, of being naked and being looked at by others. *Shame is the result of experiencing the ruthlessness of someone, and the act of reparation never came.* Persons who lack the capacity for concern induce shame, often without even recognizing the hurt they cause. Shame-related experiences are described in terms of being embarrassed, being humiliated or disgraced, feeling inadequate. We describe it in terms of shyness, "of losing face," modesty, ridicule, honor and dishonor, and to be made weak by someone stronger. We cannot maintain eye contact and we look down or to the side. Shame triggers bodily responses we cannot control such as blushing, sweating, an increased heart rate, and shortness of breath. Many of us in leadership feel inadequate after many shaming experiences and we protect ourselves against this feeling in various ways: depressiveness; arrogance; aloofness; lack of self-confidence; a "loud" voice; alienation and isolation; living a "heady," normotic life; competitiveness and exploitative power; or having a righteous attitude (or a moral defense) that assigns guilt to others.

Shame is a dynamic that keeps us from flourishing in ministry and is often a source of our destructiveness. I remember the pastor who told me: "Most often I feel as if there is something fundamentally wrong with me. I am a fraud about to be found out." He lived with a felt sense of *being* a mistake. As a song goes: "And God said the reason had hung from the tree, but I feel the reason hanging on me . . ."[16] As theologians we are stumped by shame, for shame experiences cannot be healed by atonement theories and we cannot merely pray it away.

Dietrich Bonhoeffer, the German theologian-pastor who gave us the statement "When Christ calls you, he calls you to die!" was twenty-three years old when he reflected on a shaming experience he had as a thirteen-year-old. It happened in the class of his favorite teacher, Mr. Kranz, who asked Bonhoeffer what he wanted to study. Bonhoeffer, already identified as a gifted individual, was expected to become a concert pianist and study in Berlin. His parents had already sought out a conservatory where he could pursue music. Bonhoeffer answered Mr. Kranz's

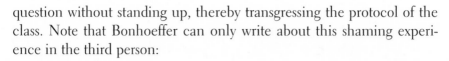

question without standing up, thereby transgressing the protocol of the class. Note that Bonhoeffer can only write about this shaming experience in the third person:

> To the question [what do you want to study] he quietly answered theology, and flushed. The word slipped out so quickly that he did not even stand up. Having the teacher's gaze and the whole class directed at him personally and not his work . . . gave him such conflicting feelings of vanity and humility that the shock led to an infringement of ordinary classroom behavior. . . . The teacher obviously thought so too, for he rested his gaze upon him for only a moment longer than usual. The boy absorbed that brief moment deep into himself. Something extraordinary happened, and he enjoyed it and felt ashamed at the same time. Now they knew, he had told them. But it did not escape him that he caused his teacher embarrassment at the same time. . . .[17]

What shaming experiences are hanging on the walls of your soul? Which specific shaming experience has a significant impact on you? Where did this experience occur and who was involved? How did you absorb this moment into your soul and how does it impact your relationships? When does shame revisit you in ministry? Who in your congregation can unleash a shaming experience in you? How do you protect yourself against the sense of shame that can be unleashed by others' ruthlessness?

Jill McNish, an Episcopal priest and theologian, writes in her book *Transforming Shame: A Pastoral Response* that shame experiences are difficult to communicate to others and difficult for others to hear, since both acts induce shame. Shame isolates us from ourselves, others, and from God. McNish reflects

> Shame . . . is an essential failure of trust in the goodness of oneself and others, and ultimately it is distrust in the goodness of God and life, distrust that we are the apple of God's eye, distrust that God is with us in the midst of suffering and adversity. Shame may be seen as a failure to trust in the essential acceptingness and lovingness of life itself. In short, shame is a failure of the experience of grace. It is a godless place.[18]

When we understand our shame and refuse to use our shame-defenses, however, we can experience new levels of spiritual, emotional, and relational maturity. In the metaphor of psychologist Gershen Kaufman, you can restore your interpersonal bridge, that interpersonal bond that ties two people together and that is severed by shame.[19] The interpersonal bridges that are destroyed are the relationship we have with ourselves, our relationship with others, our relationship with nature, and our relationship with God. Telling yourself that you are stupid, or fat, or ugly, for example, indicates a break in the interpersonal bridge you have with yourself. Likewise, an inability to live a life of grace can be the result of shame.

Since the ability to form and sustain relationships is essential to becoming a pastor, understanding and working through our shame is crucial to not only effective ministry, but also longevity of call. Kaufman carefully traces how repeated experiences of shame become internalized in such a way that one's very identity becomes "shame-based." Shame is self-referential, it wounds from within after being wounded from outside. Once internalized, shame can be perpetuated totally within the self, needing no external person or situation to induce the feeling of shame. We literally *take in* the shaming experiences we've had.

Kaufman identifies *affect-shame* binds, where a specific affect can be tied to experiencing shame.[20] Thus, if the affect is joy, surprise, or anger, you will not only experience a basic feeling such as anger or fear most of the time but will feel ashamed and guilty about those feelings. The internalization can take place if the child experiences an emotion and then the parent intentionally or inadvertently shames the child for having that emotion. Similarly, Kaufman identifies *need-shame binds* and *drive-shame binds*. Thus experiencing a need such as to be held, to be in relationship, to nurture, or to be affirmed can induce shame. Drive-shame binds are tied to our sexuality and experiencing sexual pleasure. Since feeling shame is painful, we need to protect ourselves against the shame induced by these shame binds. We use shaming or blaming others, mistrust, rage, contempt, striving for power and perfection, the transfer of blame, and internal withdrawal. Defending oneself becomes an adaptation toward outer reality.

If shame is the result of the severing of the interpersonal bridge, then Kaufman believes that shame should be addressed by the restoration of that bridge. He identifies four interrelated processes—we can call them acts of reparation—that can restore the interpersonal bridge. They are: A therapeutic relationship or a relationship of trust; reworking the devel-

opmental process; building a personal identity; and engaging in interpersonal relationships of equal power. In relationships such as these, new
affect, need, and drive binds can be established as you gain an identity
that is not shame-based. When our interpersonal bridge is restored, we
regain a sense of internal security, inner peace, and safety within the
inner life that allows us anew to risk vulnerability in interpersonal relationships. It becomes possible for us to make a contribution to the relationships we keep and to our ministries. When the shame you carry di-
minishes, you become free to love your self as you love your neighbor.

GROWING OUT OF A SYSTEM

Pastor Raymond feels called to be with persons and families who are vulnerable and dislocated. As he lives into his call, he has done much work
in restoring his interpersonal bridge and loosening shame-binds he has
around specific feelings (especially vulnerability and helplessness) and
needs (to perform and be evaluated).

Pastor Raymond was born into a family, a church, and a culture that
rarely affirmed, especially when his true self risked showing itself. His
parents, family, and the pastors that cultivated his faith relied on shame
to instill discipline and loyalty to a conservative system always under
threat by society's otherness. His compliant false self grew not only large,
but also anxious. This anxiety was awakened every time he had to
preach or teach, or visit with a person or family. Whenever people
"looked" at him or something he did was to be evaluated, anxiety would
enter his body, which became symptomatic. Learning much about his
person during his seminary education and his first years in ministry,
Pastor Raymond remains mindful of the forces that formed him, the relationships that can transform him, and his desire to have a different experience of self. Discovering who he is and who he wants to be continuously takes him back to his childhood. For as Winnicott reminds us,
home is where we start from. Here are two memories Pastor Raymond
often revisits:

> When I was eight years old, my dad began my years of "slavery" on
> the farm. I didn't want to work on the farm. I wanted to play with
> my friends. He didn't listen to me and told me, "as long as you live
> under this roof, you will work on the farm." I threatened to get a
> lawyer because slavery was outlawed and I felt like I was a slave.

Dad just laughed at me. Mom didn't stick up for me. I got trampled under the shit I had to clean every day against my wishes.

My experience of home was doing what my parents told me to do. They didn't give me freedom, and shamed me when I didn't see things or do things like they did. Mom said remarks in an accusatory tone such as, "Raymond, what possessed you to do/say that?" (As if being myself meant I was possessed by a demon). "Raymond, what is wrong with you?" "Raymond, that's not nice . . ." "Raymond, what would So-and-So think if you did that?" My parents shamed me for being different than them. They taught me to be a people-pleaser who was always nice to everyone. I grew up thinking that I have to think, believe, feel, and experience things like my parents in order to be a "good boy" or a "good son." This was the way to be nice and to keep the peace. There was no space for me to be myself.

When Pastor Raymond is not mindful, he becomes a compliant self, sensitive to what others "expect" of him. However, he has entered into significant relationships with a counselor and a spiritual director. He also remembers teachers and professors who affirmed him for who he is, not for what he did. Pastor Raymond's experience of self is changing. His body is becoming less symptomatic, finding more creative and caring ways to address anxiety. He continues his work of mourning as he grieves relationships with parents, family, and mentors that are changing and in some instances ended.

No longer tied down with shame-binds, Pastor Raymond is discovering some of the freedom he is seeking. He continues to learn what it means to be "good enough," to be free from his own perfectionist tendencies and the weight of others' expectations. One concrete example of this freedom is that he is becoming a steward of his time, limiting his preparation time for sermons, lectures, and meetings. He recognizes that the sermon is not his "best ever," but the best he could do with the time and resources he had. Another example is that through ecumenical relationships he is receiving new ways to experience and express his faith. Pastor Raymond is risking being himself, risking disagreement, and risking perceived failure. He owns his anger and destructiveness towards his parents, authority figures, and his own body. This is a vulnerable place to be in, but the only place where one can feel alive.

CULTIVATE YOUR CAPACITY FOR CONCERN

In his essay "The Development of the Capacity for Concern," Winnicott reminds us that "most of the processes that start up in early age are never fully established, and continue to be strengthened by the growth that continues in later childhood, and indeed in adult life, even in old age."[21] Do continue to grow in your capacity to repair relationships and bring restitution to others. Be guided by the following:

Examine Your Covenant with God

Examine your covenant with God. Pastor Timothy identified the divorce of his parents when he was four as a significant experience of ruthless aggression without any act of reparation. He also remembers visiting with his father, who would be visibly angry and upset but would then withdraw into silence, with his anger "hanging" in the room. Sometimes, Timothy says, his father could stay "silent" all weekend long. Timothy admits that he too can "go silent" in his marriage with Dorothy. He certainly portrays such behavior, where there is a break in the relationship but the act of reparation remains elusive, in his relationship with parishioners and with the congregation itself.

Pastor Timothy identifies his roots regarding the capacity for concern as: "The only way I experienced my father's anger growing up was that he would withdraw into a silent world. His anger was there, you could feel it in the air, but it never showed. My parents never showed me how to repair a relationship. The divorce, of course, is a good example of the break in relationship between my parents." His life prayer is: "Dear God, please keep me from getting angry, for I will not be able to control my anger." His unforgivable sin is: "To hurt others with my explosive anger." Pastor Timothy's covenant with God is: "Dear God, I will be your child if I never become angry." After careful reflection and prayer he changed his covenant with God to: "Dear God, I am your child. When I do become angry, please help me repair my broken relationships."

Think about the silent and overt communication you received from your family regarding anger, aggression, and the ability to repair broken relationships that informed covenant with God:

1. What are your roots?
2. What is your silent prayer?

3. What is your unforgivable sin?

4. What is your covenant with God?

5. What are the implications for your life, your ministry, and your relationship with God?

6. Take your findings in prayer to God and in conversation to a trusted mentor or friend.

Relationships

Engage in conversation, and possibly enter into a relationship with a mentor, a coach, a spiritual director, a counselor, or even a supervisor—someone who has worked toward achieving the capacity for concern. *Ask the person how he or she repairs relationships after distance, withdrawal, and even conflict severed the connection with someone else. How does he or she contain his or her own destructiveness? What boundary violations are especially tempting? How does your mentor or supervisor embrace her or his destructiveness, for denying it is a form of ruthlessness in itself?*

Action

Read any of the following theological works speaking to the capacity for concern:

- Kathleen Greider. *Reckoning with Aggression: Theology, Violence, and Vitality.* Louisville: Westminster John Knox Press, 1997.
- Andy Lester. *The Angry Christian: A Theology for Care and Counseling.* Louisville: Westminster John Knox Press, 2003.
- C. S. Lewis. *Mere Christianity: A Revised and Amplified Edition.* San Francisco: HarperSanFrancisco, 2001.

Revisit a significant shaming experience you had. *Where did the experience occur and who was involved? How did you absorb this moment into your soul and how does it impact your relationships? When does shame revisit you in ministry? How do you protect yourself against the sense of shame that can be unleashed by others' ruthlessness?*

Become aware of the *moment of hesitation* you experience before you engage in ruthless behavior, whether towards yourself or towards others; notice how long it takes for you before you engage in an *act of reparation.* For example, if you enter into silent withdrawal when angry and upset, how long does that state of mind last? If you used your words to cause a break in a relationship with someone, how long before you will repair the relationship? *The next time you are angry, ask yourself these questions once asked by Aristotle: Am I angry at the right person? Am I angry to the right degree? Am I angry at the right time? Am I angry for the right purpose? Am I angry in the right way?*

Scripture

Read Genesis 4:1–17(Cain and Abel). *What role do you think Adam and Eve played in how their sons related to each other?* Anger is most often a dramatization of one's inner life. *What do you think Cain's inner landscape looked like? Abel's inner life? How were these landscapes formed? What kind of transformation was Cain seeking? How do you understand God's initial unresponsiveness and then reaction towards Cain?*

Keeping in mind that the capacity for concern speaks of our ruthlessness and the ability to repair relationships, reflect on these pieces of wisdom from Scripture:

- Ecclesiastes 3:8; Ecclesiastes 7:9; Proverbs 14:17; Proverbs 14:29; and Proverbs 19:11. Notice that Wisdom envisions you becoming angry.
- Matthew 5:38–48. *How can turning the other cheek, giving one's robe or tunic, and loving one's enemies be acts of reparation? How can one love into Jesus' commands if one does not work towards achieving the capacity for concern?*
- Mark 11:15–18. *How do you understand Jesus's ruthless behavior towards the money changers and those who sold the doves offered to God?*

Prayer

Prayer itself can be an act of reparation or it can be symbolic of one's idolatrous ruthlessness. Some persons in leadership find praying *through* difficult situations helpful. It reminds them that they do not have to come up with a solution, but can depend upon the Spirit's wisdom and assistance. God Emmanuel is truly with us! Ask God to continuously show you your lack of concern and to keep you from destructive acts. Ask God in prayer to make you aware of breaks in your present relationships. Pray for God's Spirit to assist you with wisdom in acts of reparation.

Dear God, I confess that I am often destructive towards myself, towards others, towards nature, and towards you. I lack compassion and empathy and ask your forgiveness. Spirit of God, please continue to convince me of my destructiveness and assist me in acts of reparation; teach me how to turn my cheek flushed with shame, how to let go of my anger that lurks like a predator, and how to walk another mile when I want to retreat in isolation. I pray this in Jesus's name, Amen.

CONCLUSION

Developing your inner landscape and finding more creative ways to be with people include achieving the capacity for concern. When we become leaders in the body of Christ, however, we cannot remain in denial about our ruthlessness. As we used to joke as kids, "Denial is not a river in Egypt!" Effective leadership in ministry demands not only that we admit our destructiveness and find creative ways to engage our unbecoming dark side, but also that we constantly engage in acts of reparation that seek the well-being of all, including nature. It becomes a transformative moment and a life force filled with vitality when we engage our destructiveness in constructive ways. Sadly, we rarely read about these constructive acts on the front pages of our newspapers.

As in all relationships, it does not take long for us in religious leadership to realize that the majority of our ministry expectations will become disappointments and that we are not as appreciated as our congregations would like us to believe. *Being disappointed—the feeling that sets in when you spend much spiritual, emotional, and relational energy and see little results—fuels the destructiveness that lives in each of us.* Add to this the blinding dynamics of pastoral power and suddenly you have fertile soil for boundary violations and destructive acts. Since many of us experienced the shameful hate of others without reparation coming forth, we enter ministry as persons with severed interpersonal bridges. One has to be a secure "I am" and have some imagination to admit one's ruthlessness and to envision and engage in acts of reparation. The ability to repair relationships, beginning with the relationship we have with ourselves, adds depth to the Apostle Paul, who writes to the Corinthians that we are reconciled with God through Christ and that God "gave us the ministry of reconciliation" (2 Cor. 5:18). Yes, we are called to *be with* the body of Christ, rather than *do to* the body of Christ.

In this chapter I engaged our destructiveness or dark side. I also envisioned you becoming the image of God in freedom and with responsibility. Whereas this chapter addressed the lack of concern we have, the next chapter addresses how we live with the ruthlessness of others, an experience that leaves us in an isolated position, even though we are surrounded by people.

four

THE CAPACITY TO BE ALONE

The basis of the capacity to be alone is the
experience of being alone in the presence of others.

—D. W. Winnicott, "The Capacity to Be Alone"

God would forgive me
but I . . . I whip myself scorn, scorn

—Damien Rice, "I Remember"

To become a pastor is to be alone with your self in the presence of others and God. The capacity to be alone describes the ability to contain one's emotions and appetites and to enter into appropriate relationships with significant others and strangers. It speaks of a one-body relationship—yours—as well as appropriate and inappropriate two-body or multibody relationships with others. The capacity to be alone beckons some, introverts for example, to venture outside themselves, yet for extroverts, it calls for containment and guarding against spilling over into inappropriate relationships. At times, when you refrain from entering into a two-body relationship, with a mentor, spiritual director, or supervisor, for example, your soul will remain in a desert, your dreams and heart shattered, your relationships strained, and your call to the ministry in danger.

Achieving the capacity to be alone is important, for ministry is a lonely place where the majority of pastoral leaders never experience longevity of call. Sadly, being a pastoral leader can endanger others, as pastors are more likely than any other profession in the helping disciplines to be guilty of inappropriate relationships crossing professional boundaries. It is conservatively estimated that 12 percent of male pastors are guilty of sexual misconduct and more than 52 percent of clergy-

women are sexually harassed in their ministries.[1] One recent denomina-
tional study found that 67 percent of clergywomen experience harass-
ment in their ministries.[2] There seem to be forces in ministry that are not
conducive to personal health and healthy relationships.

Sociologist Erving Goffman sheds some light on forces inherent to
the ministry that can make the church a proverbial locust in the life of
the pastor (see chapter 2). In his book *Asylums*, Goffman speaks of "total
institutions"—communities that totally encompass the individual, cutting the person off from significant social interaction outside its bounds.[3]
Total institutions resocialize persons by dismantling their previously held
identities and assigning new identities with new values and behavior.
Total institutions control a person, set schedules, and monitor behavior.
In a total institution, the individual experiences a "civil death" as those
in the institution lose freedom and individuality and experience a diminished sense of self. Goffman identifies religious orders, prisons, and
army training camps as total institutions. Many pastoral leaders experience their ministries as total institutions. They have few friends who are
not within their congregation or who are not pastoral leaders themselves.
They feel controlled and rarely appreciated by the people they serve.
Others demand their time and can enter their lives at any moment. As
pastoral leaders are assigned a new pastoral identity, they find themselves
constantly under surveillance. As Parker Palmer taught us, every time
you preach or teach you expose your soul to others to look at. Ironically,
a ministry that does not function as a total institution might not be possible, for being called is about being set aside. Furthermore, we live in
the tension-field of being in this world, but not of the world. We are new
creatures in Christ (2 Cor. 5:17).

*When do you become lonely in your ministry? What identities have
been ascribed to you? How has being a pastoral leader affected your personal life? And how does it affect your relationships outside the church?
How are you grieving your "civil death"—the death of being an ordinary
person?*

A leader who knew loneliness and persecution, and who at times
lacked the capacity to be alone, was King David. In 2 Samuel 11 we discover something about David's capacity to be alone as he encounters
Bathsheba. Remember, the capacity to be alone is not about loneliness,
but how emotions, thoughts, and actions are accessed and contained in
appropriate relationships. It was a time of war and David was leading his

army from a distance as Joab was fighting on his behalf. One evening, unable to sleep, David walked on the roof of the palace and saw a woman bathing. "The woman was very beautiful," verse 2 says. Desire awakened in David. So he gathered information about the woman he saw and discovered she was Bathsheba, wife of Uriah, who was fighting with Joab. David, however, did not stop with the information he received. He used his power to arrange a meeting with Bathsheba. Still it did not stop. David had sexual intercourse with her, and Bathsheba returned to her home. Later, she sent word to David: "I am pregnant." Now wanting to hide his deed, he called for Uriah and stated he should have intercourse with his wife. Uriah, however, did not heed his king and slept at the entrance to the palace. David tried again, making Uriah drunk. This time Uriah slept among the servants and never went to his home. The next morning, David again asserted his power and commanded Joab to place Uriah in the front lines, where he was killed.

We know from Psalm 51 that David had much remorse for this transgression (51:3). The prophet Nathan, who confronted David, played a key role in David's realization. *But why was it difficult for David to contain his desire for Bathsheba? And what does it say about his person as he devises devious plans to get what he wants? Who was supporting David as he sinned? How can a man, loved by God and loving God, engage in such calculated sin? What is the role of David's power as king in these happenings? And what would have happened if David had called in the prophet Nathan to help him with his desire?*

As a pastoral leader you probably have experienced temptations similar to David's. If you are a woman it is more likely that you had to protect yourself from the inappropriate advances of someone else. The capacity to be alone in the presence of others, however, does not only speak of how you contain your sexual desire.

Imagine receiving the news that a beloved parishioner has been diagnosed with stage five cancer. You are devastated by the news and in your shock never ask permission to share the information with the rest of the congregation. *Who do you tell about the news? How does this news impact your body? When do you share the news with your partner or spouse or with the office staff?*

You are preparing your sermon or class for Sunday. You are mindful that you will stand alone in front of many people speaking God's words, not your own. It is a lonely feeling, followed after the sermon by a period of feeling depressive and depleted. *How do you invite parishioners into your preparation so that their context and lives are honored? How do you create a transitional space for your congregation and invite them to join you in the in-between world? How do you respond to comments such as "This was a beautiful sermon, pastor!" when few lives are visibly changed?*

Someone comes to seek your counsel and describes a life in chaos as wounds are given and received. The person asks: "Pastor, what should I do?" *How do you contain yourself so that you do not immediately proceed with advice? In what ways can you follow the person deeper into his or her narrative, rather than assume you know enough to help?*

Emotionally and spiritually you are in a desert. It might be depression, but you are not sure. *How will you be able to enter into your own emotional or spiritual life? Who will you seek to water your soul? Why might you delay seeking assistance? What will keep you from returning to this desolate place?*

Whether you are required to keep confidences, whether you preach, teach, or provide counsel, when you engage in self-care, a ministry without the capacity to be alone in the presence of others is highly compromised. The capacity to be alone in the presence of others speaks equally to all persons. Persons who are more introverted are often better at engaging their inner lives than extroverts, but they should not confuse the capacity to be alone with taking feelings and thoughts inward.

The capacity to be alone is closely related to the other capacities we've discussed. If you lack the capacity to believe, you will become extremely anxious as parishioners share their concerns with you. An overdeveloped false self will immediately become compliant to the expressed need of the parishioner and will answer any question without further exploration. Without imagination you will not be curious to explore a person's life and narrative. You will not ask questions or make comments that will lead a person towards deeper discovery. Rather, after a few "yes" and "no" questions or questions about medical and behavioral responses, you proceed to give counsel, read Scripture, and pray into the situation. Similarly, you need to work towards achieving the capacity for concern. For when one suspends an intervention, it feels emotionally and spiritually like hating the other and selfishly not responding to the other's needs. Without the tasks of becoming a person already identified, you probably will compulsively attempt to curb your anxiety stirred by the other person's discomfort.

This chapter first describes the unbecoming pastor who is not working towards achieving the capacity to be alone in the presence of others. Next, I argue that the capacity to be alone is not only a central aspect of one's call, but it is about being comfortable with solitude as a core spiritual task. After a discussion of how Winnicott understands how the capacity to be alone is formed within us, I argue that as a pastoral leader, you are alone with the ruthlessness of other persons; you are alone with your inner voice (or inner critic); and, you are alone with sexual beings. The chapter concludes by suggesting ways in which you can cultivate your capacity to be alone in the presence of others.

THE UNBECOMING LEADER

When you lack the capacity to be alone, ministry can become a desert where your relationships, then your spirit, and finally your body pant for streams of water (Ps. 42:1). Or you become a danger to others, having already passed the point where you are a danger to yourself and those closest to you. The unbecoming leader:

- Does not have a mentor, supervisor, or spiritual director who can speak into his or her world
- Uses a partner or spouse as a primary debriefing agent
- Cannot keep confidences
- Breaks silences with verbosity
- Responds immediately and automatically to certain stimuli
- Does not seek solitude
- Has an insatiable need for relationship
- Remains in a spiritual desert without seeking help
- Never seeks the emotional origins of psychosomatic symptoms he carries (such as asthma, migraine headaches, irritable bowel syndrome, nausea, or physical hunger)
- Emotes deep within or from a distance and hides emotions from others
- Seldom explores with another person the deeper meaning of the person's experiential world
- Experiences numbing anxiety during times of transition
- Rarely initiates conversation about uncomfortable thoughts or feelings

- Uses Scripture and prayer as a defense against further conversation
- Is ruthless towards others with the same passion with which she or he wants to be loved
- Is confused about the nature of relationships with parishioners
- Never engages the inner critic, that punitive, critical voice we all carry

Because of what was handed down to us, few of us will not be able to recognize ourselves in this brief picture of the unbecoming pastor. We visit parishioners being hospitalized and rather than asking how God is experienced right now and how the family is emotionally coping with their loved one in hospital, we ask about the diagnosis, inquire about the quality of care received, and after engaging in some small talk, read Scripture and offer a prayer without being able to contextualize both. We leave the room relieved, having taken in much information we can later share.

Where in this picture of the unbecoming pastor do you recognize your-self? When do you avoid exploration with another person of painful or difficult topics? What are the themes or issues that bring more anxiety to your person? How do you become a listening presence to persons, rather than an answering machine that dispenses theological advice? Envision growing into a person with the capacity to be alone in the presence of others, someone who can seek solitude.

FROM LONELINESS TO SOLITUDE

"Let the person who cannot be alone beware of community," Dietrich Bonhoeffer writes:

> You will only do harm to yourself and to the community. Alone you stood before God when God called you; alone you had to answer that call; alone you had to struggle and pray; and alone you will die and give an account to God.[4]

Bonhoeffer directed these words at the men who lived with him at the seminary, Finkenwalde, of Germany's Confessing Church (1936–37). Bonhoeffer warns that those called to the ministry cannot escape themselves, for by definition an ordained life is a life singled out. Many pastoral leaders, of course, are not ordained. Still, Bonhoeffer is mindful of the strains placed on those who lead.

"Let the person who is not in community beware of being alone," Bonhoeffer reverses his reflection.[5] Following our belief that we are created to be in relationship, Bonhoeffer locates pastoral leaders in a community. *There is no such thing as a pastor, one can say, only a pastor with relationships, with a congregation, with a community.* We can never dissociate ourselves from family, community, and congregation.

You are never alone, Bonhoeffer states, not even in death. The challenge thus, according to Bonhoeffer, is how to become a leader who can be alone while you are a member of a community, while you are in the presence of others. He finds the answer in spending a day alone. Bonhoeffer concludes his reflection on a day alone, saying that "Only in the community do we learn to be properly alone [*allein*]; and only in being alone [*Alleinsein*] do we learn to live properly in community."[6] This paradox, Bonhoeffer believes, originates in the call we receive from Christ.

For Bonhoeffer, being alone had practical implications as he envisioned one day each week spent alone in solitude. The overwhelming need of others, an office in disarray, or the ever present crisis prevents many pastors from resting and nurturing their souls. They physically cannot spend a day alone with themselves. The irony is, however, that the busier you keep yourself, the lonelier you will be. For, as Bonhoeffer states, you cannot escape your existential loneliness.

Henri Nouwen, who knew deep loneliness personally, argues in his book *Reaching Out: The Three Movements of the Spiritual Life* that the road to maturity leads through loneliness to solitude.[7] Following the thought of Bonhoeffer, Nouwen argues that loneliness lies so deep in all of us that the most optimistic advertisement or even substitute love items that promise conditional love cannot eradicate the feeling. We can literally work ourselves to self-destruction with Messianic expectations and continued praise from those we serve, yet remain lonely and in our overfunctioning erode the body of Christ. Loneliness suffocates and fuels violent thoughts towards self and others. Solitude, however, that inner quality that does not depend upon physical isolation, makes one receptive to God and others. It offers a creative response to life as "a place of healing from which we may reenter the fullness of life together."[8]

The journey to solitude is one of deeper engagement that speaks of your inner space. Nouwen writes:

The solitude that really counts is the solitude of the heart; it is an inner quality or attitude that does not depend on physical isolation. . . . Solitude is one of the human capacities that can exist, be maintained and developed in the center of a big city, in the middle of a large crowd and in the context of a very active and productive life. A man or woman who has developed this solitude of heart is no longer pulled apart by the most divergent stimuli of the surrounding world but is able to perceive and understand this world from a quiet inner center.[9]

Solitude, it seems, is another way to describe the capacity to be alone in the presence of others. It prevents the world from shaping us in its image. It calls us to be authentic selves and not compliant selves. Solitude, at times, will call you out of this world to prepare you to better engage the world. As one pastor told me:

I must work to self-differentiate, to resist the "shoulds," to lay my false self to rest. Sometimes this will require physical fleeing, into retreat and vacation, and I always balance life with enough quiet and rest to stay in touch with myself.

Nouwen provides a beautiful image that describes the power of solitude and the expectation of this pastor, when he says that solitude is a furnace in which transformation takes place.[10] Ministry can be a hot place, but the purification you receive from solitude's furnace will keep you from getting burnt in ministry. "With solitude we learn to depend on God," Nouwen writes, "by whom we are called together in love, in whom we can rest and through whom we can enjoy and trust one another even when our ability to express ourselves to each other is limited."[11] Solitude becomes the foundation that leads us from being hostile to being hospitable and from being sentimental to living a life of prayer.

Living into your call and growing into a mature Christian always happens in community. *How do you hear Bonhoeffer's statement that the person who cannot be alone should beware of community? How do you hold the tension that there is no such thing as a pastoral leader, only a pastoral leader with a community? If you name the faces that are your community, what do you notice? When does loneliness overwhelm you? Where do you engage in friendships? What day of the week is your day alone, your sabbatical? How is the community coming alongside you to strengthen and support you, your ministry, and your family?*

THE CAPACITY TO BE ALONE

Winnicott, a close observer of children, noticed that children, at about the age of one-and-a-half to two years, begin to play alone. In the final chapter we take a close look at the capacity to play. Here, suffice it to say that the capacity to be alone and the capacity to play are intertwined. Both need a reliable presence of a good-enough caretaker, someone who creates a benign environment and remains present in the mind of the child even if the caretaker steps out of the room for a few seconds. In his essay "The Capacity to Be Alone," Winnicott writes that "the capacity is one of the most important signs of maturity in emotional development."[12] He states that much has been written about the *fear* of being alone, the *wish* to be alone, and the loneliness inherent in defensive withdrawal, yet little on the *ability* to be alone.

The capacity to be alone is the ability to remain in a one-body relationship. Here Winnicott differentiates himself from Freud's Oedipal crisis, which implies a three-body relationship between child, mother, and father. Winnicott here is also not addressing the two-body relationship inherent in intimate relationships. To remain in a one-body relationship means that you remain within yourself. You access your true inner feelings and impulses and discover what you need or desire without becoming compliant to what others expect of you. For Winnicott, this ability, which is inextricably linked to self-discovery and transformation of one's self-experience, is an achievement. He is clear that he is not discussing the need or ability "to be alone." A person may be in solitary confinement and yet be unable to remain in a one-body relationship. "However," in words that Nouwen later echoed, "many people do become able to enjoy solitude before they are out of childhood, and they may even value solitude as a most *precious possession.*"

The capacity to be alone thus speaks to the paradox of being alone in the presence of others. Imagine a small child playing alone while mom, dad, or a caretaker quietly reads a book or listens to music. While a child is preoccupied with play activity, all kinds of emotions and tensions enter the child's body. This often scares the child. Initially the child will leave the play activity and quickly run to mother or father, only to reengage play activity. Seeking out adults implies that the tension became unbearable for a one-body relationship and for a brief moment the child enters into a two-body relationship before returning to playing alone. Slowly the child learns how to access deep emotion and how to contain excitement. Of course the same sequence of events will unfold if the child suddenly discovers that he is alone in a room or that the adults are out of sight. The child may then briefly make sure that the adults are close by before returning to being alone in the room. Winnicott referred to this seeking out of others as seeking *ego-relatedness*, "which refers to the relationship between two people, one of whom at any rate is alone; perhaps both are alone, yet the presence of each is important to the other." It is in being alone in the presence of others that the child discovers solitude and a personal life.

The presence of others at first is physical, and then the images of loved ones become internalized. Since being with those images we have internalized is more prevalent than constantly being in the presence of someone else, Winnicott states that it is important that we internalize good objects (or images), ones that can comfort, extend care, and initiate rest when we are alone. Therefore we internalize being a shepherd, someone who can take care of others. Or we see ourselves as a good Samaritan, tending to persons other leaders avoid. Internalizing bad objects, of course, will impact our lives in adverse ways. Winnicott concludes that:

> Being alone in the presence of someone can take place at a very early stage, when the *ego immaturity is naturally balanced by ego-support from the mother.* In course of time the individual introjects the ego-supportive mother and in this way becomes able to be alone without frequent reference to the mother or mother symbol.

Thank God that we were created with the ability to "take in" persons and relationships (through the process of introjection). Our Christian faith depends upon having an internalized object (and the status of object constancy), since when we say that Jesus is living in our hearts we admit that we have internalized Jesus to such an extent that we can engage him in a personal relationship. Jesus becomes alive in each of us! Sadly, we internalize not only good objects, but also punitive, persecutory, bad objects, now speaking to us in a scolding and critical voice. The bad inner object reminds you of the sarcastic joke you could have used to get back at the person who wounded you with their words. It reminds you after a meeting of the contribution you could have made, but didn't. It is the voice that reminds you that you see no visible signs that your ministry is fruitful; after all, the membership count continues to decline. It is the voice that tells you that you are a fraud about to be found out, for you really do not belong.

To say that one has achieved the capacity to be alone in the presence of other people speaks much of the individual's development. It suggests a sense of self that grew up in a caring holding environment. Good-enough parents and caretakers guarded against impingements by the environment. Furthermore, the capacity envisions a person living creatively in the world, able to contain the tensions such living brings. As Winnicott writes: "The individual who has developed the capacity to be alone is constantly able to rediscover the personal impulse, and the personal impulse is not wasted because being alone is something which (though paradoxically) always implies that someone else is there."

The capacity to be alone is closely related to emotional and spiritual maturity. It places an individual in the presence of others where initial and sustained ego-relatedness in the form of significant relationships can offer support, care, comfort, and guidance. Here, too, relationships become a holding environment that facilitates growth and well-being in allowing the person to remain in a tension field. Thus one can be apart from others, actively relating, yet neither withdrawn nor desiring the other, but simply being a relaxed, less anxious presence engaging in meaningful activity. For the capacity to be alone in the presence of others creates space for our existence. And when we can create space for ourselves, we can then create spaces where others can discover what it means to be alive in turn. Without this capacity, the individual will experience a lonely existence with a compliant false self continually seeking ways to live into other's expectations.

LEARNING NOT TO RESCUE

Elder Loretta takes her responsibilities as a caretaker of God's flock seriously. She feels called to nurture faith in people by leading Bible studies. She is the facilitator for a group Bible study of six to eight retirees. Recently, however, she sought out some guidance from her pastor because "Things are just not flowing in the Bible study." Loretta noticed that after she reads the Scripture, most often the week's lectionary text, a long awkward silence sets in, which she breaks by telling people what the text means for her. She wants others to follow her example of sharing, but only some do, leaving others mute. "This is not working," Loretta says.

Her pastor asked her what happens to her when nobody speaks. Loretta answered: "First, I notice that I have a difficult time sitting still. Nobody keeps eye contact. Then I become anxious, my mind races for ways to break the silence. When I find something to say, I speak up." She admitted that she is always the one who prays, even when she asks others to pray with her.

Loretta's pastor empathized with her frustration that "things are just not flowing." He recommended they look at a way to encourage participation and also look at her person as a leader. He introduced her to the technique of *mutual invitation*. Mutual invitation is a group format devised by Eric Law, an Episcopal priest and consultant on multicultural leadership.[13] In this format, members of the group are invited to share. They do, however, have the option to "pass" if they do not want to share anything. Mutual invitation will keep Loretta from always speaking up and invite the other members to share. The process of mutual invitation, which Loretta's pastor role-played with her, works as follows:

1. Loretta, as she prepares for the Bible study, discerns three questions to be introduced to the group, one at a time. She may call Janet, a member who often does share, and provide her with the questions in advance to empower her to share. Possible questions might be: What are you learning about God in this text? What are you learning about being a Christian in this text? Where does this text touch your personal life?

2. When they meet the next week, Loretta will explain the process of mutual invitation as described below. Most persons gain a sense of the process within a few minutes, especially if it is briefly role-played.

3. After reading the text, Janet, now empowered by Loretta, is "invited" to answer the first question. Loretta will say: "I invite Janet to share with us." All sharing is limited to two minutes and each person sharing has one of three options: 1) they can share by answering the question under discussion; 2) they can say "Pass for now" if they need more time to reflect; or, 3) they can say "Pass"

if they don't want to say anything at all as this specific question is discussed. After Janet has shared, she invites a fellow group member, probably not the person sitting next to her, to share, saying: "I invite [person's name] to share." The person who answers first can function as the time keeper for the group.

4. The second person invited to share either answers the question or responds with "Pass" or "Pass for now" and in turn invites another group member to share.

5. Members are invited to respond until every member has a chance to respond.

6. Loretta now introduces the next question and invites Janet or another person to share. The person shares, says "Pass" or "Pass for now," and then invites another member to share.

7. The process continues until all the questions have been discussed (see step 3).

Bible studies, as other group activities, especially for adults, provoke much anxiety. Law's method of mutual invitation is an effective method to lessen the anxiety, invite participation, provide freedom of response, and curb one member from dominating the discussion. After all, you can only speak when you are invited to share, and then you are limited to two minutes. Thus an atmosphere that is both hospitable and charged is created. In no group where trust has been built will individuals continue for long to "pass." The vast majority of persons, given the time, space, and the power to respond, will accept the invitation to share.

In addition to the group method of mutual invitation, Loretta's pastor suggested that while she invites someone to share, she meditatively prays in her soul: "God, let me be a listening presence. Spirit, give [person's name] the courage to share with us and help me to remain silent." Loretta was astounded by the results. By the second week everybody was sharing and some had to be reminded that they are limited to two minutes. Through empowerment—the method of mutual invitation—and creatively engaging her anxious presence through prayer, Loretta has not only facilitated an effective Bible study, but she grew towards achieving the capacity to be alone in the presence of others.

How do you respond when silence sets in during a pastoral visit or during a Bible study? What are your reactions to receiving sad or shocking

news? How do you respond when you are in the presence of someone in ob-
vious emotional discomfort? Whom do you seek out that can assist you in
being more effective in being in relationship with those you serve? When
does solitude become a precious gift?

ALONE WHEN OTHERS BECOME RUTHLESS

When pastoral leaders receive the ruthlessness of others, we feel not only
alone in the presence of others, but also lonely and isolated. Sadly, this
might happen more often than we want to admit, for many parishioners
received the hatred and ruthlessness of parents and caregivers and the
reparation never came. A task of pastoral ministry, one can argue, is helping persons achieve the capacity for concern, helping persons to live
constructively with their own destructiveness! To do so, you need to survive the ruthlessness parishioners can portray.

Imagine, for example, someone coming to you and criticizing a recent decision the congregation's governing board made. The person, in a
friendly but stern demeanor, wants to know whether you knew that your
proposal violates the path set by your predecessor for this congregation.
The person angrily asks: "Who were you talking to when you devised this
plan? Obviously not to some of us who have been here a long time and
who will have to fund *your* decision!" The person continues by saying
that he does not think you have the best interest of the congregation in
mind. In conclusion he "advises" you to revisit the proposal and inform
the congregation next week that you retract the decision that was made.

Sometimes pastoral leaders have to live with the ruthlessness of the
congregations they serve. One pastor received no salary increase in seven
years. His resentment is now almost tangible as he distances himself
from the congregation. Another pastor was told at a meeting that she
needs therapy, and then the person who told her so nominated a therapist she should visit. The elders of one congregation are blamed for the
fact that the congregation's youth never stay after confirmation.
Apparently they are not "overseeing" the congregation according to a
conservative-enough understanding of faith. In yet another congregation
deacons are told to find money to balance the budget when it is clear
that the budget that was approved at a congregational meeting will not
receive the offerings to support it.

What similar experience did you have? What feelings are churning in
you as you overhear this conversation or remember your own experience?

Where did you begin to feel like a child once scolded? How do you contain your inner dialogue and emotions to communicate with the parishioner in a manner that can facilitate a conversation? What defenses would you resort to as you engage this individual: anger; denial (the person is not attacking you, but the leaders); rationalization (explaining what really happened and the rationale behind the decision); passive aggressiveness (you cut the conversation short and say you need to go to a meeting); regression (becoming emotionally younger than your age and feeling like a child); repression (not allowing any feelings to surface); somatization (you get a migraine headache after the encounter with the parishioner); sublimation (redirecting a feeling into a socially productive activity such as exercise); or humor (joking that you are only the spokesperson for the board)? Where and to whom will you take your inner dialogue and possibly even anger that was awakened in you?

Deacon Phillip, who in chapter 2 suddenly announced: "If you cannot accept my leadership of this committee, I'll resign . . . ," no doubt experienced significant emotions and felt threatened by the two women who came forward with a request to receive financial support for a new ministry. He relied on rationalization, repression, and passive aggressive behavior to protect his vulnerable soul. The women's ruthlessness was rather benign and was limited to asking for money and claiming meeting time. When someone walks into your office, as one pastor shared with me, and demands that "your time is up at this congregation" and "you need to seek a new call," ruthless behavior by a parishioner towards a pastor receives new meaning. Another pastor shared that a few elders and deacons started spreading rumors that they considered him "materialistic" and "money hungry" when he and his wife wanted to buy their own home and move out of the rectory. Such ruthlessness unleashes powerful emotions in us.

Strange as it might sound, most of the anger and hostility you as a leader might receive is not aimed at you, but rather at the image of what a pastor should be that resides in the parishioner. This image was built up over many years by many pastors and through family comments, social images of pastoral leaders, and personal experiences. You need not take personally those attacks that feel like personal attacks, since you are not an image in someone's mind. Still, you need to live with the feelings that will be unleashed when you are hurt in ministry.

Winnicott wrote about this dynamic when he referred to a mother as someone who is both the "environment mother" and the "object mother."[14] The environment mother is someone who physically cares for her infant. She is loving and assures that the environment does not impinge on her infant. This is also the mother who hurts when her hair is pulled or when the infant bites her breast. The object mother, in turn, is the image of the mother that is alive in the mind of the infant. If the environment mother can "hold" the infant while the infant attacks the object mother, the infant can become aware that he hates the same person he loves, thereby working towards the capacity for concern. If the environment mother is destroyed and decides to return the hatred of the infant with ruthlessness of her own now directed at the infant, the infant will enter into significant despair and acts of reparation will never come. Thus when a parent spanks a child to curb the child's aggressive behavior for biting her friend, the child might become compliant and never bite again, but so too becomes a compliant self with destructiveness that looms but never is creatively engaged.

When a parishioner becomes ruthless towards you, the hostility is directed at the "object pastor" or leader and to you as the "environment pastor." Taking a few seconds to consciously divide yourself into an "environment pastor" and an "object pastor" can help you to remain present to ruthless persons and thereby facilitate their formation. Remembering the object pastor can keep you from defending yourself in ways that cause breaks in relationships, or worse, lead you to retaliate with words that wound or attitudes that do not speak of the love of Christ. In addition, allowing some of the hostility to flow to the object that resides in the mind of the ruthless person creates the space for you to appropriately engage feelings of being wounded, frustrated, or angry.

As an object leader, what are the images of being a leader that you have discovered people carry in their minds? What are the images that you can associate with and what are expectations of leadership that you cannot fulfill? How will you remain present to the next person who is hostile towards you? How will you first contain your emotions and then engage your emotional reaction appropriately?

ALONE WITH YOUR INNER CRITIC

If someone acted ruthlessly to you as envisioned in the previous section, it is very likely that you left that encounter with a familiar voice telling you exactly what you should have said, but didn't say. The voice might even have wondered why you have not portrayed more backbone and told the person exactly what you thought. Singer-songwriter Michael Kelly Blanchard sings of this critical voice we all carry. In his song, " 'Til the Terrors Are Done," he sings: "I'm stupid and slow, the worst in my class."[15] What a sad self-evaluation! Artist Damien Rice in similar fashion sings that God will forgive, but he will "whip" himself in scorn.[16] We see it in movies such as Lars von Trier's *Breaking the Waves* (1996), where Bess McNeill, played by Emily Watson, verbalizes her inner critic when she enters the chapel to pray to God. First we hear her ruthless voice, no doubt received from her conservative Protestant family town, and then she establishes ruthless relationships. We discover this voice in Job, who, in his despair, curses the day of his birth: "May the day of my birth perish, and the night it was said, 'A boy is born!'" (Job 3:3).

Achieving the capacity to be alone is impossible if you never engage your inner critic. For you are always alone with a voice that at times is punitive, vindictive, aggressive, and self-loathing. Often it raises self-doubt as it attacks the true self. Sadly, this voice never affirms, praises, or applauds you. Its only attitude is one that demeans and negates.

Object relations theorist William R.D. Fairbairn (1889–1965), a contemporary of Winnicott, names this voice we carry the "inner critic" or the "internal saboteur."[17] I prefer the latter description, for this voice sabotages our well-being and sense of feeling alive. It is the part of us that serves the false self. Fairbairn strongly differentiates himself from Freud's view that we are instinct-driven. Like Winnicott, he argues that the deepest drive we have is the desire to be in relationship with others. Humans, Fairbairn believes, seek relationships (objects) and not primarily pleasure. Seeking objects, however, leads to the internalization of those objects.

Fairbairn argues that we have different parts to the self and that each part plays a certain role and has developed according to specific relationships we had. We have an executive part, which he calls the *central ego*. It is our sense of "I" that can be responsible and rational. It observes the other parts, the latter being more imaginative, aggressive, and adventurous. The central ego grows healthy and secure when born into relationships that are accepting, loving, and caring. As was seen in chapter 1, for a large inner space to develop, one needs a facilitating environment. A sense of I that is fearful and insecure exudes those very emotions, with which others can identify at the cost of their sense of I. The central ego's work includes suppressing the remaining two parts Fairbairn identified. For we have a part that is persecutory and attacking towards our sense of I, the *internal saboteur* or *inner critic*. This part receives its energy from the culmination of all "bad" relationships we had that were frustrating, rejecting, and that withheld love and care. It is the internalized bad object we find where holding environments were inadequate. The self-contempt fueled by the inner critic is the quickest way to get a substitute sense of worth. Besides attacking our central ego or sense of I, the internal saboteur also attacks the third part of our persons, which Fairbairn calls the *libidinal ego*. This part of us is pleasure seeking. It craves excitement even as it seeks new relationships. It is an innate part of who we are, but is greatly influenced by relationships that were playful, alluring, and seductive, even irresponsible. Whereas the central ego seeks relationships with whole persons, the libidinal ego is at risk of seeing only parts of persons. The result is seeing persons as objects and not subjects, as we find in racism, sexism, homophobia, and pornography.

Although dividing the self into three parts might seem odd as we mature to be an integrated whole, and even though Fairbairn's insights are not easy to grasp, knowing more about how you function as a person can facilitate your growth and transformation. You are not a simple being. You have a false self and a true self. And you have a rational side seeking what's best, wanting to be in control. It is the part of you that can allow you to be a less anxious presence in times of crisis. It helps you keep healthy boundaries. But you also have a judgmental part that criticizes. It is the part that tells you after the meeting what you should have said, but didn't. It reminds you that you are only a fraud, about to be found out. It tells you that you are not good enough to assume the pastoral authority inherent to the position you hold. And you have a part that seeks excitement and new object relationships. It allows you to envision new ministries or ways of worship, or to speak in a prophetic voice, accepting the reaction of those around you. It is also the part of you that recognizes the beautiful parishioner and during fellowship time takes you to the parishioner under the guise of pastoral duty. Maturity asks that your rational side, the central ego, constantly engage the judgmental part and exciting part in conversation, not allowing either to experience free reign.

When your rational side is not healthy, one of the other parts will rule your life in diminishing and inappropriate ways. Also, when you do not engage these parts in significant dialogue, it is more likely that your rejecting part or your exciting part will govern your sense of being and your relationships. In those times the central ego can be called in to curb the influence of the internal saboteur or your exciting part. Mature adulthood, however, is impossible without consciously engaging the internal saboteur or the libidinal ego and returning emotional and mental functioning to the central ego.

Bonhoeffer's poem, "Who Am I?" a portion of which I cited in chapter 1, where he refers to himself as "a contemptibly woebegone weakling" and where he identifies his "lonely questions," portrays the structure of his person.[18] His central ego can observe how others perceive him and it recognizes his inner struggles. It is the part of him that "appears calm, cheerful, serene, superior" when chaos reigns in and around him. But it is also the part of his person that is "weary and empty at praying." His internal saboteur fuels his lonely questions, telling Bonhoeffer he is a fraud, "a contemptibly woebegone weakling." The poem, however, also portrays his exciting ego that is energized by bombs falling around him, through entering the fear, helplessness, and spiritual struggles of his inmates. It is the part of him that longingly anticipates his own death. These parts of Bonhoeffer originated in his holding environment, where his father, Karl, a psychiatrist, was a stern disciplinarian, but also a pacifist. Here and in other settings Bonhoeffer experienced significant shaming experiences at the hand of his father, five older siblings, and even his favorite teacher. It originated in a holding environment that was blown apart by World War I, when his brother Walter was killed in action. It is these relationships and experiences that he internalized as a voice that scolds him and a part that seeks excitement, even in death.

Paula, who discovered a "colorful God" in chapter 2, recognizes that one of the sources of her internal saboteur is her father. Here she engages the voice that suppresses her true self:

a postcard to dad

eating leftovers tonight
I hear a voice tell me to
    chew your food

how many times did
you say that anyway?
     I probably should
but then I remember
I've always eaten my
spaghetti this way

eating leftovers tonight
I learned something
     I, still, engulf my spaghetti noodles
fast, without chewing
no matter how much you
told me to slow down
     and, I still eat my chicken
with my fingers
pulling the pieces off the bone

it may not be proper
but that's the way
I like it
and maybe
the way I
always will

I don't have to wait until
I'm 80
to say, "who cares anymore,
I'm just going to do
exactly as I darn well please"
That's what I like
about 80 year olds
eating their spaghetti

But why wait?

today
I'm gonna do
exactly as I darn well please
     I'll pull my chicken
off the bone

feeling it out with my
fingers
so I know exactly what's
going in my mouth
    and I'll shovel
in my noodles
too fast to chew
because that's
what they're shaped for
to slide down
whole

and I'll mail you
a postcard
of a stomach full
of noodles
on the back it'll say
that's right, I call it art

When does your internal saboteur become active? What does it tell you? What mechanisms does the internal saboteur use to punish you: guilt feelings, a depressiveness, poor self-esteem, migraine headaches, irritable bowel syndrome, asthma, or another psychosomatic reaction? How does your central ego—your rational part—engage this critical part? Whose voices are now internalized as your internal saboteur? What can your central ego tell the internal saboteur? Imagine disowning these internalized voices; what would you then be like?

Becoming a pastoral leader assumes that your central ego will engage your internal saboteur and not allow it to govern your sense of self. Inevitably, as you serve others, your libidinal ego will become energized, and as that happens your internal saboteur will become active too, attacking your sense of self and eroding your well-being.

ALONE WITH OTHER SEXUAL BEINGS

Fairbairn helps us understand the part of us that seeks excitement. Since you were created to seek relationships and seeking relationships will activate the internal saboteur and the libidinal ego, you can expect experiences where your inner world will be persecuted or excited.

One way excitement can manifest for pastoral leaders is engaging in inappropriate sexual relationships. Without a central ego that can dialogue with the libidinal ego, the excitement the latter seeks can lead to significant boundary violations. Your central ego, as your rational component, needs to remain aware of the power you hold as a pastoral leader even as it recognizes the desire that originates in the libidinal ego.

James Poling, in his book *The Abuse of Power: A Theological Problem*, writes that power has social, personal, and religious connotations and can be used constructively and destructively.[19] Power, we are reminded, can heal and hurt, and is co-extensive to life. You cannot not exert power, and you are always being influenced by the power other persons or institutions have. Poling makes a helpful distinction between relational power and unilateral power. Relational power identifies power that functions in a web of relationships, where everyone is influenced by the power. It is power *with* people. Unilateral power, on the other hand, is power *over* people and the ability to produce an effect on another with minimal impact on oneself. Abuse originates in unilateral power, as can be seen in patriarchy, heterosexism, and abusive interpersonal relationships.

The unilateral power you have as a pastoral leader is made clear by Karen Lebacqz and Ronald Barton in their book, *Sex in the Parish*.[20] Lebacqz and Barton argue that sexual misconduct occurs in a setting where inequality of power exists between a pastor and a parishioner. Furthermore, it occurs in a setting where many pastoral leaders are struggling with various aspects of their sexuality and what it means to be a sexual person in a public role such as ministry. Although most pastoral leaders resist the thought that they hold power, Lebacqz and Barton identify powers all religious leaders share:

- The *power of freedom* (that comes from being in control of one's own schedule)
- The *power of access and accessibility* (that comes from entering homes and lives, often when people are vulnerable)
- The *power of knowledge* (as you know much about the personal and family lives of the people you serve)
- In addition, the *power of being exceptional* (as named by Donald Capps)—unconsciously meeting the needs of others (as you are perceived as being clever, a good listener, always friendly and neatly dressed, etc.)

As a pastoral leader you are in a double bind, for the more you engage persons in a relational manner, the more they share with you, the more you know, and the more power you have over them. This paradox of pastoral power plays out every time you say, "Don't call me Reverend, just call me Richard," and increases with every act of caring and compassion. It creates fertile soil for boundary violations.

How do you contain the unilateral powers of freedom, knowledge, accessibility, and exceptionality? Who can speak into your life and ministry (relational power)? When do you feel uncomfortable with the power you do have? How do you enter people's homes and lives? How do you protect persons when they are emotionally and spiritually vulnerable?

Donald Capps states that, besides the prevalence of power, desire plays a key role in being with sexual beings.[21] The Christian tradition is very ambivalent, to say the least, about desire in general and sexual desire in particular. Still, Capps notes that power and pleasure pursue each other and that these forces can fuel desire. Desire, which can be undefined, increases in strength when focused attention sets in, on, say, a female parishioner. When desire is focused, it often takes on a possessive quality. The person, now made an object by the libidinal ego, becomes "*my* . . ." This is one reason why language of "my church" is not only theologically incorrect, but relationally dangerous! Desire in ministry can cause much conflict and turmoil, for when it is not reciprocated, it turns to hate. The person who was infatuated with you or who claimed you as "my pastor," when slighted or disappointed, now spreads rumors about your conduct.

Capps argues that desire can be reappropriated by appreciating art and beauty. The energy that becomes focused on an object can be used somewhere else: music, poetry, or the arts. In addition, exercise, hobbies such as gardening or collecting, special interests or specific leisure pursuits, all can become the focus of your desire. Of course, desire can also be held in limbo, where the desire is acknowledged but not fulfilled.

What or whom do you desire? How do you reappropriate your desire for this object? What kind of music invites you into the transitional world? When did you last read poetry or visit an art museum? What hobbies can "consume" you? Whom will you contact if you sense you cannot hold your desire for an inappropriate relationship in limbo and seek its fulfillment? Which of the following danger signals can you recognize in your life and ministry: sexual arousal or heightened energy in the presence of a specific person; seeking out the parishioner more than is needed; directing the conversation towards sexual topics or using sexual innuendos; sharing intimacies that are not called for; desiring to realize the fantasy when the person has entered your fantasy life; the parishioner dominating your time; and, physical signs, such as a long hug, touching, and kissing?[22]

Finding ways to curb your unilateral power and remaining mindful of the paradox of pastoral power, as well as reappropriating desire, will assist you in being alone with sexual beings. In addition, working towards achieving the capacity to be alone in the presence of others will protect you from engaging in inappropriate boundary violations. If you are able to maintain a one-body relationship and refrain from spilling over into a two-body relationship, the potential for misconduct is greatly diminished. Stated differently, every case of sexual misconduct includes the inability to maintain a one-body relationship after the libidinal ego became energized. Especially in situations where you care for someone over an extensive period of time, you need to beware of maintaining a one-body relationship. In long-term relationships, the potential for transference relationships—those patterns of behavior that once were needed to survive relationships but are no longer accurate—greatly increases. Transference relationships support a strong argument for the use of short-term counseling techniques and for refraining from giving counsel to someone for say, more than five times for the same concern.

To what kind of person do you find yourself attracted (physical appearance, emotional and intellectual attributes, relational skills, etc.)? What boundaries have you established that keep you safe from parishioners and parishioners safe from you? How do you limit your giving counsel to a few sessions? Who will supervise you if a parishioner starts to engage you as if you were his or her abusive but seductive parent? What will you do if it feels as if you are falling in love with a parishioner? How will you protect yourself from inappropriate advances by someone? If you are a single person, how does the capacity to be alone in the presence of others impact your ministry relationships? And where will you find someone to appropriately invite into a two-body relationship?

CULTIVATE YOUR CAPACITY TO BE ALONE

As Winnicott states, achieving the capacity to be alone is central to reaching maturity. It is grace that you can continue to grow in achieving the capacity to be alone in the presence of others. Be guided by the following:

Examine Your Covenant with God

You have a covenant with God that speaks to your capacity to be alone. Pastor Timothy admits that he needs to achieve the capacity to be alone. Like many pastoral leaders he feels very isolated, even though his over-functioning nature takes him into people's homes on a regular basis. He confesses that one female parishioner, someone who sought out his counsel as her marriage fell apart, did hear about his struggles in his marriage. He enjoys her presence and believes they mean much to each other.

In examining his covenant with God, Pastor Timothy identifies his roots regarding the capacity to be alone in the presence of others as follows: "With my parents' divorce I never learned to engage my emotions, probably because it was too painful. It never felt to me that I could seek out my mother for nurture and care, for her fragile self needed those very things from me." Timothy's life prayer is: "Dear God, please give me someone who will listen to me and who would care." His unforgivable sin is: "To hurt others with my powerful emotions, especially my despair and explosive anger." Pastor Timothy's covenant with God is: "Dear God, I will be your child if I say yes to the invitation by others to enter into a two-body relationship." After prayerful reflection, he changed this covenant to: "Dear God, I am your child and even though I feel powerful emotions, they will not destroy you, me, or somebody else."

Reflect on your capacity to be alone in the presence of others.

1. What are your roots?
2. What is your silent prayer?
3. What is your unforgivable sin?
4. What is your covenant with God?
5. What are the implications for your life, your ministry, and your relationship with God?
6. Take your findings in prayer to God and in conversation to a trusted mentor or friend.

Relationships

Engage in conversation and possibly enter into a relationship with a mentor, a coach, a spiritual director, a counselor, or even a supervisor—someone who has worked toward achieving the capacity to be alone. With this person you should feel safe enough, because of the person's personality and training, to get in touch with your deepest and most powerful emotions, without any fear of dismissal, rejection, or criticism. Ask how this person learned to engage his or her own affective life and how he or she learned to become present to someone else's emotional and spiritual experiences. Also ask how this person maintains a one-body relationship and appropriately enters into two-body or multibody relationships.

Establish short-term caring relationships with parishioners.

Action

Read any of the following books addressing aspects of the capacity to be alone in the presence of others:

- Gary Harbaugh, Rebecca Lee Brenneis, and Rodney Hutton. *Covenants & Care: Boundaries in Life, Faith, and Ministry.* Minneapolis: Fortress Press, 1998.
- Henri Nouwen. *Reaching Out: The Three Movements of the Spiritual Life.* Garden City, N.J.: Image Books, 1986.
- Nancy Werking Poling. *Victim to Survivor: Women Recovering from Clergy Sexual Abuse.* Cleveland: United Church Press, 1999.
- Anthony Storr. *Solitude: A Return to the Self.* New York: Free Press, 2005.

Commit yourself to a day alone. Spend one day each week reading, reflecting, relaxing, and revitalizing your body. Communicate clearly to those around you that this day is your sabbatical day.

Foster a sense of mindfulness. Contemporary Buddhist poet Thich Nhat Hahn reminds us in his book *The Miracle of Mindfulness* that "There are two ways to wash the dishes. The first is to wash the dishes in order to have clean dishes and the second is to wash the dishes in order to wash the dishes."[23] Similarly, every act of ministry can be done in the same two ways. Become mindful of your dreams, your feelings and thoughts, the smells and tastes of food, your relationships, the pieces of Scripture you use, how you use language, and what motivates you. Be conscious of your own presence.

Draft a psalm of lament. Every leader knows disappointment intimately and experiences the ruthlessness of others. Learn the spiritual practice and discover the life-giving and life-affirming power of drafting a psalm of lament to honor your ministry. Be transcended, acknowledge the limitations of your life and ministry, and receive hope. Think of a relationship that disappointed you or a dream or expectation for your ministry that did not materialize as you draft your lament.[24]

WRITING A PERSONAL PSALM OF LAMENT

Address to God: The address to God is usually a brief cry for help, but is occasionally expanded to include a statement of praise or a recollection of God's intervention in the past (Ps. 71:1–3).

Complaint: God is informed about diverse problems or concerns that individuals (or a community) experience. In penitential psalms, the complaint can acknowledge one's sins (Ps. 71:4).

Confession of trust: The psalmist remains confident in God despite the circumstances and begins to see his or her problems differently (Ps. 71:5–8).

Petition: Filled with confidence in God, the psalmist appeals to God for deliverance and intervention. Reasons why God should intervene might be expressed (Ps. 71:9–13).

Words of assurance: The psalmist expresses certainty that the petition will be heard by God (Ps. 71:14a).

Vow of praise: The lament concludes with the psalmist's vow to witness to God's intervention (Ps. 71:14b–24).

Scripture

Read 2 Samuel 11. *How can you use your knowledge of the capacity to be alone in the presence of others to interpret David's engagement of Bathsheba? Where in the narrative did David move beyond remaining in a one-body relationship? How did David's central ego, libidinal ego, and internal saboteur function? What role does power and desire play in this text? How did David's sinful act impact his family* (see 2 Samuel 13)? *How can you guard yourself from becoming a David? And how can you protect yourself from becoming a Bathsheba?*

Read 1 Timothy 6:6–16. *How content are you at this moment* (verse 8)? *How does becoming a pastor and the capacity to be alone in the presence of others speak to "righteousness, godliness, faith, love, endurance, and gentleness"* (verse 11)? *What "temptations" or "harmful desires" are you currently experiencing? How do you protect your call to remain "without spot or blame"* (verse 14)?

Prayer

"Whatever [prayer] may or may not be," Frederick Buechner writes, "prayer is at least talking to yourself, and that's in itself not always a bad idea."[25] Prayer is getting in touch with your deepest thoughts and feelings and being alone in the presence of God. Buechner suggests that you talk to yourself about your life, what you have accomplished and what you failed to complete, and about who you are and want to be. Remind yourself of the people who loved you and those who hurt you. Talk to yourself about what matters most and what matters least. But prayer is also the odd silence when an experience surprises you; it is the wonder you experience when you see a newborn; it is being without words in the presence of someone's suffering; it is struggling through a lament. Talk to yourself or pray the lament you drafted.

CONCLUSION

The Catholic theologian Karl Rahner writes that the *experience* of self and the *experience* of God are more important than knowledge of self and knowledge of God.[26] For Rahner, these two experiences are insepara-ble. Not only do they determine how you engage the world, they make a personal relationship with God and others possible. The problem, Rahner writes, is that personal experience remains "hidden" (or unconscious).[27] Rahner sees psychologies, anthropologies, and sociologies as assisting us to reveal some aspects of our hidden nature, even if complete knowledge of our experience is not possible. Uncovering our hiddenness carries a risk, however, since we can discover aspects of ourselves that do not reflect kindly on who we are, or we can discover we know fairly little about ourselves and about God. *What if you discover that your internal saboteur and libidinal ego override your central ego too often?* Of course the opposite is also true, in that we can discover deeper ways of freedom and responsibility to engage self, other, and God.

Achieving the capacity to be alone in the presence of others beckons you to experience yourself as one created by God and invited into a significant relationship with your Creator. In addition, it urges you to accept that you are never alone, but you live with the persons and relationships you have internalized and the different parts of you that constantly engage each other even before you engage the outside world.

Cultivating the capacity to be alone in the presence of others will impact your ministry in significant ways. In this chapter I highlighted living with the destructiveness of others, dialoging with your internal saboteur, and keeping appropriate sexual boundaries. In addition, this capacity will help you to become an empathic and compassionate presence. Empathy is that capacity to contain your own world and enter into the experiential world of another. Being present to someone in such a deep and powerful way is not possible without the ability to engage your self-experience. For empathy is the imaginative act of separate togetherness.

Whereas this chapter wants to uncover some aspects of your experience of self that often remain hidden to you and to others, the next chapter addresses the capacity to discover other persons for who they are and not who you think they are or must be.

five

THE CAPACITY
TO USE OTHERS AND
TO BE USED

*To be able to enjoy another person, we must have the
experience of being enjoyed by others. To be able to use another,
we must have had the opportunity to have developed
a capacity to use others.*

—D. W. Winnicott,
"The Use of an Object and Relating through Identifications"

*The only way in which [we] achieve self-realization
is through encounters with ... persons who are not things
or matter, but human beings.*

—Karl Rahner, *Experience of Self and Experience of God*

*You'll walk beside me, I'll tell you no lies,
And then you'll see another country in my eyes ...*

—Mango Groove, "Another Country"

To become a pastor is to discover, uncover, and recover persons as subjects made in the image of God. Technically, this capacity to "use" persons and to be used is known as object usage. Far from exploiting relationships—our usual understanding of "use"—the capacity of object usage beckons you to enter into an authentic relationship with your neighbor and with God as your Creator, Redeemer, and Sustainer. It is to love God above all and your neighbor as yourself and to recognize the objective reality and otherness of another person and

God. To do so, you need to recognize, contain, and ultimately let go of any preconceived notions of personhood and of God. As a pastoral leader you are at risk of relating to people or God in a manner that simply validates the thoughts about "them" or God that you brought to the encounter. The danger is finding something that resided in you—a preconceived notion, a prejudice, or even an aspect of yourself you do not like about yourself—in the other.

Discovering persons allows for authentic relationships in which you and the other person are enriched by the experience. As Julia Kristeva reminded us in the introduction, strangers bring forth fear and often become an enemy, because the stranger reminds us of the stranger who resides in each of us. In addition, being in relationship with and worshipping God, not as an idol, a doctrine, or a theory, but as a living Person, known and yet unknown, is central to understanding your call and to feeling alive.

The cost of not discovering other people and God is high. Karl Rahner, whose words opened this chapter, warns that

> Those who fail to discover their neighbor have not truly achieved realization of themselves either. They are not in any true sense concrete [persons] capable of identifying with themselves, but at most philosophical [beings], and human beings who have lost themselves.[1]

You risk your very being, then your relationships, and then your ministry.

How do you respond to Rahner's statement that some persons cannot live into Jesus's command to love their neighbor because they fail to discover who their neighbor is? In what ways has loving someone who believes or thinks differently from you impacted your life? When do you become uncomfortable with the separate otherness of persons or groups? Maturing into a person and pastoral leader open enough to be educated by another person as to how he or she experiences self, life, and God, in short, to become a person and leader who can discover the image of God in others, is a long and difficult process.

Entering into authentic relationships is diminished since we tend to see with eyes blinded by preconceived ideas. The Jewish scholar Abraham Joshua Heschel (1907–72) states that learning what preconceived notions need to be put aside and how questions should be asked is central for discovering the prophets' (or any other) contribution. Heschel asserts succinctly:

> What impairs our sight are habits of seeing well as the mental concomitants of seeing. Our sight is suffused with knowing, instead of feeling painfully the lack of knowing what we see. *The principle to be kept in mind is to know what we see rather than see what we know.*[2]

Heschel believes that we, through our need to seek patterns and coherences, most often engage in "conventional seeing," where we interpret new experiences through past experiences. "Insight," however, which Heschel distinguishes from conventional seeing, "is an attempt to think in the present." Surely gaining insight is central to becoming a leader. Insight is not to judge, for you see the plank in your own eye (Matt. 7:1–3). It is the challenge facing Simon Peter when Jesus asked him: "Do you see this woman?" (Luke 7:44). To know what you see is being a good Samaritan, a person who can see and extend help to another person who is in need (Luke 10:25–37). It is the ability to see beyond a person's past, so that the person can reach his or her potential (John 4:1–26). To have insight and think in the present is to love your enemies (Matt. 6:44).

A contemporary of Heschel, Martin Buber (1878–1965), follows Heschel's thought when he beckons us to be mindful of the relationships we keep.[3] Rahner reminds us that persons are human beings and not things or matter. Heschel urges us to gain insight beyond convention. Buber, in turn, in his *I and Thou* (first published in 1923) envisions relationships of mutuality, openness, presentness, intensity, ineffability, and directness. He refers to such relationships of dialogue as I-Thou relationships and distinguishes them from I-It relationships.

Buber writes that the person who engages the world from an I-It stance perceives "simply things, and beings as things," and "things consisting of qualities" in an "ordered and detached world." This stance serves us well at those times when analytical thought is needed or when something is described. But analysis does not help us when it comes to relationships with persons, nature, and God, where a relationship of dialogue is needed. For analysis turns a person as subject into an object, a thing or an It. Stated differently, you cannot discover your neighbor and deepen your relationship with God in a detached way. I-It relations seek control of the other, requiring that one—the stranger easily expelled—to be who you think he or she should be (Matt. 25:35–36). These relationships are devoid of any understanding, sharing, or conversation. We protect our vulnerabilities and never make ourselves known to the other person. We turn subject-to-subject I-Thou relations into subject-to-object I-It relationships, thereby living spiritually and relationally diminished lives.

I-Thou relations view each human being (and we can add nature) as a subject with a unity of being and affirm the whole being. As a subject-to-subject relationship, I-Thou relations are direct relations, unhindered by any system of thought or preconceived notions. For Buber, they are characterized by love, care, affirmation, respect, and responsibility. The two persons or groups create and share each other's reality.

It is thus no surprise that Buber sees our relationship with God in terms of I-Thou relations. For God is the eternal Thou, the foundation for all other relations, and guides our way of being in the world. God as Thou is not sustained by a system of thought nor by our experience. God is a mystery, yet known as the One who came to give life to all. In grace, God meets us as the Thou in worship, when we love our enemies, when we engage in dialogue with persons or with their art, poetry, or music. I-Thou relations, Buber warns, never leave us unchanged.

Living authentic relationships and discovering the other person as a Thou is difficult. It requires a sense of reverie, which is an active responsive and receptive state. *Whom do you tend to see as a "thing" or "things" and not persons? What preconceived notions do you carry about persons of color, single parents, persons living in poverty or who are homeless, persons who are gay or lesbian, persons who are HIV-positive, or persons with mental illness or physical disabilities? When do words such as "Muslims," "Africans," "Mexicans," or "Hispanics" enter your speech? Whom do you objectify as "them" or "they" within I-It relationships? Where do you affirm the image of God in others? And, how can you assure that your relationship with God is an I-Thou relationship?* The capacity to use others and to be used speaks to these concerns.

In this chapter I briefly paint a picture of a pastoral leader who lacks the capacity of object usage. I discuss Donald Winnicott's concept of the capacity to use others and to be used as the capacity to discover and uncover others, to become real and to foster realness. I identify certain "games" we play, typical ways of interaction that keep us from discovering others. The chapter concludes with suggestions about how you can cultivate the capacity to use others and to be used.

THE UNBECOMING LEADER

As with the previous capacities, lacking the capacity of object usage greatly impacts your ministry. Imagine a ministry where you never discover other persons as individuals made in the image of God. Rather, you engage others as "things," from a distance, where they are kept in place by what you know of them, all along protecting your vulnerable self. Sadly, many of us engage persons and the world predominantly from an I-It stance. We see persons ("them") as "things" we fully know and who are magically under our control. The unbecoming leader:

- Objectifies persons or groups
- Uses language of "us" and "them" or "they"
- Confuses a monologue as being a dialogue
- Rarely engages in dialogue with persons different from him or her, including interfaith dialogue
- Miraculously "knows" what people think, feel, need, or how "they" should believe and live their lives
- Rarely lacks knowledge about God and persons
- Is rarely available to be engaged in or to sustain deep relationships
- Has few relationships where others can speak into his or her life
- Finds it difficult to love people for the flawed persons they are
- Does not see, and thus cannot respond to the poverty, injustice, and violence in society
- Withdraws from vulnerability and intimacy
- Portrays no respect for and does not care about nature
- Carries a sense of entitlement (for blessing, to be revered and respected, to be seen as gifted or brilliant, etc.)
- Is at risk of seeing God as an idol, something that can be handed to others

Where in this list do you recognize yourself? What words of defense or rationalizations came to you as you wanted to protect your vulnerability awakened by this list? How do you typically respond when others have a view of you that is different from the way you see yourself? What have you recently learned from someone else about yourself? What have you discovered about God in recent months that shattered beliefs you carried?

THE CAPACITY TO USE OTHERS AND TO BE USED

At the age of seventy-two, a few years before his death, Winnicott was invited to lecture in New York to a group who closely followed Sigmund Freud. The central issue of his paper was not as technical as the title suggests: "The Use of an Object and Relating through Identifications."[4] He received much criticism for the paper and later that night suffered a heart attack. Winnicott's audience heavily criticized his paper, despite discovering, uncovering, and finding another person being central themes in his presentation. The group could not put their Freudian thoughts aside and entertain new ways to think about persons and the therapeutic process. In addition, Winnicott received criticism for his choice of words, since the phrase "the use of" anticipates misuse or even manipulation. His audience, like you probably do, wondered about his choice of words, for Winnicott gave words with a common meaning, such as "use" and "destruction" and "survival," new meanings. But Winnicott states unequivocally: "By use I do not mean exploitation." Rather, by "use" Winnicott means that you can find someone "outside the area of subjective phenomena," recognizing the objective reality and otherness of a person or the world. To *use*, the dictionary reminds us, means to put into service, to employ. Winnicott anticipates a person entering into such a deep relationship with someone else—in his paper a therapist—that the person can put the therapist into service. This deep relationship, which offers a similar holding environment as parents provide their children, Winnicott argues, gives to the person seeking counseling "the capacity to use" his or her therapist.

Imagine a parishioner, Jani, visiting her pastor with a significant spiritual struggle. She wants to know whether a person who commits suicide will be saved. Pastor Frank immediately hears the question as a theological question, embarking on a long monologue of current theological thought on the issue. He is careful to summarize the different arguments around this issue as thoroughly as he can. After listening to Pastor Frank for more than half an hour, Jani leaves his office, thanking him for making it all clear to her. Pastor Frank experiences a sense of accomplishment, having answered Jani's question carefully. However, he does not notice the confusion that remains in her eyes.

Still feeling unsettled, Jani visits with her elder, Marlene. Elder Marlene tells Jani that she is asking a very good question. Marlene contains her desire to enter into a theological monologue and explores with Jani what brought the question to the fore. Jani discloses that her favorite cousin committed suicide. Elder Marlene again contains herself, resisting asking factual questions regarding the suicide, how it happened, who found her, how the family is doing, what the cousin's life history was, and what her emotional state was before the successful attempt. Rather, Marlene facilitates the grief work Jani needs to do. She invites memories as Jani recalls her youth and vacationing with her cousin. Jani cries and expresses her anger at her cousin for taking her life. "I was always there for her," she says, "Why did she not reach out to me? I could have been there for her as she sought help." After some more crying, Jani says: "She was such a kind person who loved the Lord. I know she is saved."

How do you understand the difference in the caregiving Jani experienced? Why did Pastor Frank and Elder Marlene hear the same question so differently? How did Pastor Frank view Jani? And who did Marlene discover Jani to be? What do you envision was happening deep within Frank as he heard Jani's question? And what was happening in Marlene?

Elder Marlene was put to use by Jani, leaving both with an altered experience of self. Little usage took place with Pastor Frank. He never allowed Jani to be someone different from the person he had in his mind—a person in need of a theological answer and whose concern could be alleviated by a rational, well-argued answer. He confuses good ministry with answering questions and offering solutions. Pastor Frank never imagined that the question Jani was asking was merely a symptom of significant grief work that needed to take place. He could not "play" with what he received from Jani nor could he put aside his thoughts of what she needed. *But how do you mature into a person who can play with what you receive as you contain preconceived notions?* Winnicott's concept of object usage, a concept he developed over many years, speaks to these questions.

Winnicott, echoing Buber, states that his clients must place him *"outside the area of subjective phenomena."* To clarify this statement, Winnicott differentiates two ways of engagement, the one he referred to as *object relating* and the other as *object usage*. Object relating is a natural process, for it originates in our ability to internalize relationships. Object usage, however, is an achievement. Object relating is the four-year-old telling her father that he is the strongest man in the world. Something within her—her unconscious need for protection, belonging, and security, maybe—directs the way she sees her father. Object usage, which assumes that object relating takes place, will later occur with a painful realization that her father is flawed, that he is not the strongest or the best. However, in object usage, the father becomes more real and part of a shared reality. He becomes known and a person with a flawed, but independent existence. The way in which Pastor Frank related to Jani can also be described in terms of object relating, for he only engaged her from the fixed thoughts he had about what she needed. Elder Marlene's relationship with Jani, however, can be described in terms of object usage. Marlene had to discover Jani as someone with deeper issues than the need of a theological or ethical answer.

Being placed outside the area of subjective experience is something many pastors rarely experience. Pastor Timothy, like all the pastors you met in the previous chapters, is viewed by his congregation as a self-sacrificing individual. For the congregation, a pastor is someone who is always available and ready to help; the pastor's house is always open; and the pastor never struggles emotionally, spiritually, or relationally. Ironically, Pastor Timothy too sees himself in these terms, but his views are slowly changing.

Object relating refers to the congregation placing these and other expectations on Pastor Timothy, who must be a great preacher, a creative teacher, a compassionate caregiver, an effective administrator, and someone who can invite new members into a slowly dying congregation. It never dawns on the congregation that such a "super pastor" is inconsistent with the image of the body of Christ, where many gifts are given to many persons. In the language of the previous chapter, they prefer to engage the object pastor, avoiding the environment pastor, a person of flesh and blood. The congregation does not know nor want to discover the deep-seated anger he carries towards his community as he disowns a sense of self in his overfunctioning. In this relationship, Pastor Timothy, always present it seems, rarely feels seen. This, in turn, leaves him with the feeling of not being appreciated or affirmed in authentic ways. He is reliving his relationship with his mother who remained so fragile after the divorce that he could not tell her he was struggling as well. *How can Pastor Timothy and the congregation move to a place where they can dis-*

cover each other anew—a place where he can be authentic and the con-
gregation can not only own their inhuman and unspoken expectations of
their pastor, but also love their pastor?

Winnicott argues that we discover each other through destruction
that occurs in one's imagination, in one's dream life, in play activity, and
in creativity. It is destruction and continued destruction that turns object
relating into object usage. Winnicott writes:

> The subject says to the object: I destroyed you, and the object is
> there to receive the communication. From now the subject says:
> Hullo object. I destroyed you. I love you. You have value to me
> because of your survival of my destruction of you. While I am lov-
> ing you, I am destroying you all the time in unconscious *fantasy.*

By "destroying all the time in unconscious fantasy," Winnicott meant
that the child is constantly changing (or "destroying") the image of his
or her mother and replacing it with a new understanding of who mom
or dad is. For us as adults, however, it implies that we destroy those prejudices, which are rarely conscious thought, about another person. The
best way to do so, of course, is to make the prejudices we carry conscious
thought! For example, you converse with persons living a transient existence and discover they value family life, a thought you never linked to
such persons in the past. The unconscious fantasy you carried was destroyed and replaced with a new one. Or you truly believe that God answers prayer, but after praying incessantly for healing, your health takes
a turn for the worse. Suddenly you realize that God being present to
you—God Emmanuel—is more important than the God who heals in
power. Again, the way you saw God changed.

Healthy destruction occurs in fantasy and is very different from the
actual destruction of someone, which Winnicott saw as an act of despair.
The destruction Winnicott writes about creates and has a positive con-
notation and leads to hope and joy. Annihilation (or "actual destruction")
and retaliation by the mother to her infant's ruthlessness, however, leads
to despair, hopelessness, and the birth of the compliant false self. Because
of the survival of objects, the persons in the relationship can now live an
independent and authentic life, far removed from the compliant life of
the false self. Life is enriched when one achieves object usage.

This process of destroying and discovering is an ongoing process as
layer upon layer of expectations and preconceived notions are identified

and destroyed. It takes place in every relationship. You find it in your intimate relationship where you are in love with a person and not an image or expectation of who a partner or spouse should be. It happens in caregiving where you have to find a person and not a medical diagnosis. The person being hospitalized needs to find you as a caregiver and not a friend or a miracle worker. You need object usage in your compassionate ministry as you reach out to persons who live marginally amidst personal, familial, societal, and political forces. These persons need to get to know you as a person or the congregation as a community, not as a savior or another agent of abuse and neglect. And of course, you need object usage in your relationship with God, or else risk God becoming a bundle of your projections, an idol or an It. Like Job, who had to destroy the view of God he held, admitting that he did not know what he was talking about, you have to discover God as a Thou (Job 40:4–5; 42:1–4). Every time you read Scripture and discover something new about God's person and how God engages you and the world, the dynamic of destruction, survival, discovery, and hope plays out. God becomes more real and so do you.

In developmental terms, object relating is followed by object usage. Healthy emotional and spiritual development then is seen in the capacity to discover and use another person and allowing others to use you. This capacity requires good-enough parenting and a facilitative environment. It takes a mother, a father, or a caregiver who survived the ruthlessness of the child to assure usage. In later life it takes a teacher, a mentor, a professor, or a counselor—someone whom you at first idealized or demonized, but later destroyed and discovered as someone good *and* bad, never perfect, but always fully alive and an entity in her or his own right. Winnicott reminds us that to enjoy another person takes the experience of having been enjoyed by others. And to be able to use another we must have had the opportunity to have developed the capacity to use others. It is the ongoing destruction in fantasy of persons and relationships that survive and refrain from retaliation or even disappearing when ruthlessly attacked that leads to the cross-over from subjective me-objects (object relating) to objective not-me objects (object usage).

When one has reached object usage, destruction calls forth concern and acts of reparation. The question in object usage is thus: *How can you discover the other person for who he or she is as someone fundamentally different from you? And how can you destroy the preconceived notions of personhood, life, or even ministry that you carry?* Winnicott warns us, however, that "this is a sophisticated idea, an achievement of healthy emotional growth, not attained except in health and in the course of time." Object-usage is a turning point that leads to new discoveries and deeper relationships.

BEYOND DESTRUCTION

Central to gaining the capacity to use others and to be used is destruction, which, although it takes place in unconscious fantasy, can be painful as you experience someone else's ruthlessness. Pastor Barene was surprised when the long e-mail arrived in her inbox. The day before she had preached a pastoral sermon on the dysfunctional relationships in Isaac's family (Gen. 27). She had urged her parishioners to be mindful of the family relationships they keep, especially when destructive triangular relationships are established. Today, a long e-mail from Elder Larry and his wife, Eva, which starts with the greeting "Peace," arrived in her inbox. In the e-mail, which has many references to Scripture verses, the couple finds it distressing that Pastor Barene "gossiped" and caused "distrust and insecurity" in her sermon. Larry and Eva made specific reference to Pastor Barene, who had recalled dysfunctional triangular relationships in her family of origin that she had to work through during her seminary training. The couple felt her sharing was inappropriate since the "approximate three negatives for one positive" do not honor her parents. In addition, they feel that she "demeaned" God by using the word "gosh" "no less than four times," and as she should know, "Gosh is slang/outside of standard for God." Their concerns "are not just a slippery slope toward vanity," the couple writes. They ended the e-mail saying: "Love, in Christ, Larry and Eva."

The email confused Pastor Barene, for she had received much affirmation about her sermon during fellowship time. It also angered her, for she does not see herself as someone who dishonors her parents or demeans God. Yet, she had to admit, this is how Larry and Eva, and possibly others, experienced her. Pastor Barene called her mentor to set up an appointment. The next day she first vented her anger, admitting that she was hurt by the e-mail, and named her disappointment that her sermon could be heard in the opposite manner she intended. She found it ironic that she is now in a strained triangular relationship with Larry and Eva. Then she searched for ways to respond to the couple. Pastor Barene was reminded that she is called to be a transformational agent. Together with her mentor she explored how she could engage Larry and Eva so that they discover themselves, her, and God anew. They decided that, initially, she would not respond directly to the e-mail, but rather see the e-mail as a request by Larry and Eva for their pastor to enter their lives in a significant manner.

Pastor Barene made an appointment with the couple and briefly acknowledged receiving the e-mail. She then asked the couple about their well-being and how their daughter, an only child, was doing. They informed her that their daughter had moved in with her boyfriend, a man whose divorce was not yet finalized. They found her behavior sinful and told her that she was not welcome in their home until she leaves the relationship. The couple was also contemplating changing their will and testament, bequeathing their belongings to "the work of God" and not their daughter.

Pastor Barene noticed that Larry did most of the talking. Eva sat quietly next to him with a downcast face. She asked Eva whether she missed her daughter. Eva started crying; only her body was able to say that she wanted to see her daughter and welcome her into their home. Eva's pain was palpable and Larry did not seem to notice. Pastor Barene asked Eva what she prays when she speaks with God, and Eva said: "I ask God for the opportunity to see our daughter again. I also ask God for forgiveness, for certainly we raised our daughter the wrong way." Pastor Barene asked Larry how he could respond to the sorrow his wife was expressing and experiencing. He looked puzzled by the question, but after some silence said that "I never knew Eva felt this way. Maybe we can meet with our daughter and talk with her about our concerns." He added that they can revisit his decision to forbid their daughter from entering their home and his threat to disinherit her. Eva seemed relieved by what Larry was saying. Pastor Barene offered to facilitate the meeting with their daughter when it takes place. She asked the couple if she could pray for them, naming their pains and concerns, as well as the planned meeting with their daughter. They agreed and Pastor Barene, holding their hands, prayed a brief prayer.

As their meeting was coming to a close, Larry said he thought Pastor Barene had come to see them to address his e-mail. Pastor Barene said that she was hurt and confused by the e-mail, but that the reason for her coming was not to address the e-mail, but rather to ask about their lives at this moment. Eva was able to apologize for the hurt the e-mail had caused. "I told Larry not to send the e-mail, but he insisted," she said. Larry said that even though he finds the use of the word "gosh" a modern form of cursing, he might be wrong in thinking that Pastor Barene does not honor her parents. "You obviously care about families and the relationship between parents and their children," he said. Pastor Barene accepted Eva's apology and said she was glad that Larry can see her as someone who values good family relations. She also said that she never knew about the hurt and concern they carry for their daughter and that she will hold them all in her prayers. She invited them to engage her in conversation whenever they need to and said that she would call them in a week's time to ask how they are all doing. As Pastor Barene drove to her next appointment, she thanked God for using her as an instrument to facilitate some healing in the lives of Larry and Eva. She was surprised that she was not angry with the couple, but their pain brought much compassion to her heart.

How did the relationship between Pastor Barene, Larry, and Eva develop? How are they now seeing each other through new eyes? In what ways did Pastor Barene facilitate care and restoration in her conversation with Larry and Eva? Where do you notice destruction, survival, and hope?

The relationship between Pastor Barene and Larry and Eva moved from object relating to object usage. Pastor Barene, who at first saw the couple as a thorn in the flesh out to hurt her and undermine her ministry, now sees them as a confused couple in distress, unable to relate to their daughter without her facilitative presence. Larry and Eva, in turn, who saw their pastor as someone who had little respect for her parents and for God, now see her as a person who values the parent-child relationship and loving family relations. They find solace in knowing that their pastor carries their concern in prayer. As Winnicott reminds us, the opportunity to use and to be used is a relationship-changing experience that enriches one's life.

THE GOD WE WANT AND THE GOD WHO IS

To become a spiritually mature pastor, as Karl Rahner suggests at the opening of this chapter, is to uncover and recover persons as human beings. In addition, it is to discover the Living God—Creator, Redeemer, and Sustainer. It is to recognize that you can relate to God in such a way that part of you is found in God, that God can become a thing or an It. Pastoral theologian Leroy Howe names this beautifully in a chapter entitled "The God We Want and the God Who Is."[5] Howe asks: "Could it be that we create God into our own image, and then deceive ourselves with the belief that the process is actually the reverse?" Just as we can relate to persons and never reach the stage of object usage, we can relate to God, allowing unconscious fantasies and early internalized relationships to dominate our relationship with God. "Since none of us will ever be completely free from patterns of internal object construction that we form in the earliest childhood," Howe writes, "we can expect to achieve a level of maturity sufficient to bring at least some of our representations into line with what we discover about the real other." As has been clear from the covenants with God you have discerned at the end of each chapter, the way we see God is intimately tied to family and other relationships. Howe summarizes this fact when he states that "[o]ur image of God, as well as our understanding of God's image of us, are contributed to by our internal objects, the representations we form of those who have loved us and love us still." Discovering the impact of others on the way we see God and persons, however, can be unnerving and courageous to admit.

Who is God for you? What aspects of yourself, born in relationships and a personal history, can you identify in how you see God? When does God become an idol, there to serve your needs and desires? What bargaining have you done with God regarding your personal life and your family? What are the dominant images you communicate when referring to God? And what aspects of God's being do you seldom name? How do you react when God seems to engage you in a way that does not fit your understanding of God?

These questions can be asked since we find God in the transitional space, that in-between reality that is neither objective nor purely subjective. Stated differently, God is real (objective; not-me) and illusion or fantasy (part of the me-world). God cannot be reduced to either the one or the other. For this reason, Ann Ulanov writes that we naturally believe in the God we want: "God is what I need God to be for God to be real to me, and God stands over against me as the other, external to my pictures of God and external to my control and imagination."[6] In the transitional space God never is the God offered by dogma and doctrines and never purely subjectively invoked, a product of our imagination and our psychological capacities. Faith is found in the space between your body and God's Person. In this transitional space, the question changes from truth or falsity regarding God to whether you can experience God as alive!

Ulanov writes that, "[l]ocated in the transitional space,"

> [w]e see that our religious experience arrives neither totally from outside ourselves, like a lightning bolt, nor totally from inside ourselves, as from a dream, but in the space between. In theological discourse, this means God is disclosed neither as totally transcendent to human life—apart from us, unaffected by us, untouched by human suffering, a self-closed, self-propelling being—nor as totally immanent within human experience, as found in some part of ourselves, as part of nature, the created order, a product . . . of human psychology.

Ulanov refers to the tensions between subjective God-images, those images born in personal experience and relationships, and objective God-images, those images of God coming to us from tradition. We need both, for without engaging the Transcendent God, we fall into a pantheism that finds God everywhere and in everything. God is both intimately known and a distant mystery.

That God can be reduced to human experience is beautifully portrayed in a trilogy of songs by Roger Waters called "What God Wants."[7] The songs, which open with recordings of a teenager reflecting on war and a televangelist preaching, suggest God "wants" peace and war, chain stores, as well as contributions, friendship, rain, and good and bad. Furthermore, God "wants" people to be "united financially, united socially, united spiritually . . ." The trilogy of songs, obvious parodies on how we manipulate the name of God to fit our needs, desires, and bank accounts, shows the narrow line between faith and fact, between the God we want and how we discover ourselves when we discover God.

How comfortable are you with the fact that God is neither transcendent nor immanent, but both? If you are honest with yourself, who is the God you want? What is the history of your subjective God-images? When do your subjective God-images and your internal saboteur become the same voice? What do your subjective God-images tell about who you are? In what ways are the objective God-images you receive from tradition challenging your subjective experiences of God? And when do you dismiss another person's subjective and/or objective God-image?

Winnicott is adamant that the transitional space, the only place we can find God, is a ruthless place where objects are destroyed to become real. Ulanov thus asks: "Will whatever I believe in survive my defection from it or destruction of it and come back to me, notice me, attend to me out of itself?" We find this ruthlessness in Job, who trusted God enough to attack God, only to discover that God survived the attacks and became more real and mysterious than before (Job 16:9–17). We find the destructiveness that leads to new life in Jesus' crucifixion and resurrection. After throwing all our aggression onto Jesus, so visually shown in recent films about Jesus's life, Jesus survives and returns as the Christ, loving us and offering us new life. As the Gospel of John states, the destructiveness of darkness could not overcome the light (John 1:5). We cannot find God by cautiously engaging our Creator, by being a spectator, by merely accepting the objective God-images that come to us from tradition. No, we find God through wrestling with God. In the process we may walk away limping like a Jacob, but we walk away whole (Gen. 31:22–31). Furthermore, we confess our sinfulness, sin being one more manifestation of our ruthless destructiveness.

God invites us every day to discover ourselves and God anew as we say: "Dear God. I destroyed you. I love you. You have value to me because of your survival of my destruction of you. While I am loving you, I am destroying you all the time in unconscious fantasy."[8] The destruction-survival pattern is pervasive to life and faith, where confession, receiving absolution, and celebrating the eucharist remind us that God responds with love when we admit our destructiveness and total dependence on God.

For many of us in religious leadership, wrestling with God comes to us when the objective images we received from tradition no longer give us life. Suddenly you find yourself in a spiritual desert. For others, wrestling with God begins when personal relationships end, when crisis or illness hits, when they have to admit the possibility that they are burned out, or when the deals they made with God about family and ministry prove to be idolatrous. Some religious leaders search for God and their call to the ministry when the relationship between them and the congregation they served suddenly ends. Life often helps us discover that we hold on too strongly or too loosely to the subjective and/or objective God-images we carry. Daily, it seems, we are called back to meet God anew in the intermediate area of experiencing where we can use God—where God becomes an independent reality—and where we can be used. We become co-creators and agents of God's righteousness and grace. It is in the transitional sphere where we find the spiritual, emotional, and relational energy to allow ourselves to be used.

WHY GOD?

Sometimes it feels to Pastor Lisle as if he is living into his fourth call. He taught high school for eight years before he received his call to the ministry. After nearly twenty years of congregational ministry, Pastor Lisle felt called to missions. He left the congregation for a ministry that depended on the gifts of others. And then an event happened that changed his life forever. His only son was senselessly murdered.

This experience he describes as a fourth attempt to live into his call. His son, while waiting in a parking lot of a sports stadium after an event, was shot in the stomach by an unknown man who stole only a cell phone. Later that night, during surgery, Pastor Lisle's son died. Even though it happened more than a year ago, the experience is fresh in Pastor Lisle's soul as it revisits him many times each day. The thief-turned-murderer has never been caught despite some witnesses providing the police with information. Finding closure has been elusive.

Grief and the act of violence have awakened many questions in Pastor Lisle. He describes his struggle as deeper than a lament, pleading with God daily to help him make sense of the killing. Lisle wants to believe that nothing happens outside of God's will, yet he cannot find God and meaning in the senseless killing of his son when his son was about to embark on adult living. His grief is physically eating away at him; Pastor Lisle has lost much weight the past year. Furthermore, he admits his marriage is strained, partly because his wife is engaging the grieving process in a very different way. It seems to him as if she has reached some resolution he has not and as if she is not interested in seeking justice.

Pastor Lisle states he is going through the motions, "doing what I have to do," but he experiences very little as life-giving at this moment. He trusts God enough to verbalize his distrust in God, often to the anxiety of those around him who cannot imagine an ordained person questioning core beliefs regarding God's person and presence in our world. "One thing I have discovered," he says, "is that God is a patient God who does a lot of listening. Before I used to think that God acts and calls forth acts, but now I wonder. I guess I am turning into a different missionary than I expected." Pastor Lisle furthermore admits that he does not really know what to think of people in general and society's lack of speaking out against violence in particular. He has lost his faith in humanity. "I know that not every person out there is a murderer and a thug," he says, "but my sense of trust in people has been negatively impacted by the murder."

For Pastor Lisle, the destruction/survival pattern that is inherent in life and faith received deeper meaning when someone's ruthlessness entered his life without the possibility of reparation and reconciliation. It also made the maturational achievement of object usage much more difficult and pertinent. Still, the tension in his life and spirit is opening new ways of seeing the world and seeing God, ways he can acknowledge and question. He is not dispassionate. The questioning and searching in his soul, his deep desire to find meaning for his son's life and death, his need to be a member of a healthy society, and his longing to believe in a just God propel him on a rollercoaster ride between doubt and faith. He is finding God in the space between his own subjective experience of God and the God he received from tradition, the God he feels "I should believe in, but can't anymore."

GAMES PEOPLE PLAY

The capacity to use others and to be used requires the presence of the destruction/survival cycle. Different ways of being in relationship, however, greatly hinder the achievement of usage. These ways of engagement, present in most of our relationships, not only keep us from discovering someone else's uniqueness, and vice versa, but also ensure that lives and ministry rarely blossom into life-giving and long-lasting fruit. Of course, we first learned these patterns of being in relationship in early childhood and since then we return to them frequently. I call these ways of being in relationship "games." Sadly, however, no one ever wins when we play these games, whether we play them with people or with God. Achieving the capacity of object usage is impossible if you are not mindful of these games and refrain from playing them, since the unconscious invitation to join in the so-called "fun" can be irresistible — and deeply destructive. Although these games have technical names (projection, splitting, projective identification, and extractive introjection), they are best recognized in ways of engagement you most probably have experienced.

"I Don't Want It, You Can Have It"

Pastor Joseph is the senior partner and mentor of Pastor Benjamin. Pastor Joseph is an overfunctioner—he often does the emotional, relational, and spiritual work for other people, rather than empowering them to do their own work. Due to Pastor Joseph's overfunctioning, the congregation does not function as the body of Christ, but seems to have an overdeveloped head and underdeveloped body. Since his ministry is driven by a false self that continually seeks ways to be compliant to others, Pastor Joseph is extremely busy, for being busy and getting involved in people's lives feel comfortable. He is rarely present to his family. The congregation, however, praises him for always being available. If the congregation only knew that Pastor Joseph's family has to go to extremes to get his attention!

Pastor Benjamin, ordained nearly three years, has been married slightly longer and has a one-year-old son. In his mentoring relationship with Pastor Benjamin, Pastor Joseph often questions Pastor Benjamin's way of living into his time and engaging his ministerial duties. Pastor Joseph thinks that Benjamin is not putting in the hours he needs to. Furthermore, Pastor Joseph places Pastor Benjamin in a double bind when he asks whether he is a good father to his son and a good husband to his wife. Benjamin feels caught between family and the church.

Like Pastor Joseph, Pastor Ted is also playing the game of "I don't want it, you can have it." Pastor Ted laments the presence of a few angry individuals and families in his congregations. He called these individuals "clergy killers," referring to Lloyd Rediger's description of the few very difficult persons that seem to be in every congregation.[9] According to Pastor Ted, these individuals believe they own the congregation. Recently, significant conflict has erupted between these persons and Pastor Ted. At first, Pastor Ted could not say exactly what started the conflict, but he thinks it is tied to him preaching for change in the church's worship style. Actually, he is sure it is tied to that. He admits that he has not sought the leadership's views on changing the worship style, but feels he had the mandate to go ahead and do so. As Pastor Ted names those angry with him, he becomes very animated and the arteries in his neck enlarge. Yet he will not admit he is angry. "I may be annoyed and frustrated," he says, "but I am not angry," he says forcefully.

Pastors Joseph and Ted are unaware that they are playing the game of "I don't want it, you can have it." In relational language, this is called *projection*. Projection is the operation whereby qualities, feelings, wishes, or even objects, which person A refuses to recognize or accept in himself or herself are expelled from the self and located in person (or group) B.[10] Aspects of the self are thus projected onto another object, which greatly distorts the way one perceives the other person. Around a kernel of real perception a mirror image of your own motives and feelings is formed, thereby warping the other person or persons with whom you have a relationship. We use projection as a defense mechanism to expel and then locate conflicts our souls and psyches experience in others. We can project because we internalize relationships. Since we rarely project onto all people, but a select few or a select group, we can discover something about those projected onto as we become mindful of the parts of ourselves we would rather disown.

Of course, we also project onto God. Ann Ulanov writes that "we project onto God what we cannot handle ourselves."[11] God, for example, will command the aggression we carry towards others. As we project onto God, God becomes real to us, and we can discover aspects of ourselves that previously functioned at an unconscious level. We can also discover more about God if we ask what part of God we project upon. Of course, we can project that which is good and loving, but is unintegrated in our lives, as well, often causing us to idealize another person.

What positive and negative feelings, thoughts, attributes, or attitudes do you tend to project onto others? Who are most likely to receive your projections (authority figures, the poor, the elderly, women, gays or lesbians, non-Christians, or a socially marginalized group)? How do you understand this "selection" you made?

Good or Bad

There is a second game often played in congregations. Pastor Amanda, almost a year into her new position as worship minister, has noticed that her leadership team can be placed in one of two camps. There are those who think she is the "best," even when she knows that she has made some mistakes, rushed a decision or two to still her own anxiety, or lacked in preparation due to some reason. This group, who idealize their first clergywoman, always affirm and praise. The other group, however, can find only fault. They are never excited about her proposals and can find many reasons why they should not follow her recommendations. They often refer to her predecessor by name, as if he never left the congregation. After a sermon, one or more of this group will let Pastor Amanda know what was lacking in the worship experience, why the music was too difficult to sing, how the images she used in her sermon remained abstract, or something else. Sometimes it feels for Pastor Amanda as if she cannot do anything right. She is confused, since she knows that she is not all good or all bad, but that she has certain strengths and weaknesses. Not receiving honest feedback, however, has raised doubts in her own evaluation of how she is living into her call. Furthermore, she is concerned as she anticipates the day when the praise she experiences from the first group turns into criticism and dislike.

Elder Frances plays "the game of good or bad" with her denomination. Like many denominations, hers is divided as they discuss the church's relationship with persons who are homosexual. Elder Frances is angry with those in her denomination's leadership who "obviously [have] lost their way." She believes they are not biblical in their actions, that they are leaving church tradition behind, and that they play into the hands of Satan, who wants to destroy God's church. This they do, by allowing the conversation around the ordination of gay and lesbian persons to continue. One rarely hears her say anything positive about her denomination. One can even wonder why she remains in the congregation and in the denomination, let alone on the leadership board.

Pastor Amanda is a victim of "the game of good or bad," whereas Elder Frances plays the game with gusto. "The game of good or bad," of course, is the defense mechanism called *splitting*. Splitting is the handling of anxiety or tension by seeing another person or group in either one of two ways: either good or bad, thereby splitting the loving and hurtful facets of experience.[12] We use this defense mechanism—which originated as "I am either all good or all bad"—especially when we are anxious, unsure, or feel threatened. By separating the loving (good) and hateful (bad) facets of experience and placing them into unintegrated camps, we receive the illusion of safety and clarity. However, by splitting a person or a group, we cannot discover who they are or how they understand their journey with God, for neither side of the split is closely related to reality. Thus we remove any possibility of relationships where usage can occur. Of course we also use "the game of good or bad" in our relationship with God, especially when we place the law (righteousness) and transcendence of God over against the grace and immanence of God, or vice versa.

Whom do you tend to evaluate in terms of either all good or all bad? What fears or anxieties lie behind you playing "the game of good or bad"? How is your splitting keeping you from entering into significant relationship with others? When do you split the God of grace and the God who gave us God's law?

"See What You Made Me Do"

This third game takes projection one step further. In this game, one person projects and the other identifies with the projection: Pastor Rick has a conflictual and distrustful relationship with his leadership. The break in their relationship came two years ago when his wife requested some renovations be done to the rectory in which they live. Some members on the leadership team murmured that the changes were unnecessary and that it is indicative of the materialistic nature of "our first family." The renovations were not approved and the house was painted instead. When the murmurs reached Pastor Rick's ears, he felt misunderstood and betrayed, hurt and angry, yet he has never addressed his feelings with the consistory. Last week Samuel, an elder and chairperson of the worship committee, came to Pastor Rick angered by a response given by the leadership team to the worship committee's request for moneys to install a new computer and projector system in the sanctuary. Pastor Rick, who acknowledged Samuel's frustration and anger towards the leadership team, said he will give Samuel some time during the next leadership meeting to question the leadership team's "tightfisted nature."

Here is another example of playing the game of "See what you made me do." Pastor Aaron feels self-conscious when he speaks in front of a group of people. His wife, Tammy, told him recently that he has the same mannerisms as his preaching professor at seminary. The professor would repeat a single Scripture verse numerous times throughout a sermon, placing emphasis on different words within the verse. "It works for him," Tammy said, "but not for you." These words, which he heard for the first time a few days ago, hurt him deeply and still reverberate in his ears. He is angry with Tammy but it is difficult for him to tell her. Yesterday, when he came home, Tammy was not there as expected. This upset him more than he thought it would. Later that evening, over a plate of fast food, Pastor Aaron asked Tammy why she is angry with him. Tammy denied that she was angry, but Pastor Aaron persisted, saying

"Your whole body says you're angry." Tammy again denied it, but when Pastor Aaron in a cool voice referred to "when you give me that look," Tammy burst out in anger. Not even Pastor Aaron's comment, "See, I said you were angry" could stop the argument that ensued.

The game called "See what you made me do" is technically called projective identification. Projective identification is a concept that addresses the way in which feeling states corresponding to the unconscious fantasies of one person (the projector) are engendered in and processed by another person (the recipient), that is, the way in which one person makes use of another person to experience and contain an aspect of himself.[13] It is the mechanism by which an individual inserts or projects his or her self—in part or in whole—into the object in order to harm, possess, or control it. Pastor Rick used this mechanism on Elder Samuel to engage the leadership team in conflict. Likewise, Pastor Aaron used this mechanism with Tammy, who, as she argued with him, helped him to process some of his anger at her. We discover the power of this mechanism early in life. Our parents used it to communicate their concern, fear, hopelessness, helplessness, and frustrations. You might remember playing outside. Suddenly your mother or father suddenly told you to come inside because "It is cold out there!" At that moment you were playing quite comfortably but suddenly became aware of how cold you were and rushed inside.

Where have you recently relied on the game of "See what you made me do" *to get someone else to process thoughts and feelings on your behalf? With whom do you have to engage in a significant conversation, rather than wait for your thoughts and feelings to be communicated by someone else? How do you typically respond to a person when you sense that the person has more "energy" around a certain issue than you expected?*

"I'll Give You What You Have or Know"

There is a fourth relational game religious leaders play that assures the breakdown of object usage. It is the game I call "I'll give you what you have or know (and pretend you never had it)." Mentor Justine is not listening carefully to how Pastor Ian is experiencing preaching for the first time at a funeral service for a child who died. Pastor Ian rambles somewhat as he begins to share his thoughts and feelings, his fears and doubts. Within the first minute, Mentor Justine knows what advice and guidance she can offer and tells Pastor Ian "exactly" what to do and say and what not to do and say. She rearranges Pastor Ian's feelings into a false coherence that makes perfect sense and apparently removes all Ian's anxieties. Assuming pastoral and narrative authority and power, Justine has denied Pastor Ian the struggle of engaging this first in his ministry. However, Pastor Ian has already thought quite a bit about the service that lies ahead. If Justine had only asked, she would have heard. Now Mentor Justine is giving Pastor Ian advice as if he hadn't given any thought to the service. Ian leaves the meeting with his mentor feeling indifferent about the service.

Here's another example of "I'll give you what you have or know (and pretend you never had it)": A group of students gathers to talk about issues of life and ministry. There are moments of intense conversation, of playfulness and humor, moments of intimacy, certainty and doubt, of knowing and not knowing. Sometimes one of their professors joins the conversation. Soon he does most of the talking, mimicking his classroom protocol. The professor says things the students already said or wanted to say. He points out the weaknesses and inconsistencies in their arguments. Within minutes the playful atmosphere has been destroyed and an awkward silence sets in. The students seem confused and perplexed, often looking at each other as their eyes search for connectedness. The professor continues to talk, assuming the total function of talking about what it means being a Christian in today's world. After a while students get up and leave.

In a different congregation, Pastor Joanne chairs meetings held by the leadership team. The team expresses different views and tries to think their way through to a creative solution to the problem of how to reach out to the youth in the congregation. Pastor Joanne is mostly quiet, perhaps envious of the different gifts God bestows on the body of Christ. She finally speaks up: "I think we must take this problem seriously. This is not a matter to be taken lightly." She kindly forgets that the youth is the church of today when she proceeds with a "sermonette" on how "The youth is the church of tomorrow." Up until now the leadership was serious as they engaged in responsible discernment. Through her "sermonette," Pastor Joanne appropriates for herself the elements of seriousness, responsibility, and caution. No additional ideas are raised by the leadership team and the issue is tabled to be rediscussed at a future meeting.

The game of "I'll give you what you have or know (and pretend you never had it)" is the counterpart of projective identification. In is better known as *extractive introjection,* and as the name suggests, it describes a behavior pattern where one person extracts information or feelings from another and then projects it back onto that person.[14] It is the theft of cognitive content, the theft of affective process, the theft of mental experience, and ultimately the theft of a self. When parents play this game with their children, children grow up with a deep sense of insecurity and self-doubt. Their internal saboteur will sound often and loud in their ears.

Where have you noticed this game being played? How did the people present respond? Why will you not be at risk of playing this game the next time you listen to someone else asking your counsel? How can you listen so deeply to those you love and serve that they can give you as complete an image as possible of how they experience God and their world before you risk speaking into their reality?

When we play these four games, we rob ourselves of the opportunity to discover anew ourselves, others, or God. Soon the relationships become strained and most will break down. In life-giving relationships, such as our relationship with God, we suddenly discover we worship an idol that, despite our desire to control the idol, remains lifeless. When it enters the body of Christ, the body stops functioning effectively as an agent of God's righteousness and grace.

To discover another person, the essence of object usage, is impossible without effective listening skills. It takes time, patience, confidentiality, respect, energy, and full attention to extend the grace of listening to someone else.[15] You need to be able to put yourself in someone else's shoes and become an empathic presence. Seeing the other requires your ears more than it needs your eyes. It is becoming a parent attuned to a child.

SEEING OTHERS WHEN YOU HAVE A BLIND SPOT

Kari Dodd, who gave us "A Space Large Enough" in the first chapter, reflected on her ability to see and discover others through the metaphor of having "a large blind spot" keeping her from seeing the other.

> *Driving down the highway today I saw a sign*
> *You know the kind of sign that*

Would usually say
Brought to you as a public service

Lit by many little lights in straight columns and rows
Large trucks have large blind spots

Too bad the large trucks of the world don't wear little buttons on
their lapels
That say large people have large blind spots
Therefore if you're not a large truck
I won't see you
If you're beside me or behind me
I won't see you
If you don't have a horn louder than mine
I won't see you

But with a button that size that would waste a lot of batteries and
that would have to
Be worn by an awful lot of people
People in government parents teachers pastors counselors principals
CEOs
Well you get the point, it would use up a lot of batteries

I've been hanging around with some folk lately that I wouldn't have
seen before
they were lower than me
Some were younger some use motorized wheelchairs to get around
some I can't even see enough to mention them but I've learned a
thing or two,
I'll probably forget this later but for today I've learned that large
trucks have large blind spots
And for today I'm about the biggest truck around

Remember my great idea about the signs on the buttons on the
lapels
well maybe I'm not going to push congress to make that happen
Instead I'm going to go collecting batteries for the Sharons and
Robyns of the world

Well, maybe that just shows my blindness again
Maybe I'll just be grateful to sit and listen to the Sharons and the

> Robyns as they help one another find a place that will lend them
> a battery today
> Until Medicaid and Medicare pays tomorrow
> And just allow myself to be loved and taught by them

How large is your "blind spot"? Whom does your blind spot blot out? How can you mature into a person aware of your inability to discover your neighbor? How does it impact your ministry if you go about being a big truck on a narrow road?

CULTIVATE YOUR CAPACITY TO USE OTHERS AND TO BE USED

Christian ministry and leadership depend more on the ability to enter into significant relationships *with* people than on any other skill or attribute. You might be able to speak in tongues or have the gift to prophesy; you may carry knowledge or mysteries or even give all you have to the poor or become a martyr, but without the capacity of object usage others will never experience your love (1 Cor. 13:1–3). To remain faithful to your call to the ministry, you need to work towards achieving the capacity to discover other persons, groups, and God. As you engage this task of life and ministry, be guided by the following:

Examine Your Covenant with God

"We pick up material for our personal images of God from the everyday stuff of our lives," Ann Ulanov writes.[16] Because each one of us carries different histories, we all view God slightly differently, each one of us entering into a unique covenant with God. This is also true for Pastor Timothy, whose "everyday stuff" included taking care of his mother as he became the man of the house when he was still only his mother's young son.

Reflecting on this covenant with God in light of the capacity to use others and to be used, Pastor Timothy describes his roots as: "I was raised in a house that gave me a sense of responsibility for the needs of other people. I see people as less capable than they are. As I can "sense" a person's needs, I often respond to the perceived need or needs before they are communicated to me." With this as a foundation, Pastor Timothy's life prayer is: "Dear God, let me be a helper to someone." "My unforgivable sin," Pastor Timothy states, "is not to respond to the needs of others even if they never communicate those needs to me." Pastor Timothy's covenant with God is: "Dear God, I will be your child if I respond to all the need I sense around me." Through awareness, reflection, and contemplation, Pastor Timothy is changing his covenant with God to "Dear God, I am your child, even if there are limits to how much I can get involved in the lives of other people."

Reflect on your capacity to discover and recognize the other; your ability to enter into I-Thou relationships.

1. What are your roots?

2. What is your silent prayer?

3. What is your unforgivable sin?

4. What is your covenant with God?

5. What are the implications for your life, your ministry, and your relationship with God?

6. Take your findings in prayer to God and in conversation to a trusted mentor or friend.

Relationships

Engage in conversation, and possibly enter into a relationship with a mentor, a coach, a spiritual director, a counselor, or even a supervisor, someone who can survive your destructiveness, whether in the form of aggression or any preconceived notions of who the other person must be. As you now know, such survival leads to the possibility of object usage. *Ask this transformational agent to share with you an experience of a relationship with someone else that at first had I-It qualities and then became an I-Thou relationship. Furthermore, ask this person how his/her view of God has changed over the years as he/she has discovered God anew.*

Discovering the other occurs best in relationships or trust. Invite three to five persons to enter into a covenant group with you. Address some of the questions raised in this chapter and in the previous chapters of *Becoming a Pastor*. Come alongside each other as you remain over against each other, asking difficult but pertinent questions about self and soul.

Action

Read any of the following books addressing aspects of the capacity of object usage:

- Martin Buber. *I and Thou. A New Translation with a Prologue . . . and Notes by Walter Kaufmann.* New York: Schreiber, 1970.
- Ann Belford Ulanov. *Finding Space: Winnicott, God, and Psychic Reality.* Louisville: Westminster John Knox Press, 2001.
- Mary V. Borhek, *My Son Eric: A Mother Struggles to Accept Her Gay Son and Discovers Herself.* New York: Pilgrim Press, 2001.

Volunteer at a shelter. The South African multiracial band *Mango Groove* sings that when you walk beside another person, each will find pain and loss, longing and hope in each other. "You'll walk beside me, I'll tell you no lies," they sing, "and then you'll see another country in my eyes . . ."[17] Volunteer at a shelter, a community kitchen, or similar ministry where you can enter into relationships with those often engaged in I-It relationships. Discover them as a Thou. If you vowed after chapter 1 to volunteer, take a minute to contemplate what is keeping you from following through.

Take a different route the next time you drive between two familiar settings. *What do you notice about yourself in an "unfamiliar" place? What strikes you about the new route? What surprises do you discover along this new route?* Notice people and homes, trees and animals, buildings and businesses, colors and contours. *What image is staying with you as you arrive at your familiar destination?*

Discover nature anew. Nature too reflects the face of God. Spend time in nature as a silent observer, a hiker passing by, or an active caretaker. Identify the numerous voices calling out to you; feel nature's pulse; sense your smallness under skies lit with stars; discover your significant dependence upon earth's offering.

Engage in interfaith dialogue; listen to the other. Visit with a rabbi, an imam, or someone who is a believer of a faith other than Christianity. Be educated by that person. Discover a friend in the stranger. Take note of your own reactions, fears, envy, and other responses.

Revisit a few of your sermons or listen to them on tape. Become aware of the language you use. *When do persons become objects and not subjects? Where do you use "us-and-them-language"? How do you refer to persons who are poor, women and children being abused in intimate relationships, single parents, persons who are unemployed, persons with physical or other disabilities, persons of color, Spanish-speaking persons, or any other minority group? Where did you communicate the mystery of God or go beyond the God we know from tradition? What did you communicate regarding the landscape of your soul?*

Read the lament you drafted as recommended in the previous chapter. Notice the dance of destruction/restoration within a psalm of lament. *How can this psalm of lament assist you in creating space for strangers?*

Scripture

Read the book of Job. Pay special attention to Job 16:9–17; 30:21–23; 40:4–5; and 42:1–4. *What are you noticing about Job's ruthlessness and the destruction/survival pattern of life and faith? How is Job's understanding of God changing throughout the book? Where is Job engaging his object God and where does the environment God appear? Why do you think God never retaliated for Job's aggression? How do you understand Job's confessions, especially in light of his earlier defiance? What transformations in Job do you notice?*

Read the parable of the good Samaritan (Luke 10:25–37). *Why do you think the Samaritan was able to "see" the man who fell into the hands of robbers? What do you think went on in the minds and lives of the priest and the Levite as they avoided the man they saw? Whom do you avoid like the priest and the Levite? What cost are you willing to pay to extend mercy to people?*

Read the narrative of Jesus's death and resurrection (Matt. 27:32–28:15). *What do you notice about the destruction/survival cycle and Jesus's person and ministry? Why were the chief priests unable to use Jesus? How did the survival of Jesus change the lives of the disciples? How has Jesus become your Christ? What is the nature of your I-Thou relationship with God?*

Prayer

Prayer, one can argue, is engaging both your subjective God-image and your objective God-image in conversation. Prayer is not only directed at the Transcendent God, but speaks to the deeply personal God, unique to each of us. Belief in a personal God, alongside us and immanent, but also a God that is over against us and transcendent, is central to confessing our sinful nature. Become mindful of the tension between the "God from below" and the "God from above" when you confess your sins in the words of Psalm 51:

Have mercy on me, O God, according to your unfailing love; according to your great compassion blot out my transgressions. Wash away all my iniquity and cleanse me from my sin. For I know my transgressions, and my sin is always before me. Against you, you only, have I sinned and done what is evil in your sight, so that you are proved right when you speak and justified when you judge. Surely I was sinful at birth, sinful from the time my mother conceived me. Surely you desire truth in the inner parts; you teach me wisdom in the inmost place. Cleanse me with hyssop, and I will be clean; wash me, and I will be whiter than snow. Let me hear joy and gladness; let the bones you have crushed rejoice. Hide your face from my sins and blot out all my iniquity. Create in me a pure heart, O God, and renew a steadfast spirit within me. Do not cast me from your presence or take your Holy Spirit from me. Restore to me the joy of your salvation and grant me a willing spirit, to sustain me. Amen.

CONCLUSION

As a person endowed with pastoral authority, you have at least three choices as you engage other individuals, groups, and God. First, you can choose *not to see* the other person, even when you are in the presence of someone, following the priest and the Levite (Luke 10:25–37). Such indifference, therapist Adam Phillips reminds us, can be more aggressive than any form of outright hostility.[18] Second, you can *look at* people, an act of power in itself that can be experienced by another as an attempt at subordination as the other person becomes an object. A third possible way of engagement, however, can be described as *discovering the other*. Ministry does not occur when blindness sets in or when one stares at others. Rather, ministry becomes possible when you engage someone in such a way that allows for mutual discovery of each other. Such a transformative relationship only occurs when the preconceived notions you may have of the other person, and vice versa, are destroyed. It requires a teachable spirit.

The capacity to use others and allow others to use you is an achievement of life and ministry. Sadly, it is also a capacity largely absent in the body of Christ. For us in religious leadership, it implies that we forever work under the burden of people's expectations, which most often reflect an image of leadership no one can embody. The absence of the capacity of object usage suggests pastoral relationships with parishioners where neither the parishioners nor you are growing spiritually, emotionally, and relationally. Furthermore, without this capacity we cannot prophetically engage sexism, homophobia, xenophobia, and other destructive ways neighbors and enemies are not loved. To be used as a person in leadership is truly one of the biggest compliments you can receive. It implies that you survived someone's destructive behavior, which even when it takes place in fantasy, can be hurtful. Ministry and life become rich when you and others can function as human beings and not as things.

six

THE CAPACITY TO PLAY

Satisfaction in play depends on the use of symbols. . . .
If that is loved, this can be used and enjoyed. If that is hated,
this can be knocked over, hurt, killed, etc., and restored
and hurt again. . . . The capacity to play is an achievement in
the emotional development of every human child.

—D. W. Winnicott, *Playing and Reality*

Play . . . is of a higher order than seriousness.
For seriousness seeks to exclude play, while play can
very well include seriousness.

—Johan Huizinga, *Homo Ludens*

Dance, then, wherever you may be,
I am the Lord of the Dance, said he,
And I'll lead you all, wherever you may be,
And I'll lead you all in the Dance, said he

—Sydney Carter, "Lord of the Dance"

To become a pastor means for you to playfully engage life and ministry, when alone or in the presence of others, and thereby to mature into a person who can create space where you and others can be transformed. The capacity to play is the ability to move effortlessly between illusion and reality and to lose oneself in spontaneous or purposive activity. This in-between play space, the only space where ministry can take place, is a welcoming, forgiving, and nurturing space.

149

Here souls are affirmed, restored, and enlivened. But it is also a vulnerable space, for as you attend to the lived experience of someone else, you expose the landscape of your soul.

To be(come) a playful person is to have a hobby, to read, to watch movies, to listen to music, to use your body in play, to actively contribute to and participate in culture in one way or another. It is to fly a kite; to do drumming; to surf a dune; to fly in a microlight airplane over the Victoria Falls; to do whitewater rafting while crocodiles bask in the sun; to feel your bones reverberate as an elephant trumpets close to you; to avoid hippopotami as you fish—privileged experiences I had while completing this book. Playing is to become a juggler, holding ever so loosely but with assurance knowing and not knowing, certainty and doubt, joy and sadness, belonging and alienation, pleasure and pain, or whatever other emotions crowd the landscape of the soul. Playing is to creatively engage the rich symbols of the Christian faith and to nurture the Christian tradition in a world come of age. It does not deny reality, nor does it rob the imagination of vitality.

Pastor Andrew (see the introduction) played with the thought that a teen's suicide attempt can be a burden he has to carry; and that he is at risk of being a thief, stealing another's sense of responsibility. Likewise, Pastor Cassie was encouraged to playfully "disappoint" persons so that she can reclaim a self smothered by someone else's need for perfectionism.

Pastor Timothy (chapter 1) discovered that the compliant false self cannot play, since playing requires responsiveness, not reactivity. Pastor Ken played with words and wrote a song both to lament his small inner space and also to acknowledge the growth he had already experienced in becoming a pastor. Michael Newheart played with "wine" and discovered he is a "whiner," and that the bread he longs for is the bread of self-acceptance and self-confidence. Likewise, Kari Dodd is playing with numbers and expanding her inner space as she asks what "the Jesus math" means for her.

Playing is to seriously engage the miracle question given in chapter 2. It is being Paula, who envisions a multicolored, "colorful God." Deacon Philip, however, firmly rooted in the objective world, could not dance with the women who wanted to respond to the childcare needs in the community.

When we refuse to bring tensions and unspoken words into play, ministry is greatly diminished, as Pastor Natalie discovered (chapter 3).

Also, when we overfunction, as Deacon Pete did, we deny others the space to grow. Sometimes, as Pastor Raymond discovered, becoming a pastor implies revisiting old playgrounds where words wounded, where lives were lessened, and where looks killed.

All players know that sometimes one plays alone and other times it is appropriate to play with others. Elder Loretta played with Scripture and learned how to create a space so that others could join her (chapter 4). To become a pastor is to play with your internal saboteur, for that is more fun than being blamed, criticized, or judged. Therefore you engage your inner critic in playful conversation, refusing to play the game of blame-your-inner-critic that you have learned to play so well. You say: "Surely not everyone who affirms me has it totally wrong? I cannot be the fraud I feel I am, can I?"

In chapter 5, Pastor Frank could not play with Jani, but Elder Marlene did when she invited Jani to bring her loss and sorrow into a creative space where meaning and healing could be found.

Playing requires all the capacities we've discussed thus far. You need the sense of security that comes with the capacity to believe, since playing brings excitement and vulnerability to one's being that needs to be held. Furthermore, the true self can play with spontaneity and wild abandon, both forms of playing that the compliant false self rarely experiences. Playing requires the capacity to imagine, for it best occurs in the intermediate area of experiencing and relies on the use of symbols. For a child, a broom becomes a horse; you as a leader can see the water that flows from your church into the neighborhood, where families and individuals are watered like a valley of acacias (see chapter 2). Suddenly your congregation is becoming a river! And you experience the vulnerability when you playfully tell the congregation, "We are a river that needs to water our neighborhood! How are we water and where are we scorched land?" And since playing can easily escalate into violence, it benefits from the integration of love and hate and the act of reparation within the capacity for concern. The wooden gun the child carries become a "smart bomb" in adulthood. The play sparring between two friends ends in fighting and one nose bleeding. So in addition to everything else, you need to discern whether you will play alone or with others, for both can be unbecoming of being a pastoral leader. And, if you cannot use others and be used, if persons remain things and never persons created in God's image, play space is relocated to the real world, where winners live at the cost of those who lose.

A sense of playfulness permeates Scripture, with wordplay, riddles, strange reversals, irony, and the rich use of metaphors and parables carrying Scripture's message. Jacob, for instance, whose name carries connotations of deception, becomes the deceiver (Gen. 22). God's playfulness with life is seen in giving a baby to an old couple, causing even Sarah, the mother-to-be, to laugh (Gen. 18:12). Numbers 22 tells the story of Balaam and his talking donkey, with the donkey more attuned to God's reality than Balaam. Samson asked the Philistines a riddle, yet even after three days they cannot solve it (Judg. 14:14). Elijah playfully showed the prophets of Baal that they are worshipping an idol, urging them to cry out louder to their god (1 Kings 18:16–46). In chapter 2 we discussed the playfulness of Elisha, who moved an army effortlessly between blindness and sight, and who fed the enemy when others wanted to kill. The Psalms tell us David loved to dance and sing and in Psalm 104 God creates a frolicking leviathan. The Book of Proverbs envisions an ant as a teacher (6:6) and a pig with a gold ring through the nose (12:22). The dance of desire of the lovers in Solomon's Song of Songs leaping upon mountains and skipping over hills has raised considerable anxiety among Christians (2:8). The Book of Isaiah is filled with wordplay, with Isaiah looking for judgment (*mishpat*), but seeing oppression (*mishpah*); he looked for righteousness (*tsidaqah*), but heard cries (*tsaaqah*; 5:7). The prophet Amos calls wealthy women who oppress "cows" (4:1). Jesus turns water into quality wine when everyone expects the quality to diminish (John 2).

Furthermore, in the Gospel of John, the blind see and the sighted are blind (John 9). Peter, as described in Acts 12, after he miraculously escapes from prison, is left outside a closed door by a very excited Rhoda, who forgets to invite him in. The apostle Paul definitely has a playful spirit: In the first letter to the Corinthians, he beckons the people to become foolish so that they might become wise (3:18). Writing to the Philippians, he first addresses Euodia (*Euodian*, 4:2) and then in 4:18 describes the congregation as a fragrant offering (*euodias*). He admonishes the idle Thessalonians for being busybodies (2 Thess. 3:11). Throughout Scripture, one sees and senses the playfulness of God as God plays with creation, in offering salvation, and with God's people. These few references celebrate the playfulness of the Book we love.

It is thus no surprise that we've been created to be *homo ludens*. We've been created to be playful beings! Not even warped Christian piety and a misunderstood work ethic can repress playfulness. *Homo sapiens*, at times, might be intelligent. And *homo faber* might be able to make things, even instruments that destroy. But *homo ludens* can play, practicing the classic Aristotelian virtue of *eutrapelia* with wit and flexible resourcefulness. Theologian Hugo Rahner, brother of Karl, writes in his book *Man at Play* (1967) that *eutrapelia* implies a lightness of spirit midway between boorishness and frivolity.[1] One can see the trapeze artist in this word. *Eutrapelia* is graceful playfulness; it is playing for the sake of seriousness. We can laugh at ourselves and with others yet remain accountable to a God who demands worship and love of God, love of self, and love of other. Playing, then, is walking a tightrope between the virtue of graceful playfulness and the vice of "obscenity, foolish talk or coarse joking" (Eph. 5:4). Falling off the tightrope is not the real danger. Rather, the danger is in how long you will be left behind before you continue to walk the line. But walking this line creates possibility and offers discovery.

Playing is an attitude, a way of living more than an activity in which you engage. So every aspect of ministry can be a form of playing. You play when you engage in preaching, teaching, caring, or completing administrative tasks. You play with words and metaphors, with symbols and rituals. Furthermore, you invite others to join you in the intermediate area of experiencing. For us as pastoral leaders, the paradox is that there is nothing we can *do* to *be* playful. Yet, we can cultivate an attitude of playfulness that permeates everything we do.

In this final chapter, we first look at the unbecoming pastor as a pastoral leader who lacks this playful attitude. Next, we move to D. W. Winnicott's thoughts on the "capacity to play." I suggest that the "wise fool" offers an appropriate self-understanding for pastoral leaders who want to be playful, and that as pastoral leaders we need to develop a theology of play that can inform our lives and ministries. The chapter concludes with suggestions of how to cultivate an attitude that makes playing possible.

THE UNBECOMING LEADER

Since playing draws on all the capacities already discussed, the vast majority of the unbecoming leaders in the previous chapters will lack the capacity to play. As was stated in the preface, the unbecoming leader is someone whose leadership is greatly compromised, even inappropriate. The unbecoming leader:

- Sees ministry and life as "serious business"
- Is burdened by perfectionism
- Rarely laughs when a mistake is made, when misunderstanding sets in, or when invited by others into a play space
- Spends much time daydreaming or engaged in "soft addictions," such as watching television, surfing the world wide web, playing "mindless" computer games, and being in unproductive meetings
- Accumulates the thoughts of others in the form of books, but rarely allows those thoughts to inform life and ministry
- Responds to people asking how things are with, "I'm busy…"
- Believes life is lived according to fixed rules
- Desires to control others
- Rarely uses or appreciates the richness within metaphorical language
- Resists the multiplicity of meaning within language
- Seldom engages families-as-a-whole, but prefers to split the family into age groups and then avoids the younger generation
- Resists being enriched by the imagination of members in the body of Christ
- Gives persons facts (such as theological truths, tradition, or dogma) and expects persons to creatively respond to (or play with) them
- Finds liturgy restrictive and thus of no use or has a normative, suffocating approach to liturgy
- Does not recognize the facilitative and liberating potential of ritual
- Confines imagination to solitary sexual activities such as masturbation and pornography
- Finds play in inappropriate relationships and in risky behaviors
- Never lets a supervisor, mentor, or group of peers see his or her play activity

To which of these statements above did you immediately react? Why this statement in particular? How would you describe your spirit of playfulness to someone else? When are you most likely to be responsive (versus being reactive) to life and ministry? In which areas of your ministry can you become more playful? Who is helping you to become more playful?

THE CAPACITY TO PLAY

D. W. Winnicott was a playful person. He loved rolling on grass and riding his bicycle with his feet on the handle bars. He liked reading and singing, playing the piano, and spending time in the kitchen. He played team sports and liked being an athlete. He appreciated the Beatles and Beethoven and loved going to movies, art galleries, theaters, or the symphony. He would make his own Christmas cards. He wrote poetry (from the Greek *poien*, to create), drew sketches, and created therapeutic games to assist him in his work with children. He was such a friend of children that the children of a Danish colleague believed he spoke Danish when he could not speak Danish at all! Likewise, when he met a young French boy, being unable to communicate in French, he purred and meowed like a cat. At times, he drew the ire of police by driving his car with his head poking out through the roof and his walking stick on the accelerator. Furthermore, he found his friends among artists, musicians, dancers, painters, and sculptors. He saw himself as a person who wanted to experience everything to the fullest, even his own death. In notes on an envisioned autobiography, Winnicott starts with the prayer: "Oh God, may I be alive when I die."[2] It is certainly no surprise that he emphatically said that "the capacity to play is an *achievement* in individual emotional growth."[3]

Winnicott liked *playing*, the experience of creating play symbols, more than *play*, a form of symbolic communication, even if he used both. He got interested in playing when he discovered transitional objects and transitional phenomena, which we discussed in chapter 2. Since playing depends on some achievement of the five capacities discussed thus far, much has been said about the developmental process that leads to an attitude of playfulness, which can be summarized as follows:[4]

Stage 1: Playing occurs best in situations where a good-enough holding environment, supported by similar parenting, welcomes the infant into the world. In this holding environment one finds trust—the establishment of confidence—within the infant and between the infant and the caregiver. Of course, this environment greatly determines the capacity to believe. In the holding environment, the baby lives in a me-world, with the loving mother or caretaker providing objects to be found by the infant. Since playing originates in the inner space created by the facilitative environment, Winnicott writes that playing "becomes an expression in terms of external materials of inner relationships and anxieties."[5] One's playing is not determined by toys nor by opportunities to play, but by the quality of one's inner space, home to our anxieties and insecurities. The way we play tells something about who we are, especially the size and condition of our inner spaces.

Imagine a baby being held by loving caretakers who remove impingements such as loud noise, sudden movements, extreme temperatures, and hunger or other forms of deprivation. Also imagine a pastor who, only after careful listening and after a trusting relationship (or working alliance) has been established, probes for deeper meaning or confronts with loving care. Whether the issue at hand is the joy and disorientation of being new parents or the disorder and despair of a major illness or loss, an environment is needed before a pastoral leader and congregant can engage in this form of holy play. Therefore we have pastoral conversations in places that offer some privacy or are welcoming and comfortable.

Stage 2: Even as playing comes from the inner space, this is not the place where playing is found. Playing, for Winnicott, has a specific place. It is neither inside (the me-world) nor is it outside (the not-me world). Rather, playing, as an experience occurs in a potential space between baby and the mother or caretaker, that interpersonal and intrapersonal space between reality and fantasy, and dependent upon both. It is in this space that Winnicott believed we become alive, for living exclusively in the inside me-world and the outside not-me world implies reactivity to internal or external stimuli, which are, but do not symbolically represent anything. Through playing in the potential space, that space between the interpreting self, one's symbols, and raw sense data, we become alive, interpreters of fantasy in terms of reality and reality in terms of fantasy. We give meaning, becoming creators and cocreators.[6]

In the intermediate area of experiencing a child becomes preoccupied with other-than-me objects. It is the space between an infant and a breast or a bottle. This is the place where transitional objects reside and where creative imagination roams. It is this place where objects are destroyed and restored, hurt and mended, dirtied and cleaned, and killed and brought to life again. Later it becomes the space between the child and the soft toy, and later yet the space of play activity and of symbols and culture. Here, in the potential space, the infant learns how to manipulate objects and discovers the limitations of personal power and skills and the unlimited scope of the imagination. In play activity, however, a child also discovers that it is probably the only true free space, tolerated by caring individuals. A good enough parent, for example, will not respond to a child's imagination that turns a wood block and a rope into a fire truck and a hose, saying: "No, that is not a fire truck and a hose, it is a wood block and a rope." Nor will a parent negate a child's comment that the doll she is holding is her baby. In play, physical objects get private meanings.

Pastoral leaders often enter into the potential space between themselves and others. We do so when we preach and pray, when we teach and care. We also enter that space when we engage in ritual and when we celebrate communion or baptism, all aspects of ritual rich in metaphor and paradox. In this space we learn that we should not make promises we cannot keep, that God's Spirit can enter into lives and situations, and that meaning and hope can be found, not given.

In the potential space we honor the freedom of a personal faith. Where one person might respond to a personal crisis with "I am being punished for my sins" (Job 4:7), another might respond by saying, "It was God's will" (Ps. 16:5). Another person yet might find solace in: "Christ died for my sins. I am a new creation" (John 3:16). And another person might respond angrily, saying, "Why did this happen to me?" (Ps. 3:1–3); or the person might accuse God: "Why did you bring this upon me, God?" (Job 21:2–4).[7] The playing pastoral leader will not view one response as more theologically correct than the other, but will be able to work (or play) with each response, offering care and facilitating transformation and healing as the person's experience of self and the experience of God changes. However, the pastor who sees a parishioner's response as a theological statement that needs to be challenged and corrected collapses the play space and, in doing so, destroys the opportunity for fruitful ministry.

Stage 3: "Play is always exciting," Winnicott writes. "It is exciting *not* because of the background of instincts but because . . . it always deals with the knife-edge between the subjective and that which is objectively perceived."[8] Furthermore, playing is exciting because it involves one's body. Stated differently, playing is exciting since in the potential space, you and your body, with other things, come alive. Since being alive includes ruthless feelings, one depends on the capacity for concern and the integration of love and hate into one's person to be playful.

One youth pastor remembers how excited the youth became when they decided to have an event called: "Rock the boat with the Rock of Ages." This event, however, threatened the elders of the church, for the elders did now know whether "rock" meant "rock music" or "to shake." Neither meaning appealed to them. They could not envision a rock concert in the church hall, not did they want things to change in the congregation. As Sydney Carter's famous hymn states, the elders could not dance with the youth!

Or you may have felt the energy and excitement that comes to you when you are called to a home in crisis, only to return home depleted, as if energy flowed from you as you counseled the family. In addition, as a playing pastoral leader, you discover powerful emotions that flow between you and a parishioner: helplessness, anger, frustration, or care, concern, love, and erotic desire.

Stage 4: The next stage in the development of playing is playing alone in the presence of someone else. Here the child learns how to hold emotions within a one-body relationship or to enter into appropriate two-body relationships. When tensions become unbearable due to frightening images or feelings or due to bodily excitement, the child briefly spills over into a two-body relationship by running to a parent or caretaker. Running to mother will diminish the fear or excitement, and the child can retreat to a one-body relationship and playing alone. "Responsible persons must be available when children play," Winnicott writes. But since a child must learn how to play alone, a parent of caregiver should not always insert himself or herself into the child's play activity. Being present is often enough to communicate care and safety. When the child has reached this point of development, play will have form, with a specific beginning, middle, and a natural end. It will be imaginative and without repetition, exciting but not overexciting or disorganized.

For playing pastoral leaders, play best occurs if you have a mentor, a supervisor, or a group of peers who can listen in to the experiences you are having. Most pastors, however, do their ministries with no one close enough to speak into their lives and ministries. A supervisory relationship can assist you in becoming a confidential person, comfortably holding much knowledge about individuals and families, with little risk that you will inappropriately "spill over" and break confidences. Furthermore, one can learn to play in conversation and in giving counsel. One can gain the skill to keep a conversation exciting, yet not overexciting or disorganized.

Stage 5: Finally, the child learns how to play with others, how to play along with others, how to play according to rules, and how to allow for complexities in terms of leaders and followers. The child learns how to "enjoy an overlap of two play areas." Suddenly the younger sister is also interested in dolls, and if the oldest sister's doll is cold and in need of a blanket, the younger sister's doll needs a blanket too! As the dolls lie next to each other, covered with small blankets, the dolls—and sisters—become friends. As a leader you invite others into the decision-making process, and even though it slows down the process, suddenly you are informed in ways you never could have imagined. Playing with others implies that you take the contributions of others into consideration when you ask for input or feedback.

To play with others, of course, implies that the child must view her mother or caretaker as a subject, someone also able to play, and not merely an object with which to play. The mother does this by not only playing with her child, but by introducing her own playfulness and play activities to her child. If the child never discovers the mother as someone other-than-me, and thus never develops object usage, play space is either relocated to the real world, where winners live at the cost of those who lose, or is found exclusively in the inner world, where play has a compulsive, anxiety-driven, and even autistic nature. Playing together in a life-giving and life-affirming relationship that enriches both persons and all participants is impossible in I-It relationships.

Pastoral leaders who are quick to provide advice and even biblical counsel, as some contemporary pastoral counseling methods suggest, cannot play in the "overlap of two areas." Within minutes an assessment is usually made. No exploration of meaning already found is done. The person is never asked how or what he communicates with God regarding his concern, or how she experiences God's presence in her life at this moment. Rather a selected "biblical truth" is offered as counsel, while often not taking the context of Scripture or the context of the parishioner into consideration. Omnipotently, the pastor attempts to change the experience of the other person or burdens the person with a "should" they need to live into. All one finds is compliance or acquiescence, no spontaneity or deep transformation. Such failure in confidence limits the potential space, which in turn inhibits a person's play capacity.

You can portray an I-It relationship with those you serve when you refer to the congregation as "them" or "they," as if all within the congregation think, believe, and act alike. If we cannot allow others to use us, playing in ministry is greatly diminished. Unfortunately the biblical image of a congregation as a flock of sheep can be disadvantageous, since most us think of a sheep as an It and not a Thou. Pastor Patterson, for example, who sees his congregation as a "blue collar congregation," resists the idea that a sermon group, consisting of members of his congregation, can help him become a better preacher, pastor, and person, for the parishioners—he silently thinks—"are not highly educated." And Elder Rita, who has not earned the pastoral authority she claims for herself, becomes angry when members in the congregation question the decisions of the leadership team. "This is not a paid position," she often says, "and what do *they* know; they are not at the meetings where we discuss things." In addition, if your congregation cannot discover you for who you are but engages you from preconceived notions of who a pastor should be, your congregants will trust you only as far as their preconceived notions correspond with their experience of you.

For children and adults alike, the functions of play are to assist us with aggression and existential anxiety; to give us an experience of self, of other, and of the outside world; to find and establish friendships; and, to move toward personal integration. Furthermore, Winnicott believed that playing itself has therapeutic and revelatory value because it is a creative experience and informs one's living. "It is in playing, and only in playing," Winnicott writes, "that the individual child or adult is able to be creative and to use the whole personality, and it is only in being creative that the individual discovers the self." Even as you can reflect on what is created to see how it reflects the landscape of your soul, the false self can keep us from discovering such truths spoken from deep inside.

Pastor Herman, a "preaching pastor," spends much time each week on the sermon he creates for Sunday. Rarely, however, does he ask himself: *Why am I using these images and not others? How can I play more with images and words? What is this sermon saying about the landscape of my soul? How does the congregation experience me? What will I gain if*

I invite others into the sermon-writing process with me? Why do I tend to offer one point of view in my sermons, rather than offering many perspectives and allowing the parishioners to find an image to play with?

The act of creating—whether a poem, journal, sculpture, pottery piece, pastoral conversation, or sermon—cannot heal a poorly developed self in itself. First you need to look at your creation from a critical distance, asking how your creation mirrors the landscape of your soul. And if the wounds we carry have been received in relationship, the restoration we seek must come through relationship as well. Therefore, take the assessment of the landscape of your soul in conversation to a mentor, your covenant group, or another transformative relationship. Playing, however, even if it does not heal us in itself, does invite us to be a participant in culture. "There is a direct development from transitional phenomena to playing, and from playing to shared playing, and from this to cultural experiences," Winnicott writes. Thus, whether you coach Little League, enroll in dance or art classes, go to the movies or to the symphony, tell Bible stories to a group of four-year-olds, take the youth group on an intercultural immersion trip, or volunteer at a shelter—all forms of play— you also participate in culture, that expansive word describing training, development, refinement, but also nurturing and cultivation.

Cultural experience, including participating in the Christian faith, thus begins with creative living first manifested in playing as infants and as children. This relationship between individual play as a child and cultural experience further implies that playing in itself is a satisfying experience. "It leaves me invigorated, even when I paint late into the night after a long day," states one pastor who paints large abstract paintings. Another pastor tells that in play she discovered that "being introverted does not mean being inhibited." Playing can be free-form or structured meandering that renews us, bringing balance to our lives. *If playing is the result of a developmental process, what can you gather about you becoming a person in light of your current forms of playing? How does your playing reflect the landscape of your soul? Since playing continues all our lives, where in culture and in life do you find a playground? What needs to happen before the creative impulse, which includes playing, can enliven you?*

Playing is a bridge between the inner and the outer, between self and other, between sense and non-sense, between you and a life to be lived. It is the dramatization of the landscape of your soul, even as it brings possibilities and rearranges current understandings. The grace is that it is a bridge that can be rebuilt over and over again, even as one can recognize the gap between this and that.

PLAYING WITH GOD

Pastor Randy, in his third year of ministry, has accepted the challenge and responsibility to become a pastor and to live into his call. Here, in "God-Wolf," he plays with what he calls "a sleeping theological platitude," his longing to be united with God. The reflection was written in winter, and one can sense the back-and-forth movement between self and Other/God; the sense and non-sense, and the destruction and restoration inherent to play activity:

> God-Wolf
> Haunt me, hunt me, have me God-gray wolf.
> Snarl and sink into my foundering flesh.
> Inhabit the forest of my dreams
> and Prowl and stalk until you rest behind
> the knowledge tree—one eye on me, one set on deeper things.
> Pursue until sated foreteeth find their moist home within your muzzle,
> until reverie and lapping savor the last of me
> and I have been devoured into the fur clad heaven of your stomach.

In what ways are you playful in your relationship with God? Scripture sees God as a lion, a leopard, and a bear (Hos. 13:7). The Spirit of God is seen as a dove (Matt. 3:16). *What animal would symbolically represent God for you? And why? How would you currently describe your relationship with the Lamb of God (John 1:29)? And with what animal can you associate yourself?*

BECOME A WISE FOOL

What model of pastoral leadership best fits playfulness and encourages the capacity to play? I believe the answer to this question is *the wise fool.* Alastair Campbell, in his book *Rediscovering Pastoral Care*, argues compellingly that the tradition and image of the wise fool needs to complement the pastoral leader as a good shepherd and as a wounded healer.[9] In a world where a business model of leadership has been exposed as corrupt and exploitative, reclaiming the image of a pastoral leader as a wise fool can redeem Christian leadership, even as it encourages a sense of playfulness. The wise fool is not in competition with the shepherd or the wounded healer as if one can be a leader with a single self-understanding, or as if one model is wrong and the other right.

The shepherd, Campbell writes, speaks of tenderness (Isa. 40:11), skill (Ezek. 34:16), and self-sacrifice (Zach. 12:10). The shepherd is courageous (1 Sam. 17:34ff) and has personal and professional integrity (1 Pet. 5:2ff). It takes a pastor-as-shepherd to care for the sick and dying, to expose and address social injustices, and to welcome the marginalized into the fold. For much of the Christian tradition, the shepherding model of pastoral leadership had been the primary model. This changed in 1972 when the Catholic priest-psychologist Henri Nouwen published his book *Wounded Healer: Ministry in Contemporary Society*.[10]

The wounded healer, in contrast, deepens pain so that healing can come. It is the suffering servant (Isa. 53:5) who speaks "the language of wounds," rooted firmly in the crucified God (Col. 1:20; 2 Cor. 1:5). The wounded healer can admit personal vulnerability and invite the vulnerability of others by not being "a pastoral bulldozer." It is the leader who has reclaimed an inner sense of security so that he can remain less anxious in the midst of others' chaos. It is the pastoral leader who knows how loss has impacted her life, and has done the work of mourning so that she can help others grieve. It is the person who has worked through personal trauma, so as not to become traumatic to others. As such, wounded healers can live in the broken reality as they hopefully anticipate the coming of God's reign.

Since ancient times and in all cultures, court jesters have mediated societal forces and liminality. Out of the tradition of the jester, often associated with the Middle Ages and the later works of William Shakespeare or Fyodor Dostoyevsky, comes the wise fool. The wise fool, Campbell states, "is especially vulnerable to those who hold earthly power: easily derided and exploited, used as a scapegoat . . ." The image follows Paul, who writes that one should be a fool to become really wise (1 Cor. 3:18). The wise fool is someone who can, through simplicity, expose insincerity and self-deception. It is the person loyal to the point of *foolhardiness*, who embodies the paradox that the person who wants to save his or her life will lose it (Matt. 16:25). It is the wise fool who is strong in personal weakness (1 Cor. 4:9–13).

Campbell identifies the wise fool as the prophet who speaks into our reality, who exaggerates our hopeless sinfulness, who encourages us to defy legalism (Luke 6:1–11). The prophets broke down political and societal structures (Isa. 1), spoke in a language that most could not understand (Jer. 5:3), and acted with a sense of pathos that reflected non-sense (Hos. 3). The prophets even broke down the structures of time and space. Similarly, the wise fool is someone who can respond with creative spontaneity, often when relationships are strained or when conventional language breaks down. It is someone who, existentially, experiences what it means to be in the world, but not of it.

Campbell recalls the story of Mulla, in Idries Shah's *The Exploits of the Incomparable Mulla Nasrudin*, who moved back and forth between Persia and Greece riding a donkey. Each time he carried two panniers of straw with him. The guards thought he was smuggling contraband but could never catch him red-handed. To their question: "What are you carrying, Nasrudin?" Mulla would answer "I am a smuggler." Years later, obviously having gotten into wealth, Mulla moved to Egypt. One day, a guard met him and asked him what he was smuggling all those years. Living out of the jurisdiction of Greece and Persia, Mulla answered, "Donkeys." Mulla, a wise fool, could exploit the overlooked and reveal the unexpected.

The pastoral-leader-as-wise-fool:

- Loves his or her enemies by sincerely telling the person who is "a thorn in the flesh": I do not know why, but God has placed you in my prayers often the last weeks. How are you doing? And how are your children (Luke 6:27ff)?

- Deflects the anger and impasse amongst the leadership team by saying: "I wonder if I too will be sacked like Coach M, despite my successes on and off the field?"

- Exposes the conflict and dysfunction between mother and father by asking: "What is happening between you two that Jet has to steal a DVD to get your attention?"

- Realizes that lament is life-giving and does not lead to despair: "God, my ministry is currently plagued by locusts . . ."

- Finds a connection between physical illness and faith: "In what ways is the cancer that is destroying your healthy cells also tearing away at your faith in God?"

- Distinguishes between difficulties and problems: "Tell me again how we turned the fact that people are leaving rural areas into self-blame that we have lost our Calvinistic roots?"

- Plays with paradox amidst a worship war. "Friends, we cannot worship without restraint if we are not held by faithful liturgy."

- Remains loyal to a denomination despite decisions by the denomination's leadership or corporate body that do not reflect one's personal values.

- Listens often and uses words sparingly: "I have much more to say, but my desire to hear how you are experiencing what is happening is bigger than my desire to speak"; "I can recite what I learned about this topic in school," or as a famous poet said, "Yes."

- Sees the humor in everyday life, in slips of the tongue, in scenes from nature, and in those who are too serious to be humorous.

Furthermore, the leader-as-wise-fool is the leader who offers love foolishly when others want to condemn or when love becomes conditional. It is the leader who speaks to the true self in another person, rather than soothes the false self. The pastoral-leader-as-wise-fool is the pastoral leader who brings to the fore the multiple motivating factors behind an appeal to embark on a building project, for she knows that if persons feel heard, then the likelihood of them supporting the project increases. And the wise fool colors liturgy and worship with rituals such as Holy Communion, since he knows that ritual communicates at a level deeper than any spoken word and that worship is a hallowed playground.

What prompts you to believe that some of your role models and mentors are wise fools? Thinking of recent ministry experiences, where do you notice the shepherd, the wounded healer, and the wise fool within you? What counsel will the wise fool give the business leader or someone who adopted only one model for ministry? How can you sustain the inevitable tension-field the wise fool enters? What is your theology of play that can guide your ministry?

TOWARDS A THEOLOGY OF PLAY WITH DEUS LUDENS

The wise fool is someone who upholds a playful spirit. But can we be playful when Jesus says: "Woe to you who laugh now, for you will mourn and weep" (Luke 6:25b)? Theologians Hugo Rahner and Jürgen Moltmann ask the same question: "May a Christian go on merrily playing when a stern and strict choice has to be made for eternity?" And "Is it right to laugh, to play and to dance without the same time crying out and working for those who perish in the shadowy side of life?"[11] These theologians, as you do, see the suffering and injustices in the world. The answer that Rahner and Moltmann give to these questions is a persistent and loud "Yes." For if one never discovers the freedom that lies in playing, one never claims one's full humanity and remains cold to suffering and injustice.

Every person carries some ability to play. We've been created, Rahner writes, with "a kind of mobility of the soul . . . a spiritual elegance of movement" that allows for playfulness and seriousness. When we do play, we are "softened by the pleasure of play," Thomas Aquinas once said. We need to play, for as our bodies "cooperate in the activities of the soul," we are revitalized to feel alive.[12] The virtue of *eutrapelia* mentioned earlier in this chapter suggests the ability to "[stand] between two extremes," to be a "well-turning" person.[13] Only the wise fool can stand in the gap created when you are healthy and you take your jacket off in the presence of someone dying to spend time with that person; or when you reach out to persons who live in poverty while you return to your comfortable life tonight.

If "play is at least half of life," as Hugo Rahner insists, then we need to reclaim the playfulness we experienced as children, the playfulness our Creator places in us, or else risk never living at all.[14] We can play and dance, inside and outside the church, because we were created by God as *Deus ludens*—a God at play. God played when creatively the earth and the skies above were formed, and this cosmic dance continues. God played when Adam and Eve were sculpted from dust, bone, and breath, when God freely invited God's people into a covenant. God plays when Wisdom roams the streets as the Proverbs tell (8:27–31); when God sent Light to illumine the darkness. Furthermore, God's freedom of play broke through when Christ was raised from the dead and became a new creation, at first unrecognizable to the disciples. God plays as the Triune God. We dance with God when God meets us in worship and as God's reign comes to our lives, our relationships, and to our cities and societies. Every time we experience God's grace—acts of pure freedom—we also experience our God at play. And so we play throughout the church year, wondering if we can dance on Good Friday, but anticipate leaping in the air Easter morn. Certainly any reflection of us being and becoming playful persons and pastoral leaders finds meaning only in the fact that we were created by, and believe in, a God who can play, *Deus ludens.*

"Is it right to laugh, to play and to dance without the same time crying out and working for those who perish in the shadowy side of life?"
Moltmann asks. The answer is yes, for God is a God who laughs *and*
cries. We can be playful and become childlike (and not childish) because the ground of our being is the reality of God (Matt. 18:3). And we
can become a serious, compassionate presence to others, for we have received God's compassion first (2 Cor. 1:3b–4).

If play is an attitude, a way of being, and not something one does or
needs to master, as we believe, then Rahner's and Moltmann's question
has to be rephrased to ask "How do you play when you find yourself in
the shadowy side of life? Or, How do you play when you are in the light
and others are in shadows?" And here the answers might be to discover
that freedom is something deeply personal, determined by the capacity
to believe and the other capacities mentioned in this book, and freedom
is something freely given by God. The personal creates space for the theological, and vice versa. "How can we sing the songs of God in a foreign
land?" the psalmist asks (Ps. 137:4). We can play, even in the shadowy
side of life, because we can lament, and lament is a form of play. Thus,
whether we engage in lamenting-as-play or in rejoicing-as-play, we experience "a temporary suspension of the normal state of affairs," which is
hope.[15] Our souls and selves are transformed by a playful and creative response to life. Play invites hope.

How does Deus ludens *speak into your life? What rituals and traditions inform your theology of play? How do you remain playful in a world
that is crying out in hunger and poverty; a world overflowing with interpersonal and political violence; and a world that is HIV-positive? Whom
does your congregation invite to their playground? What forms of playing
will welcome these strangers-to-be-friends? How can your community become a body of Christ that creates space for all — including their leaders —
to play?*

A PASTOR IS SOMEONE WHO PLAYS[16]

A pastor is somebody who can play and who does so alone, with others and
with God, and in sacred places such as hospitals, funeral homes, classrooms, offices, meetings rooms, television rooms, and of course in front of
pews. This may sound obvious or even effortless, but do not be fooled.

Many pastors want to lead, lecture, and then leave, but that is leading, lecturing, and leaving. Pastoral ministry, however, is playing and not

leading, lecturing, or leaving. Almost anybody can learn to lead and lecture, and ultimately everybody leaves, but no one can decide to play. Whenever you lead, lecture, or leave, you are compliant to persons and politics, but the moment you play, you are a true self, spontaneous and responsive. To be a true self in a church that prefers reactivity more than spontaneity and creativity requires confidence, imagination, concern, solitude, curiosity, and playfulness.

The only way to be a true self is to become one, even if it takes a lifetime to accomplish. Ministry as playing is about being and being with, not about doing. Surely you have to work harder than any leader, lecturer, or someone leaving can ever imagine. Of course, your false self can convince you otherwise, urging you to lead, lecture, and leave.

After you have played in various places with those accustomed to being led, lectured, and left behind, remind yourself that you are still becoming a pastor! Therefore, should you discern the call to become a pastoral leader, think of doing something else unless you are willing to become a true self who can play alone, with others, with God, and in sacred places such as hospitals, funeral homes, classrooms, offices, meetings rooms, television rooms, and in front of pews. Few other vocations offer such a large playground with so much reward. So become someone who can play!

CULTIVATE YOUR CAPACITY TO PLAY

We live in a world where we watch others at play—and are willing to pay large sums of money for the experience—but we rarely engage in play activity ourselves, despite the fact that most forms of playing are *gratis* and grace. We go to NASCAR races; we attend football, soccer, and baseball games; we watch others play poker with decadent amounts of money. Or we gamble; buy expensive exercise equipment we never use or books we never read; seclude ourselves with a PlayStation or computer; or find a playmate in the host of the shopping channel on television.

Since play occurs best in a safe, trustworthy place, which ministry offers only at times, conscious effort is needed to nurture the capacities that make playing possible. For many pastoral leaders the deliberate onset of playing is when stress in their lives forces them to *do* something about it. Such reactivity, however, rarely induces the responsive attitude of playfulness. Rather, playing becomes one more burden to be measured for its excellence. *GRASP* can help you understand yourself as a *homo ludens* and identifies ways to reclaim the playful self you are.

Examine Your Covenant with God

Our covenant with God identifies the God we internalized with the relationships and the environment that was our holding environment in our formative years. Pastor Timothy cannot think of himself in terms of playing or being playful. On the brink of burnout, he states: "I am too tired to do anything. Where will I find the time to go to the gym three times a week? I've tried that, by the way. I lasted two weeks." Pastor Timothy also says that the guilt feelings he experiences when disappointing others are enough to keep him from taking time for self-care and exercise. Like some pastoral leaders, Pastor Timothy equates playfulness and good self-care with hard work and fruitless ministry. Reflecting on his covenant with God in terms of the capacity to play, Pastor Timothy describes his covenant as follows:

My roots: "Becoming the man of the house at an early age, I was robbed of my childhood. I remember being complemented by adults for being *so responsible, so mature beyond my years.* Whenever I wanted to act my age, I received the silent message that I was letting my mother down." My life prayer: "Dear God, please let me be serious and responsible—mature beyond my years." My unforgivable sin: "To show people the hurt, but also playful self I am." My covenant with God: "Dear God, I will be your child if I am always responsible and always serious about life." In conversation with his mentor and after he studied the Apostle Paul's references to being foolish to this world, Pastor Timothy changed this covenant to: "Dear God, I am your child even as I learn to love myself, something that is foolish in the eyes of the world."

Since Pastor Timothy already enjoys going to fast food restaurants, he decided that he will only frequent those restaurants with a children's play area. He will take special notice of how the children play, how the parents or caretakers engage their children, and how much he is eating while doing so. Pastor Timothy told his mentor that he can do this at least twice a week, but probably more, since he often finds himself in such restaurants.

Reflect on your capacity to play:

1. What are your roots?
2. What is your silent prayer?

3. What is your unforgivable sin?
4. What is your covenant with God?
5. What are the implications for your life, your ministry, and your relationship with God?
6. Take your findings in prayer to God and in conversation to a trusted mentor or friend, or to the covenant group to which you belong.

Relationships

Engage in conversation, and possibly enter into a relationship with a mentor, a coach, a spiritual director, a counselor, or even a supervisor, someone who has worked towards achieving the capacity to play. Ask this person how he or she came to be a playful person. *How does playing manifest in his or her personal and professional lives? Why would this person see him- or herself as a wise fool, someone who can stand in the tension-gap between extremes?*

Ask your covenant group, the one you created having read the previous chapter, how they understand themselves as playful selves. *Where have they experienced playfulness recently? What discourages or even prohibits them from embracing playing as an attitude? How does playfulness manifest in their lives and ministries? What is the cost to themselves and to others when they rarely engage in playing?*

Action

Read any of the following books addressing aspects of the capacity to play:

- C. S. Lewis and Pauline Baynes. *The Complete Chronicles of Narnia.* New York: HarperCollins, 2000.
- Eugene H. Peterson. *Christ Plays in Ten Thousand Places: A Conversation in Spiritual Theology.* Grand Rapids: W.B. Eerdmans, 2005.
- Margery Williams. *The Velveteen Rabbit: Or, How Toys Become Real.* New York: HarperFestival, 2005.
- Donald Winnicott. *Playing and Reality.* London: Tavistock, 1993.

Spend time with children, even if they are your own. Visit and observe a children's playground. Or visit a children's home or volunteer at the pediatric ward of a hospital. Let those who can engage in natural play reawaken your capacity to play.

Creativity without playfulness does not exist, and vice versa. Please revisit the suggestions in chapter 2 and create by bringing something into existence or engaging the creativity of others. Play with words and ideas and create something, whether it is a poem or a prayer. Awaken the "original poet" within you.

Engage in any play activity: Participate in a sport or just exercise; take up dance lessons; learn to play an instrument or pick up the one you never touch; discover your vocal cords as an instrument, and read a children's story giving each character a unique voice, or sing a familiar song in different voices (high, low, with an accent, in an "opera voice," etc.); act a favorite story from Scripture, literature, or life; play with words as you write a poem, a creative reflection, or a sermon; invite others to create, with you, your next sermon; introduce paradox to your speech; play games, some with few strict rules, but asking improvisation; fly a kite; or lie on your back and spot the animal, face, or shape in the clouds or look for shooting stars.

Scripture

Read Psalm 104, a psalm that portrays God in playful terms, creating creatures that "frolic" (verse 26) and playing "hide-and-seek" with people (verse 29). *What images of play come to you as you read this psalm?* Notice how God is playing with creation. *What metaphors describing God's majesty speak to you? And why? How can creation itself be seen as an act of God's creative playfulness?*

Read Solomon's Song of Songs. *How does the interaction of the lovers speak of two persons' playing together?* Identify the many ways the lovers play with words to communicate their love for each other. *What feelings did you notice, what thoughts came to you, and what physical excitement or anxieties entered your body as you engaged this rarely read portion of Scripture? Who is the God veiled behind the playful engagement of the two lovers?*

Read Romans 12:3–8. *How can the functioning of the body of Christ with its many members be seen as a form of playing together? As a leader, how can you encourage such playing? How can you be playful with the specific gift you received from God? Why are some pastoral leaders so reluctant to invite the gifts of others to enrich a congregation?*

Prayer

There is significant similarity between praying and playing. Both praying and playing contribute to our ability to live an embodied existence *with* the unknown/Unknown. Praying and playing sustains, nurtures, and provides a means to live in a broken world. Furthermore, through praying and playing we can discover other persons, the world, and God, in a new way. Pray this Helen Salsbury poem that appears in Leslie Flynn's book, *Serve Him with Mirth*.

> *Dear God, we make you so solemn,*
> *so stiff and old and staid.*
> *How can we be so stupid*
> *when we look at the things you've made?*
>
> *How can we miss the twinkle,*
> *that must have been in your eye*
> *when you planned the hippopoto*
> *And the rhinoceri?*
>
> *Who watches an ostrich swallow,*
> *then doubts that you like to play,*
> *Or questions your sense of humor,*
> *hearing a donkey bray?*
>
> *Could the God who made the monkey*
> *have forgotten how to laugh?*
> *Or the one who striped the zebra*
> *and stretched out the giraffe?*
>
> *How could an oldish person*
> *fashion a pelican*
> *Or a perfectly sober Creator*
> *ever imagine man?*
>   *Amen.*[17]

CONCLUSION

"Become like a child, [Jesus] said,"

> if you want to mature as an adult. To play the ultimate game, don't rely on will, belief, denial, or reason alone. Play. Play in a

Godly way. Play with the Creator. Enter the existential game with imagination, wonder, and laughter if you want to become new without end.[18]

"Play," Jerome Berryman continues, "makes us young when we are old and matures us when we are young." It is thus no surprise that the best play can occur with God and in ministry, where what is and what is to come create one another—dialectically a pure form of playing. Play takes place in the overlap of two areas of playing, that of the pastoral leader and that of the parishioner, that of the preacher and that of the text, or that of the pastor and the congregation. Ministry, however, is not simply playing alone, playing with others, and playing with God, it is also the conscious cultivation of an attitude of playfulness within self and others. And this attitude is especially asked for when we hit the limits of life.

Playing, especially for children, is rewarding in itself. In a world and a church that is purpose driven, where pastoral leaders are ever conscious of "numbers" and "programs," and where goals and outcomes define even play, the pleasure inherent to play is not valued. Play becomes work. One more thing to do that can be evaluated for its successfulness. It is no surprise that most attempts to play are not sustained and that playing as an attitude cannot be reached through specific activities. Rather, cultivate a play-filled life!

To play in ministry is to become a wise fool. A wise fool knows when laughter, a form of play in itself, is wanted or warranted. When behavior becomes immoral and harmful to others, even disrespectful, it ceases to be play. Likewise, a wise fool can recognize deviations of play that reflect either an autistic or a realistic view of reality, such as the sexualization of play, seeking domination in play, engaging in play only when strict rules are in place, and seeking play in excessive physical exercise.[19] Without the capacity to play, it is impossible to engage the space between you and a thought, between you and a text, or between you and another person.

May you achieve the capacity to play, may you become a wise fool, and as Aristophanes wrote about the dance we do around truth, may your soul be able to say:

Let me never cease throughout the day,
To play, to dance, to sing.
Let me utter many a quip,

let me also say much meant in earnest.
And if my playing and mockery be worthy of Thy feast,
Let me be crowned with the garland of victory.[20]

To play, sing, and dance, to bring the rich meanings of words to the fore, all partake in giving us a sense of feeling alive, a sense of being real. Envisioning ministry in any other way is sad indeed, even unbecoming!

Conclusion

ENDINGS AS BEGINNINGS

There is no such thing as an infant.

—D. W. Winnicott,
The Maturational Processes and the
Facilitating Environment

The person who walks with the wise grows wise,
but a companion of fools suffers harm.

—Proverbs 13:20

[It] requires greater courage to preserve inner freedom,
to move on in one's inward journey into new realms, than to
stand defiantly for outer freedom.

—Rollo May, *Man's Search for Himself*

Y ou are someone who wants inner freedom. You resist being compliant to the desires of others or being someone who wears a persona like a mask to hide a hollow soul. You intuited psychologist Rollo May's (1909–94) comment that society needs persons with an "indigenous inner strength."[1] May continues that "not new ideas and inventions, important as they are, and not geniuses and super [human beings], but persons who can *be*, that is, persons who have a center of strength in themselves," will change our societies. *Becoming a Pastor* is a book that shows you sources for how to *be* a transformational person. This book's basic assumption is that who you are determines the way you lead. Therefore, you are becoming someone who:

- Has an inner space secure enough to be hospitable even as you acknowledge your own insignificance
- Imaginatively and creatively participates in the reign of God in a world obsessed with radical, autistic individualism and extreme reality determined by corporations
- Lives close to your own destructiveness as you continue to facilitate the reparation of lives and relationships
- Is comfortable being alone while in the presence of individuals, a community, God, and other internalized persons
- Discovers persons without necessarily finding safety in "knowing" or "understanding" them
- Remains playful, even in serious moments such as where death and destruction enter the lives we live

You are becoming the image of God you were created to be—someone who carries much potential for inner transformation and outer contributions. Potentiality, however, is worthless in itself if it is not nurtured within you and around you. Potential without fulfillment is like a flower that is never watered.

Becoming a Pastor refuses to accept a homogeneous or idealistic understanding of pastoral leadership, yet envisions a way of being in ministry that is different from, and at times more fruitful than, other ways of pastoring or leadership. The capacities discussed speak into character traits of effective leaders, such as being charismatic, collaborative, inclusive, ethical, prophetic or visionary, pastoral, passionate, prayerful, and welcoming.[2] The capacities, however, cannot be reduced to these traits, for they describe a path of becoming a self who, among greater things such as being a mature person, a loving partner, or a nurturing parent, is also a pastoral leader in the body of Christ.

To engage the book in critical conversation, you need to recognize the relationship between childhood experiences and the call to the ministry. Your compliant false self prepared you well to live into the many expectations your congregation and its parishioners have of and for you. However, your compliant false self can prevent you from discovering life as a transformational journey or from becoming a pastor. And as it hinders formation, the false self can energetically and effectively allow you to burn yourself out, never to experience any spontaneity or freedom in life or in ministry, or worse, the false self will watch you and those around you go up in flames. Sadly, ministry can become a repetition of a life first lived in childhood. For compliancy, reactivity, and the apathy that follows are not easily laid to rest. As James Dittes, a theologian with a passion for pastoral ministry, reminds us, ministry is not about answering questions or having questions answered, but it is a creative responsiveness of continually formulating questions and reshaping answers; recalling, reforming, and revisioning life and community with God's redemptive Spirit.[3] If you have read this far, no doubt, you have found that you can look at and tell about yourself without being overwhelmed. You are not putting self and soul as risk, for you are becoming. As May writes:

> The human being cannot live in a condition of emptiness for very long: if [a person] is not growing toward something, [the person] does not merely stagnate; the pent-up potentialities turn into morbidity and despair, and eventually into destructive activities.[4]

VOCATION AND THE TELLING OF SELVES

A pastoral leader is someone who can tell about himself or herself in appropriate ways and relationships, since, theoretically, you can only hear and see what you are able to say. Thus the congregation of the pastor who cannot preach on domestic violence is a statistical anomaly. Since no one ever shares his or her painful reality with their pastor, the pastor believes that such evil does not happen in the congregation. The elder who cannot mourn personal losses cannot lead the congregation in lamenting the often radical change that occurs in ecclesiastical contexts. And the deacon who cannot imagine poor parenting never sees the abandonment some children experience in the congregation. Since we can only hear and see what we can verbalize in helpful ways, knowing oneself is extremely important, for every person knows destructiveness intimately, has experienced significant losses, and knows the pain of abandonment.

The ability to tell about oneself, to gain self-knowledge, should not be confused with self-centeredness or ego-centricity. Self-centeredness is a form of self-exaltation and idolatry, whereas a person with a secure inner space has a nurtured soul available to be used by others and by

God. In seeking self-knowledge we follow the God who searched us, who perceives our thoughts from afar (Ps. 139:2). Self-knowledge and the growth that can come from having transformational persons and experiences in your life allow you to be truly present to yourself and to others. In this freedom one can become a leader who makes space for others or the congregation to grow. Telling about yourself, obviously, leads you to your autobiography.

In his book *The Social God and the Relational Self*, Stanley Grenz (1950–2005) discusses the importance of autobiographical work in order to discover who one truly is. "Self-expression," Grenz writes, "presupposes an awareness of one's unique self, which in turn arises by means of observing and cataloguing one's personal thoughts and feelings."[5] Self-knowledge, which is often sought with a passion equal to the fear of discovering who you really are or the fear that others might discover that you are a fraud, does not guarantee spiritual or emotional growth. Nor does it bring personal power, happiness, contentment, or even success. Self-knowledge can, however, indicate the kind of transformational relationships and experiences you need as you mature as a person and as you become a pastor.

Becoming a Pastor thus provides a framework that guides significant self-exploration and the telling of your self and your relationship with God. All of us can tell something about the capacities, which ones are well-developed in us and which ones are not. As a leader in the body of Christ it is your task to discover the extent to which the capacities have been nurtured in your person. Furthermore, it is your task to continually cultivate all the capacities, or risk putting your pastoral leadership at risk. As you keep these capacities in mind, the way you tell about yourself, the way you become present to others, the way you lead, and the way you *believe in* God, continually changes. Surely a personal and spiritual autobiography has to be retold often, or else it becomes a sad testimony of a life and soul not reaching its God-given potential. Retelling, however, can help us mend the "gaps" that entered our person, those moments where "[e]ither something unspeakable happened to us—abandonment, assault, appropriation of parent's needs—or something that should have happened did not—a warm holding, loving handling, object-presenting."[6]

When you learn to tell about yourself, you truly live into your call to be a pastoral leader, a call you received and discerned and that was affirmed by a gospel community. The word "calling" has its roots in the

Latin word *vocare,* hence the close relationship between the words "calling" and "vocation." The dictionary states that the word "calling" can mean "the summoning or inviting into a spiritual office or to the pastorate of a church," or "to call up a memory of the past," as in evoking a memory. You said yes to the first meaning of call when you were ordained or acknowledged by your faith community. *Becoming a Pastor* challenges you to call up memories of the past. For receiving and accepting the call to be a leader in the body of Christ brings a commitment to take a careful look at who you are as a person. Becoming a pastoral leader requires you to call on your self in "sober judgment" (Rom. 12:3), even as you are called by God and a faith community.

BECOMING EMBODIED, BEING "ENSOULED"

To become a pastor is to be an embodied person. It is to know your body's longings and desires, its warts and wounds, its potential and its limitations. It is to be comfortable with your body's shape and sounds, a body you care for, for you need to be a body to live into your call. The prophet Isaiah describes his call in terms of being embodied when he states, "The Spirit of the Sovereign [God] is on me, because [God] has anointed me to preach good news to the poor" (Isa. 61:1). At first glance you might think that leadership is about preaching or teaching, as if you are called to say something. The translation of the word as "to preach," however, is a rather poor one. The Hebrew word used is *basher,* from the stem *bashar,* which literally means "meat" or "flesh." Isaiah thus says: "The Spirit of the Sovereign [God] is on [you], because [God] has anointed [you] to *enflesh* good news to the poor." Preaching elicits visions of speaking. Enfleshment is about embodiment and a way of being with people and seeing the world. Enfleshment reminds us that we have bodies made of dust. Such bodies leave imprints of all who touched us, or worse, walked over us. But bodies made of dust can also be transformed!

Becoming a Pastor, however, is not just about embodiment. It calls forth the nurturing of your soul. For bodies without "watered" souls speak of the sins of the fathers and mothers that visit the next generation.[7] Bodies have to be "ensouled," to use the language of the Australian pastor-theologian and artist Douglas Purnell.[8] Ensouling experiences are to give soul to something or to nourish the soul of someone. It is to be unconditionally loved and affirmed. These experiences typically acknowledge a life lived or life as it unfolds. Ensouling experiences naturally include people, food and wine, laughter, music, and good conversation. They can leave you in a tired state, yet your mind and soul is energized and rekindled.

Ministry too can be ensouling—to you and to others. It includes the conversations or prayers or Bible studies that awaken your spirit. Purnell, for example, takes his congregation to art museums; they discuss movies and have jazz concerts. He empowers his families to engage in difficult conversations and to become present to each other, or to remember with authenticity a loved one who has died. He is actively involved in nurturing the next generation of pastoral leaders. Purnell covenanted with the congregation that:

- He seeks to live honestly, deeply, and openly as their spiritual leader
- He will love the people given to his care
- He will lead the best possible worship that he can
- He promises to listen to the people and to the community
- He will not succumb to popular models of ministry, but together with the congregation will seek for an authentic way of being the body of Christ

Personally, he grieves the losses and disappointments of ministry and covenant relationships that break down. He paints and journals regularly. He lives creatively and is being watered as he becomes water to others.

When you nurture the capacities described in this book, you might discover that you become more embodied—that is, more aware of what happened and is happening to, in, and through your body. I hope that you might also discover that you become more soulful, that you discover yourself, others, and God anew, and that you will be engaged in deep and significant relationships that are truly ensouling.

No doubt you have discovered you cannot become all by yourself. In writing about parents and their infants, Winnicott states that "there is no such thing as an infant."[9] By this paradoxical statement, Winnicott meant that there are only infants dependent on parental care. There are only infants *and* a mother, father, or caregiver. Only infants *and* a community. Only infants *and* a society that protects children against harm. To say that there is no such thing as an infant is a different way of talking about our baptismal vows, where parents and a faith community covenant to facilitate the embodiment and ensoulment of a new member to the community.

Likewise, in the body of Christ, there is no such thing as a pastor. One only finds a pastor *and* a family that informed a way of being in the world; only an elder *with* an interior space determining the way the elder leads; only a deacon *and* formative relationships and experiences that are now seen in the decisions the deacon makes. Furthermore, there is only a pastoral leader *and* a congregation; only a pastor *and* a covenant group to hold you accountable to transformative *and* ethical leadership and that encourages the creative nurturing of your person. Ultimately, there is only you *and* God, the One who called you to ministry, who created you with the capacity to internalize relationships; the One who created you with the capacity to be renewed, revitalized, and transformed; the One who gave you the ability to take a step back and assess the condition of your self *and* soul or the nature of your leadership. Thus, in the body of Christ, the paradox of pastoral leadership is that transformation for ministry comes from within and from without. You are responsible for your own formation, yet the only way to become a pastor is to be in transformational relationships with teachers, mentors, counselors, and with the triune God.

TRANSFORMING SELF AND SOUL IN THE CLASSROOM

Becoming a Pastor encourages the nurturing of future leaders who are spiritually and emotionally mature. It wants to challenge and inform Christian and especially theological education. Surely education has as a primary goal the formation of mature Christians and leaders. Where education is reduced to the giving and receiving of knowledge, transformation of self and soul is greatly diminished. *What* one knows and thinks—knowledge—is important, and knowing *when* tradition addresses a contemporary concern can be helpful. Furthermore, *how* one discerns has a significant impact on leadership. However, the effective cultivation of persons and leaders requires that we ask *who* is the leader? The tension in education between inquiry or knowledge and the ability to live-within-the-situations with reflective wisdom—the latter often referred to as a *habitus*—remains.[10] *Habitus* implies profound, life-orienting, identity-shaping participation in the constitutive practices of the Christian life. Therefore, the cultivation and transformation of lives—which the Greeks called *paideia*—is the goal and focus of Christian education. Whether students are taught the classic languages, history, theology, or even the arts of ministry, the root goal of each is the transformation of selves and souls.

Classrooms have to invite the learners to become more personal in their learning. Writing rational and well-researched papers, even if it serves the academy in gaining knowledge, may also serve a false, normotic self that finds safety in abstract thoughts. Furthermore, it strengthens a clergy-only paradigm for pastoral leadership at the cost of lay leadership, even as it ill prepares leaders to be responsive to a world in crisis. Rather, education is best understood as "an act of walking with, sharing with, acting with, remembering with, and constructing meaning with people in a learning community."[11] Education perceived as such is spiritual and personal formation, the deepening of a personal and spiritual autobiography, the transmittal of tradition and doctrines, and professional training for pastoral leadership. It cultivates wisdom, a way of being and seeing things, more than providing knowledge and information. Effective pedagogy chooses qualitative formation over quantitative learning without denying that knowledge informs, but cannot be equated with wisdom. Furthermore, transformational teaching and experiences cannot be passed on to other agents, such as the supervisors of clinical pastoral education programs, where, typically in a hospital setting, the person of a pastor (the who) is being challenged and transformed. Or theological educators cannot distance themselves from their transformational task by saying that it is the church that is responsible for cultivating a mature personal and pastoral identity.

Rather, in congregations, in colleges, and in seminaries, teachers and mentors are all transformational agents facilitating the maturation of persons. Classrooms, therefore, need to:

- Facilitate the capacity to believe and expand the inner space
- Cultivate a pastoral imagination comfortable in the in-between world between autistic subjectivity and objective reality
- Address the destructiveness we all carry and help students to achieve the capacity to repair relationships
- Empower persons with ways to access their emotional and spiritual lives

- Invite persons to discover where they come from, who they are, and what they know about persons, life, and God, as if for the first time
- Encourage and affirm a playfulness that informs all aspects of life and ministry

Classrooms that seek the transformation of self and soul reclaim the sacramental nature of life and of teaching. Such a model envisions teaching as leading persons on an amazing journey of exploration, discovery, and change. Christian educator Mary Elizabeth Moore writes in her book *Teaching as a Sacramental Act* that Christian education needs to be re-envisioned as sacred teaching—mediating the Holy. Moore writes, "The more specific assertion is that Christian teaching needs to be envisioned as sacramental, with the purpose of mediating God, and with approaches that mediate God's grace and God's call to the human community for the sake of human sanctification and creation's well-being."[12] Sacramental teaching creates an atmosphere where you can feel real, where you can find a way to relate to your self, where you can discover others and the world, and where you can participate in the coming of God's reign. It draws on your cognitive abilities even as it requires you to respond imaginatively to history and tradition.

Just as we leave a communion table fed and nurtured, good-enough education leaves students with a sense of being revitalized and a sense of feeling alive. The learners know that they will be effective facilitators as they create space for themselves and others to grow, even if they do not know how to "do" everything and or even if they cannot meet every situation with the security of past experience. A mature leader knows that he or she is fundamentally unprepared and ill-equipped, yet prepared enough to be fruitful in ministry. Mature leaders can hold the tension such knowledge brings without fleeing to false solutions such as unearthly piety, narcissistic grandiosity, or just complaining about their inadequate seminary education for years. It is accepting that you can do very little ministry, yet can accomplish much, since ministry is done *with* sisters and bothers in Christ and *with* the participation of the Spirit.

FAN INTO FLAME THE GIFT OF GOD

The apostle Paul, writing to a young Timothy, states "train yourself to be godly" (1 Tim. 4:7). Paul compares this training to physical conditioning but states that becoming godly holds promise for today and for the life to come. He then continues to urge Timothy to be secure in himself, despite his youth, to be an example, to be prophetic (and we can add imaginative) in preaching and teaching, and to watch his self and soul. When we are called to be leaders in the body of Christ, we are called, like Timothy, to be godly. But being godly, after the Word became flesh and made a dwelling among us (John 1:14), is always one body, yours, reaching out and connecting with other bodies, some rich and some poor, some healthy and some ill, some young and some old, some content and some in crisis. Paul states that Timothy has to "fan into flame the gift of God" (2 Tim. 1:6). I am grateful that Paul beckoned Timothy to accept responsibility for his own formation, for one can easily succumb to the false self's apathy to seek transformation or to be transformed. Expanding the inner space, a central dynamic in becoming godly, is far too uncomfortable for the false self to tolerate.

I expect that the promise to yourself to *become* occurred often as you read these pages. Remember, you were created with the desire to transform your self-experience, on our own and with the help of teachers, mentors, counselors, and spiritual directors. But besides the ability to recognize areas of our person where growth and learning will help us become mature persons and leaders, we also received "a spirit of power, of love, and of self-discipline," not a "spirit of timidity" (2 Tim. 1:7). Sometimes, however, the spirit of timidity is present. We make promises to ourselves and even to others our anxiety does not allow us to keep. Or we embark on a journey of self-transformation and self-care but cannot sustain the attention needed. In times like that (which, thanks to our false self, is the experience of most persons), seek out a transformational agent who can fan your flame, who can awaken your spirit of power, love, and self-discipline. "The person who walks with the wise grows wise, but a companion of fools suffers harm," the Proverb says (13:20). Walk then with the wise, mature, and those who are becoming. You will be transformed in ways not imagined, but truly inspired by God's Spirit and in service of the body of Christ. As God promises those living into their call: "I will lead the blind by ways they have not known, along unfamiliar paths I will guide them; I will turn the darkness into light before them and make the rough places smooth" (Isa. 42:16). God will not forsake you.

ENDINGS AS NEW BEGINNINGS

The poet T. S. Eliot (1888–1965) writes in his "Little Gidding" that "[w]hat we call the beginning is often the end and to make an end is to make a beginning." He continues, saying that

> *We shall not cease from exploration.*
> *And the end of all our exploring*
> *will be to arrive where we started*
> *and know the place for the first time.*[13]

How does one conclude a book if the end is where we start from, as Eliot suggests? As the prodigal son discovered, we eventually have to go home, but home will never be the home we once knew. Yet it is also true that it is never too late to become. Like peeling an onion, you either remove one layer after the other to discover who you are, or you add layers of protection and reactivity. Inevitably your exploration in these pages led you deep into yourself, back to your family of origin and to formative experiences and persons. And, as Eliot intuits, when we go back there, we often discover self and other, including God, anew. Singer-songwriter Peter Mayer, reflecting on how he experienced church as a child and how he listened to miracle stories, discovers that "everything is holy now"—a child's face, the arrival of a new day, a bird singing.[14] Miracles are everywhere and holiness abounds, no longer confined to certain experiences and places such as the miracles of Moses and Jesus or the sacraments. To become a pastor is to revisit the familiar and to discover it anew. It is to discover holiness in oneself and the stories one can tell, and to discover holiness in others, in life, in creation. To become a pastor is to rediscover, every day, that God is the Other, the holy Thou.

Six centuries before the birth of Christ, the Greek philosopher and mathematician Pythagoras said that people are most honest and most truly show who they are when they pray in privacy to their gods. Our prayers portray something of who we are, but more importantly, we become what we pray. *Becoming a Pastor* envisions the reign of God coming to you as a pastoral leader and to the gospel community you serve. It hopes for a life of freedom empowered to bear fruit and to be lived to the full (John 10:10). As you move on with your inward journey, as you become a pastor, this is my prayer for you:

Creator, Redeemer, Sustainer,
Be the Thou that informs my self and soul.
Create space for me to grow
so that others can grow through me,
in this life and into the next.
Stretch my inner space, cultivate my imagination, and feed my body.
Repair my relationship with you severed by my sin.
Help me be responsive where other relationships are in need
     of reparation.
Keep me alone in the presence of others.
Let me not become destructive to myself,
and allow me the grace to discover others.
For you reign in freedom and with power.
This is your playground. Amen.

ENDNOTES

PREFACE

1. All dictionary references are taken from *The Oxford English Dictionary* unless otherwise indicated: *The Oxford English Dictionary*, CD-ROM, 2nd ed., version 2.01 (London: Oxford University Press, 1987).

2. All scriptural quotations are taken from The New International Version unless indicated: *The Holy Bible: New International Version* (Grand Rapids: Zondervan Publishing, 1984).

INTRODUCTION: Created to Seek Transformation

1. Claus Westermann and David Green, *Genesis: A Practical Commentary, Text and Interpretation* (Grand Rapids, Mich.: W.B. Eerdmans, 1987), 23.

2. Adriaan Van Selms, *Genesis: Deel I*, De prediking van het Oude Testament (Nijkerk: G. F. Callenbach, 1979), 67. "Maar the vrouw voelt de begeerte naar een kortere weg to geestelike ontplooiing, verlaat de weg der gehoorsaamheid om sneller tot het doel te breken" Author's translation of Van Selms's Dutch commentary: "But the woman felt a desire for a shortened path to spiritual growth, and left the path of obedience to achieve her goal faster."

3. Daniel N. Stern, *The Interpersonal World of the Infant: A View from Psychoanalysis and Developmental Psychology* (New York: Basic Books, 1985).

4. Christopher Bollas, *The Shadow of the Object: Psychoanalysis of the Unthought Known* (London: Free Association Books, 1987), 13–29. Bollas writes about "the transformational object."

5. See Question 75: "What is sanctification?" The Westminster Larger Catechism can be found at: www.reformed.org under Historic Church Documents.

6. To protect and maintain confidentiality, all the cases in this book are true, but not factual. Many composites were created, which does not make them less real. Where appropriate, the permission of individuals was received.

7. Simon A. Grolnick, *The Work and Play of Winnicott* (Northvale, N.J.: Jason Aronson, 1990), 3.

8. D. W. Winnicott, *Human Nature* (New York: Schocken Books, 1988), 34.

9. Martin Buber, *I and Thou. A New Translation with a Prologue "I and You" and Notes by Walter Kaufmann* (New York: Scribner, 1970).

10. Julia Kristeva, *Strangers to Ourselves* (New York: Columbia University Press, 1991).

11. Ibid., 20.

CHAPTER ONE: The Capacity to Believe

1. Brooke Hopkins, "Winnicott and the Capacity to Believe," *International Journal of Psychoanalysis* 78 (1997).

2. Paul Tillich, *The Courage to Be* (New Haven: Yale University Press, 1980). Tillich knew personal anxiety intimately and was hospitalized three times for "nervous breakdowns."

3. Parker J. Palmer, *The Courage to Teach: Exploring the Inner Landscape of a Teacher's Life*, 1st ed. (San Francisco: Jossey-Bass, 1998), 2.

4. Margaret S. Mahler, Fred Pine, and Anni Bergman, *The Psychological Birth of the Human Infant: Symbiosis and Individuation* (London: Hutchinson, 1975).

5. Erik H. Erikson, "Womanhood and the Inner Space," in *Identity, Youth, and Crisis* (New York: W.W. Norton, 1968).

6. Erik H. Erikson, *Childhood and Society* (New York: W.W. Norton, 1993), 248.

7. Erik H. Erikson, *Insight and Responsibility: Lectures on the Ethical Implications of Psychoanalytic Insight* (New York: W.W. Norton, 1994), 118.

8. Donald Capps, *Deadly Sins and Saving Virtues* (Philadelphia: Fortress Press, 1987).

9. Frederick Buechner, *Wishful Thinking: A Seeker's ABC* (San Francisco: HarperSanFrancisco, 1993), 35.

10. Sarah Blaffer Hrdy, *Mother Nature: A History of Mothers, Infants, and Natural Selection* (New York: Pantheon Books, 1999).

11. D. W. Winnicott, "From Dependence towards Independence in the Development of the Individual (1963)," in *The Maturational Processes and the Facilitating Environment: Studies in the Theory of Emotional Development* (Madison, Conn.: International Universities Press, 1994).

12. Harry Guntrip, *Mental Pain and the Cure of Souls* (London: Independent Press, 1956), 137.

13. The poem can be found at: http://tennysonpoetry.home.att.net/45.htm.

14. D. W. Winnicott, *Home Is Where We Start From: Essays by a Psychoanalyst*, 1st American ed. (New York: Norton, 1986), 68.

15. Dietrich Bonhoeffer, *Letters and Papers from Prison* (New York: Macmillan, 1972), 347.

16. Winnicott, *Home Is Where We Start From*, 143.

17. Emil Brunner, *Truth as Encounter* (Philadelphia: Westminster Press, 1964), 148.

18. Michael Willett Newheart, *Word and Soul: A Psychological, Literary, and Cultural Reading of the Fourth Gospel* (Collegeville, Minn.: Liturgical Press, 2001), 63–64.

19. Dennis E. Kenny, "Clinical Pastoral Education: Exploring Covenants with God," *The Journal of Pastoral Care* 34, no. 2 (1980).

20. Eunice Tietjins, quoted in H. Richard Niebuhr, *The Responsible Self: An Essay in Christian Moral Philosophy* (New York,: Harper & Row, 1963), 137.

21. Buechner, *Wishful Thinking*, 23.

CHAPTER TWO: The Capacity to Imagine

1. Christopher Bollas, *The Shadow of the Object: Psychoanalysis of the Unthought Known* (London: Free Association Books, 1987), 135ff.

2. For a reader-friendly discussion of how the brain functions and its relationship to religious experience, see David Hogue, *Remembering the Future, Imagining the Past: Story, Ritual, and the Human Brain* (Cleveland: Pilgrim Press, 2003).

3. D. W. Winnicott, "Ego Integration in Child Development," in *The Maturational Processes and the Facilitating Environment: Studies in the Theory of Emotional Development* (Madison, Conn.: International Universities Press, 1994), 56.

4. D. W. Winnicott, "Transitional Objects and Transitional Phenomena," in *Through Paediatrics to Psycho-analysis: Collected Papers* (New York: Brunner/Mazel, 1992), 239.

5. Ibid., 230.

6. Ibid., 239.

7. Quoted in: Don Postema, *Space for God: Study and Practice of Spirituality and Prayer* (Grand Rapids: CRC Publications, 1997), 24.

8. Winnicott, *Home Is Where We Start From: Essays by a Psychoanalyst*, 1st American ed. (New York: Norton, 1986), 39.

9. Ibid., 44.

10. Michael Eigen and Adam Phillips, *The Electrified Tightrope* (Northvale: Jason Aronson, 1993), 77.

11. Shaun McNiff, *Creating with Others: The Practice of Imagination in Life, Art, and the Workplace*, 1st ed. (Boston: Shambhala Publications, 2003), 104.

12. Paul W. Pruyser, *The Play of the Imagination: Towards a Psycho-analysis of Culture* (New York: International Universities Press, 1983).

13. Paul W. Pruyser, *Between Belief and Unbelief* (New York: Harper & Row, 1974), 111. See Paul W. Pruyser, "Psychological Roots and Branches of Belief (1979)," in *Religion in Psychodynamic Perspective: The Contributions of Paul W. Pruyser*, ed. H. Newton Malony and Bernard Spilka (New York: Oxford University Press, 1991), 162ff.

14. Pruyser, *The Play of the Imagination*, 65.

15. Walter Brueggemann, *Interpretation and Obedience: From Faithful Reading to Faithful Living* (Minneapolis: Fortress Press, 1991), 2. In this section I rely heavily on Brueggemann's contribution. Other quotations from this book are taken from pages 12, 13, and 21.

16. Margaret Guenther, *Holy Listening: The Art of Spiritual Direction* (Cambridge: Cowley Publications, 1992), x.

17. Dykstra's ideas, including quotations, in this section are from Craig Dykstra, "The Pastoral Imagination," in *Initiatives in Religion* (2001).

18. Dietrich Bonhoeffer, *Letters and Papers from Prison* (New York: Macmillan, 1972), 279. Italics added.

19. From Emily Dickinson's, "Behind Me—dips Eternity—" as quoted in Simon A. Grolnick, Leonard Barkin, and Werner Muensterberger, *Between Reality and Fantasy: Winnicott's Concepts of Transitional Objects and Phenomena* (Northvale, N.J.: Jason Aronson Press, 1988), 464.

20. Winnicott, *Home Is Where We Start From*, 49.

CHAPTER THREE: The Capacity for Concern

1. Kathleen J. Greider, *Reckoning with Aggression: Theology, Violence, and Vitality* (Louisville: Westminster John Knox Press, 1997), 8.

2. Christie Cozad Neuger, "Narratives of Harm: Setting the Developmental Context for Intimate Violence," in *In Her Own Time: Women and Developmental Issues in Pastoral Care*, ed. Jeanne Stevenson Moessner (Minneapolis: Fortress Press, 2000).

3. This phrase was taken from Marc Cohn's song "The Things We've Handed Down," from *The Rainy Season*, CD, © 1993, Atlantic Records.

4. Kathleen M. O'Connor, *Lamentations and the Tears of the World* (Maryknoll, N.Y.: Orbis Books, 2002), 89.

5. Andrew D. Lester, *The Angry Christian: A Theology for Care and Counseling* (Louisville: Westminster John Knox Press, 2003), 115.

6. Ibid., 206.

7. Ibid.

8. Greider, *Reckoning with Aggression*; David W. Augsburger, *Hate-work: Working through the Pain and Pleasures of Hate* (Louisville: Westminster John Knox Press, 2004).

9. Lester, *The Angry Christian*, 128.

10. Frederick Buechner, *Wishful Thinking: A Seeker's ABC* (San Francisco: HarperSanFrancisco, 1993), 2.

11. D. W. Winnicott, "The Development of the Capacity for Concern," in *The Maturational Processes and the Facilitating Environment: Studies in the Theory of Emotional Development* (Madison, Conn.: International Universities Press, 1994).

12. Regarding persons having an innate morality, Winnicott is supported by the Christian apologete, C. S. Lewis. See Lewis's *Mere Christianity: A Revised and Amplified Edition* (San Francisco: HarperSanFrancisco, 2001).

13. D. W. Winnicott, *Human Nature* (New York: Schocken Books, 1988), 70.

14. D. W. Winnicott, *Deprivation and Delinquency* (London: Tavistock Publications, 1997), 92.

15. Harriet Goldhor Lerner, *The Dance of Intimacy: A Woman's Guide to Courageous Acts of Change in Key Relationships* (New York: Harper & Row, 1989), 103–04.

16. This phrase was taken from "Adam and Eve," a song by October Project, from *Falling Farther*, CD, © 1995, Sony Records.

17. Eberhard Bethge and Victoria Barnett, *Dietrich Bonhoeffer: A Biography* (Minneapolis: Fortress Press, 2000), 40.

18. Jill L. McNish, *Transforming Shame: A Pastoral Response* (Binghamton, N.Y.: Haworth Pastoral Press, 2004), 36.

19. Gershen Kaufman, *Shame: The Power of Caring* (Rochester: Schenkman Books, 1992), 13–14.

20. Ibid., 43ff.

21. Winnicott, "The Development of the Capacity for Concern," 101.

CHAPTER FOUR: The Capacity to Be Alone

1. Karen Lebacqz and Ronald G. Barton, *Sex in the Parish* (Louisville: Westminster John Knox Press, 1991), 69, 145.

2. Find a summary of this study at: http://www.gcsrw.org/newsarchives/2005/05032.htm.

3. Erving Goffman, *Asylums: Essays on the Social Situation of Mental Patients and Other Inmates* (Chicago: Aldine Publishing, 1962).

4. Dietrich Bonhoeffer, *Life Together* (New York: Harper & Row, 1954), 76.

5. Ibid., 77.

6. Ibid., 83.

7. Henri J. M. Nouwen, *Reaching Out: The Three Movements of the Spiritual Life* (Garden City: Image Books, 1986).

8. Ibid., 16.

9. Ibid., 37–38.

10. Ibid., 8.

11. Ibid., 19.

12. D. W. Winnicott, "The Development of the Capacity to Be Alone," in *The Maturational Processes and the Facilitating Environment: Studies in the Theory of Emotional Development* (Madison, Conn.: International Universities Press, 1994), 29. This section often references this paper. Other pages quoted are (sequentially) 30, 31, 32, and 34.

13. Eric. H. F. Law, *The Wolf Shall Dwell with the Lamb: A Spirituality for Leadership in a Multicultural Community* (St. Louis: Chalice Press, 2003), 79–88.

14. Winnicott, "The Development of the Capacity for Concern," in *The Maturational Processes*, 75–76.

15. Michael Kelly Blanchard, "'Til the Terrors Are Done," *Watered: Reflections on Nurture*, CD, © 2005, Gotz Music.

16. Damien Rice, "I Remember," *O*, CD, © 2003 Damien Rice, under exclusive license to Vector Recordings.

17. W. Ronald D. Fairbairn, *Psychoanalytic Studies of the Personality* (New York: Routledge, 1996), 101, 102–06.

18. Dietrich Bonhoeffer, *Letters and Papers from Prison* (New York: Macmillan, 1972), 347.

19. James N. Poling, *The Abuse of Power: A Theological Problem* (Nashville: Abingdon Press, 1991), 24ff.

20. Lebacqz and Barton, *Sex in the Parish*, 93ff.

21. Donald Capps, "Power and Desire: Sexual Misconduct Involving Pastors and Parishioners," in *Women, Gender, and Christian Community*, ed. E. Jane Dempsey Douglass and James F. Kay (Louisville: Westminster John Knox Press, 1997).

22. Lebacqz and Barton, *Sex in the Parish*, 57.

23. Thich Nhat Hahn, *The Miracle of Mindfulness* (Boston: Beacon Press, 1987), 7.

24. This form for lament was taken from Donald Capps, *Biblical Approaches to Pastoral Counseling* (Philadelphia: Westminster Press, 1981), 74.

25. Frederick Buechner, *Wishful Thinking: A Seeker's ABC* (San Francisco: HarperSanFrancisco, 1993), 86.

26. Karl Rahner and Geffrey B. Kelly, *Karl Rahner: Theologian of the Graced Search for Meaning*, The Making of Modern Theology (Minneapolis: Fortress Press, 1992), 174.

27. Karl Rahner, *Foundations of Christian Faith: An Introduction to the Idea of Christianity* (New York: Crossroad, 1982), 26.

CHAPTER FIVE: The Capacity to Use Others and to Be Used

1. Karl Rahner and Geffrey B. Kelly, *Karl Rahner: Theologian of the Graced Search for Meaning*, The Making of Modern Theology (Minneapolis: Fortress Press, 1992), 178.

2. Abraham Joshua Heschel, *The Prophets* (New York: HarperPerennial, 2001), xxiv. Emphasis added. In this section on Heschel I rely heavily on the introductory pages to his book.

3. Martin Buber, *I and Thou. A New Translation with a Prologue "I and You" and Notes by Walter Kaufmann* (New York: Scribner, 1970). All references to "I and Thou" refer to Buber's book.

4. Winnicott addressed the New York Psychoanalytic Society. D. W. Winnicott, "The Use of an Object and Relating through Identifications (1968)," in *Psycho-Analytic Explorations*, ed. Clare Winnicott, Ray Shepherd, and Madeleine Davis (Cambridge: Harvard University Press, 1994). Additional references to "The Use of an Object" come from pages 219, 226, 225, and 231.

5. Leroy T. Howe, *The Image of God: A Theology for Pastoral Care and Counseling* (Nashville: Abingdon Press, 1995), 77ff. Additional references to Howe's book come from pages 91, 95, and 112.

6. Ann Belford Ulanov, *Finding Space: Winnicott, God, and Psychic Reality* (Louisville: Westminster John Knox Press, 2001), 36. Additional references to Ulanov's book come from pages 20 and 19.

7. The songs "What God Wants, Parts I–III" can be found on Roger Waters, *Amused to Death*, CD, © 1992, Sony Records.

8. Winnicott, "The Use of an Object," 222.

9. See G. Lloyd Rediger, *Clergy Killers: Guidance for Pastors and Congregations under Attack* (Louisville: Westminster John Knox Press, 1997).

10. Jean Laplanche and J. B. Pontalis, *The Language of Psycho-Analysis* (New York: Norton, 1974), 356.

11. Ulanov, *Finding Space*, 105.

12. Thomas H. Ogden, *The Matrix of the Mind: Object Relations and the Psychoanalytic Dialogue* (Northvale: Aronson Press, 1986), 50.

13. Christopher Bollas, *The Shadow of the Object: Psychoanalysis of the Unthought Known* (London: Free Association Books, 1987), 243.

14. Ibid, 157ff; 165–66.

15. Sarah A. Butler, *Caring Ministry: A Contemplative Approach to Pastoral Care* (New York: Continuum, 1999), 30–31.

16. Ulanov, *Finding Space*, 23.

17. Mango Groove, "Another Country," on *Another Country*, CD, © 1993, Gallo Records.

18. Adam Phillips, *Promises, Promises: Essays on Literature and Psychoanalysis* (London: Faber and Faber, 2002), 127.

CHAPTER SIX: The Capacity to Play

1. Hugo Rahner, *Man at Play* (New York: Herder & Herder, 1967), 99.

2. Michael Jacobs, *D. W. Winnicott*, in Key Figures in Counseling and Psychotherapy (London: Sage Publications, 1995), 23–24.

3. "The capacity to play" is used in "Notes on Play," found in D. W. Winnicott, *Psycho-Analytic Explorations* (Cambridge, Mass.: Harvard University Press, 1994), 59.

4. In this section on the capacity to play, I rely heavily on: D. W. Winnicott, *Playing and Reality* (London: Tavistock, 1993). For a brief summary of the developmental process that leads to playing, see pages 41–48ff. See also 41, 51, 54, 100, 104, 109.

5. Winnicott, *Psycho-Analytic Explorations*, 60.

6. Thomas H. Ogden, "Playing, Dreaming, and Interpreting Experience: Comments on Potential Space," in *The Facilitating Environment: Clinical Applications of Winnicott's Theory*, ed. Gerard Fromm and Bruce L. Smith (Madison, Conn.: International Universities Press, 1989), 257.

7. These different ways of responding to the theodicy can be found in Johannes Van der Ven and Eric Vossen, *Suffering: Why for God's Sake?* (Kampen: Kok, 1995).

8. Winnicott, *Psycho-Analytic Explorations*, 205.

9. Alastair V. Campbell, *Rediscovering Pastoral Care* (Philadelphia: Westminster Press, 1981), 47–64.

10. Henri J. M. Nouwen, *The Wounded Healer: Ministry in Contemporary Society* (New York: Image Books, 1972).

11. Rahner, *Man at Play*, 92; Jürgen Moltmann, *Theology of Play* (New York: Harper & Row, 1972), 2.

12. Rahner, *Man at Play*, 100.

13. Ibid., 93–94. For a discussion of how *eutrapelia* was understood by the early church fathers (such as Aquinas, Clement, Ambrose, and Augustine), and how the tradition got lost to Christianity, see pages 91–105.

14. Ibid., ix.

15. Moltmann, *Theology of Play*, 9.

16. A short reflection by e.e. cummings (1894–1962), entitled "A Poet's Advice to Students" motivated this reflection. e.e. cummings, A *Miscellany Revised* (New York: October House, 1965), 325.

17. Helen Salsbury quoted in Leslie B. Flynn, *Serve Him with Mirth: The Place of Humor in the Christian Life* (Grand Rapids: Zondervan, 1960). The

book can also be read in electronic format at http://guide.gospelcom.net /books/ServeHimwithMirth.htm.

18. Jerome W. Berryman, *Godly Play: A Way of Religious Education* (San Francisco: HarperSanFrancisco, 1991), 1.

19. Winnicott, *Psycho-Analytic Explorations*, 61.

20. Aristophanes, as quoted in Rahner, *Man at Play*, 31.

CONCLUSION: Endings as Beginnings

1. Rollo May, *Man's Search for Himself* (New York: Norton, 1953), 80.

2. Adapted from http://www.divinity.duke.edu/programs/spe/articles /200508/marksofexcellence-list.html.

3. James E. Dittes, *Re-calling Ministry*, ed. Donald Capps (St. Louis: Chalice Press, 1999), 27.

4. May, *Man's Search for Himself*, 24.

5. Stanley J. Grenz, *The Social God and the Relational Self: A Trinitarian Theology of the Imago Dei* (Louisville: Westminster John Knox Press, 2001), 100.

6. Ann Belford Ulanov, *Finding Space: Winnicott, God, and Psychic Reality* (Louisville: Westminster John Knox Press, 2001), 140.

7. "Watered" is a metaphor used by singer-songwriter Michael Kelly Blanchard. It speaks of a person who was and is loved, cared for, nurtured, affirmed, encouraged, and carried in good-enough relationships.

8. Shared in personal communication with the author.

9. D. W. Winnicott, *The Maturational Processes and the Facilitating Environment: Studies in the Theory of Emotional Development* (Madison, Conn.: International Universities Press, 1994), 39.

10. Edward Farley, *Theologia: The Fragmentation and Unity of Theological Education* (Philadelphia: Fortress Press, 1983), 35. Farley defines *habitus* as a "cognitive disposition and orientation of the soul, a knowledge of God and what God reveals."

11. Mary Elizabeth Moore, *Teaching as a Sacramental Act* (Cleveland: Pilgrim Press, 2004), 13.

12. Ibid., 5.

13. From T. S. Eliot's "Little Gidding," in *Four Quartets* (New York: Harcourt, 1943).

14. Peter Mayer, "Holy Now," *Million Year Mind*, CD, © 1997, Blue Boat Records.